THE ORDEAL OF CONVOY NY 119

by Charles Dana Gibson II

Published by: South Street Seaport Museum
16 Fulton Street
New York, N.Y.

A detailed accounting of one of the strangest
World War II convoys ever to cross the North Atlantic

Dept. of Army Clearance under "Freedom of Information Act."

Dedicated to those who lost their lives while serving on the small craft of the Army Transportation Corps— Water Division while enroute to or within the European Theatre of Operations 1944-45.

TABLE OF CONTENTS

FOREWORD

World War II was probably the last global war that will have been fought on land, sea and air with involvement of all the great powers of the world. The Ordeal of Convoy NY 119 was not a major military incident of that war, yet it was unique, heroic at times, and its story exemplifies the lessons of all wars. Its reading will give an insight into national attitudes and human nature that throughout history have undergone little change. It chronicles an episode that may not be repeated even though its lessons will be. This is history in its most valuable form. Furthermore, it has been told from the viewpoint of all hands, with the fascination of an historical novel.

Democracies have never been prepared for the bold military moves of dictators of other nations, citizen-soldiers or sailors or airmen are never trained for the best performance of which they are capable, professional military personnel exhibit a steadfastness and dedication to duty of which their nation can be proud, and the individual citizen draws on inner sources of strength to display courage and to overcome obstacles with intelligent adaptation to the situation. The saga of NY 119 reaffirms these truisms. In today's emergencies the public attitude seems to be such that we may doubt that history is likely to repeat itself, but read this story and be reassured that the attitudes and conduct evident in today's generation gap have existed before, yet did not eliminate displays of moral and physical courage.

At the time of Pearl Harbor, detailed preparations for moving a large American expeditionary force had not been made. Current inventories of transport, construction schedules and operating procedures for the use of the total U.S. transport capacity were hastily prepared. The United States Army that then included the Air Corps with its Air Transport Command also operated the troopships of the Army Transport Service. Thus the Army was heavily involved in water operations and all the efforts to develop the capacity to deploy and support the U.S. forces overseas. Logistic support of the forces already deployed overseas added to the burden of moving additional forces with their equipment and accompanying supplies. Two and one-half years after Pearl Harbor the support of the cross-channel invasion of Normandy placed an urgent requirement for means to unload the many ships awaiting discharge at their anchorages. In some cases of critical items, it was easier to ship another clearly documented load from the U.S. than to locate the items already aboard ships swinging on the hook just off shore. The tugs and barges of the convoy of this story would contribute substantially to easing the critical situation that had developed. This knowledge was known to the principals of this convoy and obviously motivated them in making sacrifices.

Although not so evident to those involved, release of the cargo ships awaiting discharge would also benefit the worldwide shortage of shipping needed to support other campaigns in Italy, in the Pacific, and in the China-Burma-India theaters of operation, as well as the movement of lend-lease material to our allies.

The inter-relationship of small unit actions and global strategy is well illustrated by Convoy NY 119. As a unique operation, one of a few of its kind, it deserves the painstaking research and interesting recital by Charles Dana Gibson.

Having been a transportation staff planner for the Joint Chiefs of Staff during World War II, and a commander of Army and Joint Commands since, I appreciate the translation of plans into reality, something that frequently seems miraculous. The part played by the participants in Convoy NY 119 illustrates the importance of the individual to the total picture of global strategy. Had the delivery of the convoy been more successful, other subsequent events could have been influenced for the better. It is never too late to learn, and The Ordeal of Convoy NY 119 offers many lessons. It can also be read for its interesting story alone. Small boat enthusiasts will find it describes what is probably an unknown experience to them and one they would not wish to repeat for themselves. The involvement of the U.S. Army in what might appear to be an exclusively naval matter will probably surprise some, but it was so, and adds still another dimension to the breadth of the story.

Rush B. Lincoln, Jr.
Maj. Gen. U.S. Army, Retired

Wellesley Hills, Massachusetts

ACKNOWLEDGEMENTS

The author gratefully acknowledges the assistance of the following persons without whose help the task of preparing the history of Convoy NY 119 would have been impossible.

Foremost: Captain Alfred L. Lind, USNR Retd. who spent many hours at his desk writing voluminous replies to my questions and acting as an instigator to prompt former members of TG 27.5 to jot down their recollections; Dr. Dean Allard, Office of Naval History for giving me that 'above and beyond assistance' which came in so handy to a novice historian; Colonel J.F. Smith, Chief, Transportation Resources, General Staff, for his expert knowledge of the art of untangling red tape; Mrs. Emma Jo Davis, Historian, Transportation Corps Museum for her aid in research and the giving of advice; Helen Becker, for the hours spent over a hot typewriter; Irene E. Gibson for her help in wading through cases of records at The Modern Military Record Center at Suitland, Maryland; Elizabeth K. Spruill, for her expert assistance in proofreading, typing and editing the fourth and final draft; last but not least, Carl Evers for a most accurate and dramatic cover painting.

* * * * * *

My gratitude goes out also to the many officers and men who gave of their time in order to provide me with first hand accounts of their personal experiences and photographs. They are arranged here by order of the ships on which they served—ranks are given if the person listed still has a known Reserve affiliation:

CTG STAFF: Sabin P. Sanger

USS ABNAKI (ATF 96): Robert Crowl. *Crowl was not on the ship at time of the Convoy but he helped give me a valuable insight into the command situation aboard that ship.

USS JOHN M. BERMINGHAM (DE 530): Reginald Auchincloss, H.H. Hannaman, Ambassador Robinson McIlvaine, Kenneth Trulsen.

USS EDGAR G. CHASE (DE 16): Russell V. Bradley (CO), Maurice B. Baker.

USS MASON (DE 529): Commander W.M. Blackford—USNR Retd (CO), Monroe J. Bails, Leonard Barton, Gordon Buchanan, Cassin W. Craig, Manuel De Cuir, Lorenzo A. Dufau, Byron F. Whitford.

USS MAUMEE (AO-2): Commander Hollis C. Ballard USNR Retd. (CO), Bruce Beagly, Julian Bobbitt, Lt. Commander John Dodson USN Retd., Dr. Aaron Z. Oberdorfer.

USS O'TOOLE (DE 527): Commander V.S. Mauldin USN Retd. (CO), Ethan A. Adams, John C. Boutall, Walden Bryant, Charles B. Dayton, Captain Edward P. Edmunds, USNR, Commander Marshall D. McDorman USNR.

USS POWERS (DE 528): Bailey Cowan, Lt. Commander Arthur McCarthy USN Retd., Lt. Commander Kendall C. Valentine USNR Retd., Henry G. Wenzel III.

USAT Y 34: William A. Purchase (CO)

LT 784: My thanks to the brother of Captain Clarke (deceased), Mr. B.W. Clarke who remembers some of the events which Captain Clarke had spoken of prior to his death.

USAT ST 510: Stanley Pasko

USAT ST 718: Wallace S. Olivey (CO)

USAT ST 719: Valentine B. Swartwout (CO); Clarence V. Harding, Ridgeway C. Leonard, John A. Thebus, Jr.

USAT ST 720: Charles Howard Buswell

* * * * * *

In addition to those that participated in the voyage of NY 119 and who provided me with recollections, I would also like to thank the following who either were involved in the shore side support of its preparation or arrival and who assisted me in assembling information relative to the history. Listed also are others whose assistance was invaluable:

Captain V.F. Prideaux of Truro Home Guard Forces; Lord Mayor of Plymouth, E.D. Nuttall, W. Best Harris (Librarian City of Plymouth), Col. Perry C. Euchner USAR Retd., Lt. Commander D.R. Benson RN, Col. C.F. Moninger USAR Retd., Martin J. Tuczinski, Thomas Hohmann, Col. Jean Gray USA, J.C. Bratten, William Nelson, Col. Emmett Scott USA Retd., Col. C.A. Noble USAR Retd.; Alexander Brown; Raymond Nurme; Anthony Nucci; Frank Braynard; Harvey Brouard; Marion L. Gibson; Harriette Winterer.

AND a number of others which space does not allow me to list, but to whom I am very thankful for their interest and help.

C.D.G.

AUTHOR'S NOTE

The Army vessels within Convoy NY 119 represented but a minuscule percentage of the 12,466 small craft and units of floating equipment that the United States Army Transportation Corps listed in August of 1945.

The Army then inventoried:

      510 freight supply boats

      104 Y-class tankers

      746 tugs of the LT, ST, and CT classes

    4,597 barges

      499 rescue boats

The Army, in World War II, was not only a large user of vessels classified as small craft, but they also operated a sizeable fleet of troop transports and large ocean-going freighters. These larger vessels were totaled on 31 July 1945 as 186 ships.

In the early 1950's the large vessels which then belonged to the Army were taken over by the Military Sea Transport Service, an agency operated by the Department of Navy. The Army however retained its small craft, the mission of which was to directly support the Army's logistical efforts although their role was to be restricted to that of rivers, harbors, and coastlines.

During the Vietnamese War, Army small craft not only performed a coastal and harbor supply role but also, equipped as gun barges and armed patrol craft, made up a large portion of the "River Assault Force" operating in the Maikong Delta.

The Army Transportation Corps currently operates a center at Fort Eustis, Virginia, for the training of both officers, warrant officers, and enlisted men, in the operation of the small fleet of tugs, freight supply ships, small troop-carrying craft, and patrol vessels which still remain under its control.

THE PROLOGUE

For those who are about to read of the preparation for Convoy NY 119 and the story of its crossing, it would be helpful to be aware of the situation as it existed in the Atlantic at the time of the Convoy's planning as it is extremely doubtful whether such a convoy would have been planned, much less executed during the height of the Battle of the Atlantic. To convoy such a slow speed conglomeration of unwieldly vessels during the dark days of 1942 and 1943 would have been to say the least, an over-consumption of a scarce commodity, namely escort vessels. Secondly, even with a large number of escorts, getting such a potpourri of ships past a wolf pack of German submarines would have been nearly impossible.

* * * * * * *

Following is a somewhat sketchy but I trust comprehensive portrayal of the Atlantic battle prior to September of 1944:

The War in the Atlantic was well underway for the United States long before it made a formal declaration of hostilities. It really started for the Americans when the SS ROBIN MOOR, a U.S. merchantman en route from the United States to South Africa with a general cargo was sunk by a German submarine on May 21, 1941. The United States Navy became directly if unknowingly involved when the U 203 tried unsuccessfully to sink the battleship TEXAS on June 20, 1941, although this incident was undiscovered by U.S. authorities until after the end of the War when a search of German naval documents disclosed it. The U 203's log records her attempts to gain a favorable attack position which she failed to do despite sixteen hours of effort.

On the 7th of July 1941, the United States relieved the British garrison then stationed on Iceland and it was with this act that although neutral, the U.S. started a sequence of steps which soon led it toward becoming a beligerent in the Atlantic blood bath.

On September 4th, the USS GREER, a destroyer en route from the United States to Iceland, was warned by aircraft of a German U boat across her path whereupon she lowered her sound gear and began tracking the submarine. The plane, a Britisher circling overhead, asked the GREER's skipper whether he was planning to attack. Being told that the GREER did not intend to do so, the British plane dropped a cluster of depth charges on the head of the German. The sub Captain, naturally unknowing as to who had dropped the charges, launched a torpedo toward the GREER which missed. The American then counter attacked with depth charges and ten minutes later the U boat fired a second torpedo which again missed. The destroyer eventually lost sound contact and abandoned the hunt.

The episode involving the GREER was just what the doctor had ordered insofar as President Roosevelt was concerned since he badly needed a justification for the United States' action in garrisoning Iceland. Swiftly the State Department propaganda machine went into high gear accusing Germany of "piracy on the high seas", this being shortly followed by what Roosevelt had intended all along which was an Executive declaration that; "from now on, if German or Italian vessels of war enter waters, the protection of which is necessary for American defense, they do so at their own risk."—The United States deemed these waters to be the entire western half of the North Atlantic. In September the U.S. Navy even went so far as to secretly tell the British that they would bottle up the Denmark Straits against incursion by German surface raiders. The British were also privately informed that the U.S. would lend them some ships from the Atlantic Fleet should the German pocket battleships break out into the open ocean.

On the 15th of October 1941, the American destroyers PLUNKETT, LIVERMORE, KEARNY, GREER and DECATUR participated in repelling a U boat "wolf pack" attack against a convoy south of Iceland. So engaged, they themselves became the recipients of German retaliation—the KEARNY being badly damaged although able to reach Iceland under her own power. Following this episode and some fifteen days later the USS REUBEN JAMES was torpedoed while escorting a convoy 600 miles west of Iceland— all her officers and over two-thirds of her men were lost.

By the time of our official entry into the War on December 8, 1941, the United States Navy was not new to the combat role it was to play but it is doubtful that at that time anyone anticipated the heavy sinking of ships with accompanying loss of life which was to follow. The victims were to be mainly from the American and Allied Merchant Marines; the British Merchant Navy alone losing over 29,000 men, the American Merchant Marine approximately 5,000 (although this number does not include civilian seamen employed by the U.S. Army Transport Service). Additionally there were hundreds lost from the Naval Armed Guards and from the escort forces.

Casualties during the first two months of the War were unimpressive but business picked up for the Germans somewhat in February when Convoy ON 67 had six ships torpedoed out of a total of thirty five. The next ON convoy lost two more. If it is asked, "Where were the expected heavy attacks against the transatlantic convoys—where were the submarines?", the answer is that they, the Germans, were preparing themselves for the real assault that was to follow which was not to be in the North Altantic but rather along the United States Eastern Sea Frontiers and in the Caribbean.

* * * * * * *

The first attack along the United States coast was when the CYCLOPS, a British steamer, was torpedoed some 300 miles east of Cape Cod. During the following months much hostile activity occurred directly off our shores, where, due to an acute shortage of patrol vessels, the Germans operated with almost complete immunity. When the attacks began in earnest, the submarines would often launch their torpedoes from the surface on which the attacker had drifted awaiting a vessel to pass between it and the lights ashore, thus silhouetting the victim. The civilian communities, apparently having no comprehension of what it was like to be a merchant seaman dying in a pool of flaming oil, were unresponsive to pleas from the Navy to dim the lights of coastal cities. In fact, when such a proposal was made along the southern Florida coast, screams of protest arose claiming that the "tourist season would be ruined". This was an area particularly hazardous for southbound shipping as ship Masters in order to escape the full northerly set of the Gulf Stream were forced to hug the coastal reefs thus putting them in some areas within three to five miles of the lights of "pleasuredom". It wasn't until mid-April that the government finally got tough and ordered waterfront lights and advertising signs extinguished, meanwhile many seamen died unnecessarily. The slaughter along our Atlantic coast was then being carried on in such safety for the attackers that the submarines in full daylight would lie on the surface watching their victims die while they in turn took photographs.

To fight off this onslaught, the Navy in April of 1942 had at its disposal only twenty-three large patrol craft and forty-two small ones less than eighty three feet long. Additionally there were three almost useless World War I PCs and twelve old "Eagle Boats" along with a few converted yachts. Reciprocating by coming to our aid, the British lent twenty-two converted trawlers crewed with experienced officers and men which helped, but fell far short of what was needed.

Things were so bad for the merchantmen that the tanker O.A. KNUDSEN was attacked three times in twelve hours by three different U boats, the final attack sinking her—all the time she had been frantically sending out distress signals, yet not one patrol vessel or plane was available to come to her rescue. All sorts of vessels were being sunk including sailing ships and tug boats towing barges. Those who weren't torpedoed were being shelled and machine gunned. Even proximity to port was no guarantee of safety as a tanker was torpedoed while maneuvering to pick up a harbor pilot off Cape Henry.

Meanwhile anything the Navy could fly or float, whether it was military or civilian was being thrown into the breech. This included Civilian Air Patrol (C.A.P.) single engine planes armed with hand grenades and home-made bombs. The small civilian crewed planes, strange as it may seem, were highly effective, not because of their potential destructive power against Germany's U boat arm but rather due to their usefulness in keeping subs below the surface. The C.A.P. although never having a confirmed sub kill, was invaluable for the reason already given plus that of providing sighting reports of submarines and merchant ship survivors—they continued doing yeoman service up to the end of the War while losing twenty-six planes and many of their personnel in the process.

* * * * * * *

Starting in May and continuing into the summer, submarine activity began shifting from the Eastern Sea Frontier into the Gulf of Mexico and the Caribbean. A concentration of shipping near the entrance to the Straits of Florida and to that of the Mississippi Delta were major attack centers—in May, June and July there were twenty-two reported sinkings near the mouth of the Mississippi alone.

* * * * * * *

From February on, U boat action shifted mainly to the Caribbean where it concentrated against the petroleum and bauxite trades. One hundred and fourteen ships were sunk there between the end of January and the end of July. During June, the U boats claimed more tonnage sunk in the Caribbean and in the Gulf of Mexico than they had sunk over the entire world during any month previous to 1942. One submarine, the U 161, had the audacity on March 10th to enter the Harbor of Castries, St. Lucia, now a popular West Indian tourist resort, where she torpedoed the Canadian steamer LADY NELSON and another ship, both of whom were lying lit alongside the dock. An American tanker, her skipper more cautious in his policies, was nearby at anchor but blacked out thus missing the lethal attention of the submarine. Off Port of Spain, Trinidad two cargo vessels were sunk while at anchor in the roadstead—afterwards the cocky German skipper defiantly steamed out on the surface with his running lights brightly lit.

During the early months of 1942, the War at sea in the Atlantic was pretty much one-sided as it wasn't until March that the first U boat was sunk—this off Newfoundland where it was the recipient of an air attack, being one of the few kills made during the first half of the year.

* * * * * * *

By the middle of the summer, American flag vessels were joining British merchantmen in the great convoys then being sent to Murmansk in an attempt to supply the beleaguered Russians. These were classified with a PQ numeral designation of which some of the more unfortunate ones had over half of their vessels torpedoed or bombed. PQ 16 was attacked for six days straight being on the receiving end of continual daylight aerial bombing from German planes operating out of Norway, the planes being aided and abetted by submarines which continually probed for weaknesses in the convoy's escort screen. Another, PQ 17, lost so many ships that when it was all over it was estimated that waiting ashore along the Russian coast for rescue were over 1,300 survivors, 581 of them being Americans.

To his lasting credit, it must be remembered that the American merchant seaman who was the major victim of the bloodletting was a civilian volunteer whose "enlistment" ran out with the termination of each voyage—yet the ships which departed American ports into this bloody cauldron were being crewed by seamen fully aware of what lay before them and who were being compensated at a rate not in excess of what the war production industry was offering ashore. Sailing with them went the "Armed Guard", a force of Navy gunners (in the early days some Army personnel were included in the gun crews). The Navy boys were usually commanded by a young naval reserve Ensign or Lt. jg and when an officer was not available, then a petty officer. The job of the Armed Guard was to man the deck guns of each merchantman, although at the beginning of the War since most of the Armed Guard detachments were skeletal in strength, they had to be heavily augmented with merchant mariners, none of which had any gunnery training whatsoever.

By the late summer and the early fall of 1942, the United States was being faced with a serious shortage of merchant vessels and the personnel to man them thus causing the balance of power in the Atlantic to begin tilting in favor of Admiral Dönitz and his submarine force. Yet within a few months the American genius for mass production began to turn out replacement ships at a hitherto before unbelievable rate. The men to man them were being trained and put aboard before the paint on the ships' decks was completely dried. As the war progressed and the manpower situation became acute the age minimum for merchant marine personnel was dropped from seventeen years of age to sixteen. Even men in their late sixties who had prior experience at sea were asked to return and many of them did.

* * * * * * *

The trans-Atlantic convoy routes, unlike the eastern seaboard and southern waters were relatively safe, at least until early August of 1942—a date which marked the advent of the German tactic of full scale "wolf pack" attack. Although this method of offense had been in the planning stage for a considerable period of time, it wasn't until the Germans had accelerated their U boat production capabilities that the plan was put into widespread use. The reason that the Atlantic convoy routes were selected by Admiral Dönitz for this new offensive, was that unlike the Eastern Sea Frontier, the Gulf, the Caribbean and the south Atlantic, the northern and middle Atlantic were the only areas in which his packs could operate without overexposing themselves to Allied air surveillance and attack. The United States and Britain were hoping that negotiations then being carried on with the Portuguese would allow the basing of patrol planes in the Azore Islands which could fill this gap—the Portuguese however were jealously guarding their neutrality, still not sure as to who the victor would be so nothing came of the talks.

The German "wolf pack" attack system had as its scouting arm, wide ranging single operating reconnaissance submarines, which upon sighting a convoy would broadcast its location to German Submarine Headquarters (at that time located in western France)—orders would then be beamed out from HQ to any "Pack" within interception range which would then collectively converge upon the convoy. The system worked so well that not one single trans-Atlantic convoy escaped attack during the month of August. The following month the losses were not quite as serious yet eighty-eight ships went down in the Atlantic zone.

Those submarines still operating individually had moved their areas of operation away from the east coast and the Gulf and Caribbean to the west coast of Africa where in the Gulf of Guinea alone, fourteen vessels were sunk. Around the neighborhood of the Cape of Good Hope, twenty-four went down—all in the month of September. There were still not enough escorts to handle all the shipping routes and many of the merchant ships sailed alone which was the case with the African trade. Occasionally vessels southbound down the west coast of Africa with routing around the Cape of Good Hope to Suez would be convoyed, but this was far from offering complete safety as one Admiralty group designated as SL-25, lost eleven ships during October.

Back on the North Altantic convoy route, Convoy SC 107 in a three day action suffered the loss of fifteen of its ships. Another trans-Atlantic convoy following a more southerly route, lost fourteen ships out of forty-four—this in November.

* * * * * * *

What was to follow has been referred to in a number of ways: Admiral Morison has called it "The Mid Winter Blitz"; Captain John M. Waters, Jr. USCG, has referred to it in a book which he wrote, as the "Bloody Winter"—whatever the term, it was hell to those who participated. The months of January, February and March of 1943 were to the Germans that period in which they hoped to strangle off the life blood of the Allied effort toward the goal of building up troop and material strength in the British Isles preparatory to the Allied invasion of "Fortress Europe" which was to come in June of the following year.

For a seaman who loses his ship during the winter in the North Atlantic, his life expectancy is but a very few minutes in waters which often hover below 30° Fahrenheit. Unless a man is fortunate enough to abandon in a life boat he is as good as dead. Some of the merchant vessels provided their crews with survivors suits—heavy rubber one-piece garments which were designed to not only keep out the water but to keep the body's heat in—these worked fairly well but the problem was that the issue of them had been somewhat limited. Even with a suit on, one had to be picked up, not always possible under convoy attack. Fortunately for human life the heaviest toll of shipping consisted mainly of cargo vessels and tankers. Very few ships carrying troops were torpedoed, thus the loss of life that winter was kept from becoming astronomical.

One reason for the safety record of troop carriers, was that beginning in August of 1942 most troops were shipped overseas on large and very fast ex-luxury liners such as the EMPRESS OF BRITAIN, the QUEEN MARY, the QUEEN ELIZABETH and the United States merchant ship SS MARI-POSA. Later in the War the U.S. Army Transport Service and the United States Navy were to put many more vessels into this usage. In the case of the QUEENS because of their excessive speed, escorts could not pace them; therefore they traveled alone.

There were some unfortunate exceptions to the safety records for troop ships on the North Atlantic run, one disaster being the Army transport DORCHESTER which was torpedoed en route to Iceland with a total complement including merchant crew, Armed Guard and troops of over nine hundred fifty men; only two hundred and twenty-nine of them were saved. Another trooper that didn't make it was the SS HENRY R. MALLORY which was carrying a total of three hundred and eighty-four troops and Navy passengers along with one hundred and eleven in her crew and Armed Guard, bound also to Iceland. According to the record, sixty percent of her total complement went down with her.

All through this terrible winter, scores of ships, many of them with their entire crews were lost, yet by March the pendulum was beginning to swing back. More escorts were being added for convoy protection and science was bringing forth new techniques for use against the Germans; but before the winter was over Dönitz had racked up 337,852 tons of Allied shipping for the six months ending March 1943.

One of the saddest things during the battle that winter was the needless loss of life on merchant vessels due in part to a lack of centralized doctrine and poor individual ship discipline. A case in point was that of the SS PUERTO RICAN which was sunk to the north of Iceland in the early part of March. The one survivor who was picked up managed to save his life by taking the time to go below and put on his rubber life suit—obviously the Master of this vessel had not seen fit to mandate that these suits be worn at all times or at least that they be in the possession of an individual crew member no matter where he be.

An interesting anecdote concerning the independence of merchant seamen which sometimes led to their downfall is told by Admiral Morison in Volume I of his series: "The officers and crew of SS MATTHEW LUCKEN-BACH were so disgusted at the Convoy's not changing course after five ships had been torpedoed that they held a meeting and decided to straggle. But the U boats got her just the same."

* * * * * * *

The date April 6, 1942, marked the start of a change in the Battle of the Atlantic as it was on this date that the United States Navy unified its anti-submarine warfare command and it was out of this change in command structure that the famed "Hunter Killer Groups" emerged—each group to have as its nucleus one of the small escort carriers, their cargo so deadly to the submarine in waters where hitherto aircraft had not been known. Additionally, task group escort forces had now reached a numerical strength wherein in addition to providing a tight screen for a convoy, they could dispatch vessels to hunt down and stay over a submarine until the kill had been made. In August of 1943 funds were allocated for the production of 1,000 of new destroyer escorts (DE), vessels designed for the specific purpose of killing submarines. Actually only 178 of these sleek warships were commissioned in time to put to sea before the end of the War, however those that did played a most essential role toward tipping the balance. The addition of the DEs plus the submarine chasers and corvette class vessels which were being added to the Allied Navies in the Atlantic, created a less suicidal environment for the merchant mariner. By 1944, should a merchant ship become a straggler, no longer would she find herself along in a hostile ocean. Instead her crew members would discover what real happiness was—that of having a high-speed gray hull standing between them and the enemy below.

If there was any time that could be termed the turning point in the balance of power for the Battle of the Atlantic, it would probably be late April of 1943. The German submarine fleet was still strong yet Allied capability not only began to counteract it but was capable of blunting force with counter force. A case in point would be the story of Convoy ONS 5 which departed England on the 22nd of April and which consisted of forty-three merchantmen initially escorted by a Royal Naval group consisting of two destroyers, a frigate patrol vessel, four corvettes and two rescue trawlers. Abeam of Iceland they were joined by a third Royal Navy destroyer. On April 28th the Convoy was reported by a German scout the U 650 which was reconnoitering for a "wolf pack" of fifteen boats—fortunately for the Convoy the alerted "wolf pack" members sending in their positions and status reports to Admiral Dönitz gave away their locations to the escorts. The Commander Task Group, Commander T.W. Gretton RN sent out his flankers on sweeps to keep down and hopefully scare off the undersea attackers. Since the sub commanders were jabbering at a sustained rate over their radios, it wasn't difficult through the use of high frequency direction finders (at that time a secret weapon of the Allies) to locate one sub after another forcing them to submerge, thus reducing their speed substantially. Unable to communicate further, the submariners began their attacks in an uncoordinated manner which lost them the advantage of a simultaneous assault, which had it occurred, would have been extremely difficult for the escorts to counteract. During the night of the 28th and 29th of April, two U boats were badly damaged by depth bombs which forced them to leave the Pack and head toward base for repair. At dawn on the 29th, the Pack made its first kill sinking the American freighter SS McKEESPORT—all but one man was rescued by one of the trailing trawlers.

That night, a U.S. Navy patrol plane operating out of Iceland and off to the Convoy's flank, spotted a submarine on the surface. Executing a fast bomb run it caused a third damaged German to "chuck it" and head for the repair yard. By now a heavy gale had blown up bringing with it blinding snow. Under the storm's cover, one of the subs, the U 192, tried breaching the convoy screen but was driven off.

The following day and the next the Convoy was saved from attack by two factors: the extremely bad weather and the air cover provided by bombers flying out from Greenland and Iceland, effective in keeping the submarines submerged; thus severely reducing their approach speed which meant that the U boats were unable to arrive at an attack posture.

By May the 2nd, the gale had blown itself out whereupon two escorts were sent to round up the stragglers. No sooner had the escort vessels bunched ten of these stern followers into an assemblage of order than a heavy fog set in preventing a close-in return to the Convoy. The two escorts then stayed with the stragglers.

The "Achilles' Heel" of the escort group now began to become apparent; that of its short battle speed endurance as many of its ships were reaching the point of exhaustion insofar as their fuel capacities were concerned. Subsequently threatened, Gretton detached two of the neediest escorts to Iceland and Nova Scotia respectively. One of the ships was DUNCAN, the flagship of Gretton, so the overall commmand now went to Lt. Commander R.E. Sherwood RN.

By the morning of the 4th of May there were only seven vessels left in the screen, all right under normal circumstances but not now as there appeared to be an extraordinary build-up of German radio transmissions indicating a large concentration of U boats zeroing in on the Convoy. What the Allied group didn't know was the large number of U boats. Fifty-one wolves were then being routed in by Dönitz to feed off ON 5.

Fate was with the Allies as the Convoy had by now progressed far enough to the westward so that it came under the long range protection of a Canadian air umbrella. The planes, (Catalinas) taking over from the Greenland squadron, continued to successfully keep the U boats submerged thus blunting their attack capabilities. One Catalina, spotting a German on the surface sunk the U 630 on its first bombing run. Thirty of the fifty-one U boats were organized into group "Fink" which had had the time to distribute itself so as to close in from all four directions. Working in groups of two's and three's they were able to sink some stragglers the night of May the 4th and although unable to penetrate the escort screen they did fire torpedoes into the main body of the Convoy. The German score for the evening's work was seven merchantmen.

One of the rescue trawlers, the NORTHERN SPRAY having taken aboard a hundred and fifty survivors which was her capacity, left the Convoy and headed into St. Johns, Newfoundland to unload.

By mid-morning "Fink" closed in again and before the day was over it had sunk five more merchant ships—a corvette trying to get revenge killed one of the wolves.

That night with the Convoy in close proximity to Newfoundland, fifteen U boats began their attack approach but fortunately a heavy fog descended making the shooting conditions very poor for the Germans. The Pack paced the Convoy waiting for a let up in the poor visibility during which time Sherwood sent his escorts out to track down every radar and sonar contact that could be made. Another submarine, the U 638, was sent to the bottom by this method. Leaving the screen perimeter some time during the night, HMS ORIBI on her way to assist one of the corvettes which was depth charging a submerged U boat, sighted the U 125 within fifty yards of her bow. The ORIBI rammed just as the U boat was beginning her crash dive and an hour later the damaged U 125 was on the surface astern of the Convoy in the process of trying to call in another U boat to take off her crew. She was sighted by an escort and finished off with gun fire.

By the time the sun had come up to lighten the foggy mist, a Canadian surface escort group rushing out from Newfoundland arrived to give needed re-enforcement. At this point ONS-5's remaining screen was dangerously low on depth charges. With the arrival of the newcomers, two more U boats were destroyed and two more damaged. Before the noon hour had passed, Dönitz still in radio contract with his Pack and not liking the odds, called off his wolves.

Freed of the peril from submarines, the Convoy was still a long way from being in the clear as she was to proceed for the next two days and nights in a dense fog, her merchant ships (none of them equipped with radar) keeping station by whistle signals and by following raft lights towed astern of the vessels ahead of them. When it was finally over, the Convoy, merchantmen and Navy men alike, received via radio from Winston Churchill the following understated praise: "The Prime Minister compliments the Convoy on steady courage during the late attacks."

If what the Germans had thrown at ONS-5 in late April and early May of 1943 had been committed to battle two months before, there is little doubt because of the then existing Allied strength, that the entire unit, both (merchantships and escorts) would have been annihilated. Yet faced with the awesome odds of what had been sent against it, only thirteen of the merchantships had been lost out of a total of forty-three. Despite the fact that just six submarines were destroyed by the escort force, ONS-5 can be tactically counted as a victory on the part of the Allied Navies.

* * * * * * *

The convoy that followed, westbound from the British Isles, was ONS-6. Reconnoitered by a submarine on the 6th of May just south and east of Iceland, a "Wolf Pack" was alerted to close in. No sooner had the skippers of the Pack surfaced their craft to run an intercept than they sighted aircraft overhead thus forcing their boats down. None of them got even close to the Convoy. On the morning of the 9th, ONS-6's escort joined by a carrier group which insured its safe passage for the rest of the way to Canada.

The next convoy, ONS-7 lost one of its vessels on the 17th of May but this was to be the last Allied ship sunk either eastbound or westbound in the North Atlantic until mid-September.

* * * * * * *

Meanwhile convoys bound to the European Theater from New York and taking a more southerly route along the latitude of the Azores, did receive some lethal damage but this kept getting less and less as the escort carrier groups not only reinforced the close screens but acted as independent "Hunters-Killers".

Adding to the Germans' woes, the British were then carrying on a concentrated offensive in the Bay of Biscay off the west coast of France making it almost impossible for a submarine to take the open sea without either being actually attacked or at least forced to crash dive in the shallow waters. In May, the Germans had forty-one of their submarines sunk, most of them with total crew losses. It should be noted that because of the nature of underseas warfare, the majority of the U boats which were sunk had their pressure hulls ruptured by depth charges while beneath the surface, thus fatalities were more often than not one hundred percent. At the end of the War the Germans claimed that they had lost by enemy action over 32,000 submariners and over 650 subs, yet because of extraordinary leadership on the part of Dönitz, the morale of the Nazi underseas fleet remained high up to until the very end of hostilities.

By July of 1943 there was little doubt left as to who was winning the war at sea—in that month thirty-seven German and eight Italian subs were sunk by Allied action in the Atlantic area while at the same time and in the same area, only twenty-four Allied merchantmen went down. (Admiral Morison the Historian, compares this score to that of May 1942 when only four U boats were sunk. But the loss to Allied merchant shipping was one hundred and twenty vessels.)

The Germans began to try counter balancing innovations in order to equalize Allied strength. One of these was the use of "milch cow" tanker submarines which were designed to refuel U boats at sea thus prolonging their war cruising time. This tactic helped, yet the radio traffic necessary to home in the subs towards their "milch cows" would very often give their positions away to the Allied "Hunter-Killer" groups thus further jeopardizing the already strained resources of Admiral Dönitz. (Here it might be noted that earlier in the War the Germans often used conventional surface tankers to refuel their submarines at sea but most of these had been sunk by 1943 as had the German blockade runners many of whom had the capability of refueling submarines.)

The reader should not get the false impression that the summer of 1943 was all honey and roses for the Allies insofar as submarine attacks were concerned. There was activity aplenty but in parts of Oceania other than in the North and Central Atlantic. The South Atlantic and Mediterranean were still losing shipping and in the Indian Ocean things were quite serious from the standpoint of Allied losses, caused not only by the German underseas fleet but also from some Japanese subs which were working as close as Zanzibar off the East African coast.

* * * * * * *

On the 20th of September the Germans put to trial one of their new inventions specifically designed for use against naval escorts—the acoustic torpedo which successfully crippled the destroyer HMS LAGAN. In the same convoy attack two freighters in ballast were sunk, one of which the DOUGLASS, was an experiment in mixed racial crews having as a matter of fact, a black Master. An intriguing side light was that the DOUGLASS had aboard a girl stowaway; fortunately she was rescued.

During the same month, other trans-Atlantic convoys were attacked but none of them took the punishment that had been meted out to their counterparts the previous winter.

* * * * * * *

Early 1944 was historic for the Germans, not because of successes but because of the experimental introduction of the "Schnorchel"; a device whereby a submarine could travel submerged while breathing through its "Schnorchel" which had the appearance of an exaggerated periscope—the device also served to exhaust diesel engine fumes thus allowing a submarine to run at top speed on her diesels while partially submerged consequently preventing a commander from having to risk his vessel on the surface. The early "schnorchelers" were employed on nuisiance raids against the east coast of the United States but this campaign was quite limited and unsuccessful insofar as tonnage sunk; Yet it did achieve the purpose of tying up a large number of anti-submarine vessels which could have been beneficially used elsewhere. For the Germans, it also proved, that particularly in shallow waters, a "Schnorchel" equipped sub could operate with relative safety even in heavily patrolled enemy seas.

The invasion against "Fortress Europe" commencing June 6th, mandated Dönitz to put what few "Schnorchelers" he then had against the trans-Channel convoys. The Germans were to discover that this traffic was so heavily and efficiently escorted and the German submarine force despite its new device, then so numerically weak, that little damage could be done to the Allies.

* * * * * * *

By mid-September of 1944, which was the time that NY 119 was being readied, there were probably not more than half a dozen German U boats at large in the open Atlantic. Those that were on patrol were laying quietly, their captains and crews not only anxious to avoid testing the efficiency of an escort's screen but also of exposing themselves to almost certain death from the "Hunter-Killer" groups. NY 119 was thus privileged to make its crossing and entry into the English Channel at a time when Germany's underseas fleet was at its lowest operational level since 1940.

This peaceful scene was shortly to change, specifically in northern European waters when commencing in mid-December (approximately six weeks after the Convoy's crossing) Admiral Dönitz unleashed his newly launched "Schnorchelers". What would have happened to NY 119 had it entered the Channel as late as January 1945 is a matter for speculation.

There is little doubt though that had the Convoy been conceived and sent across the Atlantic any time from the summer of 1942 on through the winter of 1943, it most probably would have been rendered inoperative before it reached mid-Atlantic—imagine if you will as you read on what would have been the situation had the MAUMEE (the Convoy's oiler), been torpedoed and sunk somewhere between the east coast of the United States and the Azore Islands. This would have stopped not only the LT tugs in their tracks along with the barges but also the escort vessels leaving the whole assemblage less the Y Boats in the position of clay ducks in a shooting gallery. The Convoy or most of it could have been destroyed and most probably would have been. Even if it had made it safely to off the Western Approaches, then E Boats which were then based in force at north-western French ports (these flotillas were sent to Channel ports further to the east following the invasion in June) would have torn NY 119 to shreds.

In summary, it is inconceivable that a convoy such as NY 119 could have been routed trans-Atlantic unless the Battle of the Atlantic had been at a very low peak insofar as German naval strength was concerned.

End of Prologue

INTRODUCTION

NAVAL MESSAGE   NAVY DEPARTMENT

DRAFTER   F — 313

FROM COMINCH (Commander in Chief)   PRIORITY
                                          RUSH

DATE   14 AUGUST 1944   COMEASTSEAFRON
                                   (C.O. Eastern Sea Frontier)

FOR CODEROOM   0009/15   CINCLANT
                                   (Cmdr. in Chief Atlantic)
                                   PD NEW YORK (Port Director USN)
                                   ADMIRALTY (British Navy)
                                   COMNAVEU (USN Europe)
                                   P D CHARLESTON (Port Director USN)

COMEASTSEAFRON SAIL IN CONVOY 5 SEPTEMBER OR AS SOON THEREAFTER AS READY THE FOLLOWING ARMY CRAFT FROM NEW YORK TO UNITED KINGDOM:

     7 — LARGE TUGS, EACH TOWING 2 CAR FLOATS
     1 — LARGE TUG TOWING 1 CRANE BARGE[1]
     2 — UNENCUMBERED LARGE TUGS AND FROM 10 TO 15
            SMALL 85' TUGS
   15 — SMALL TANKERS (Y BOATS)

CHARACTERISTICS OF ABOVE CRAFT SIMILAR TO CORRESPONDING TYPES SAILED IN CONVOY NY 118. COMEASTSEAFRON ARRANGE DETAILS OF CONVOY ASSEMBLY DIRECT WITH COMMANDING GENERAL PORT OF EMBARKATION NEW YORK, WHO WILL FURNISH HULL NUMBERS OF VESSELS TO BE INCLUDED IN CONVOY. CINCLANT PROVIDE ESCORT AND ESCORT OILER.

S E C R E T

COMINCH   ORIG

39.....FX 37.....ARMY CHIEF OF STAFF.....ADM STARK.....

Thus began the short gestation period of a special convoy which was to be born and named NY 119 on September 23, 1944. On that date Commander Alfred L. Lind[2], a Reserve Officer, was to become its guardian and given the overall responsibility to shepherd it safely to its port of delivery—Falmouth, England.

Lind commanded Destroyer Escort (DE) Division 80 and flew his pennant in the USS O'TOOLE. Other DEs of his group were the USS POWERS, USS MASON, USS BERMINGHAM, and the USS CHASE. For the mission of escorting Convoy NY 119, Lind's escort group was designated Task Group 27.5 and was initially enlarged by the addition of a fleet oiler, the USS MAUMEE and later, the Navy seagoing fleet tug, USS ABNAKI.

It was not common even as late as 1944 for a reserve officer such as Lind to commond a Destroyer Escort Division. Of the 68 naval officers commanding Atlantic groups, only 14, or about 20%, were reservists. A reservist, given such a responsibility, had to be an extremely able officer with the capability to function tirelessly and efficiently in situations not ordinarily encountered under fleet operational conditions. Not only was there the enemy below to reckon with, but there was the equally difficult task of moulding the civilian vessels within a convoy command into a controllable entity. Lind had been tried and proven, but the assignment of NY 119 was something else again, and a cause of worry from the onset. It was fortunate for his peace of mind at the time, that he was unaware that NY 119 was to become "the worst of them all."

The journey of NY 119 was to traverse 3539 nautical miles during a period of 30 days. Its rate of advance was to average 4.74 miles per hour. It was to encounter winds gusting to 90 mph and seas that roared down from crests estimated at heights up to sixty feet. Of the 65 vessels named within the convoy, 14 of them were small 85 foot harbor tugs designed to go no further than a harbor's entrance. Fifteen more were "Y" tankers built for short coastal runs and inland waterway use and not to face the violent temper of the North Atlantic. The 14 pick-a-backed barges were mostly of a condition unfit for the rigors of the open ocean. Some of them had been built sixteen years before. The Army Transport Service (ATS)* civilian crews that were to man this incredible armada, were in part, the last scrapings available from the exhausted wartime manpower pools. Some of them were misfits, unable to find further employment on conventional merchant ships. Others were too old or too young for military service. Many, both officers and seamen, were untrained in the basic elements of seamanship. Fortunately there were a few, mainly Scandinavians, who, attracted by American pay rates, provided the talents and abilities that were to prove essential to

*By the Fall of 1944 the name of the Army Transport Service had been officially changed to that of Transportation Corps, Water Division (civilian), but its members still referred to themselves as A.T.S.

survival.[3] There were others, good men, though at first green, who learned seamanship enroute and gained a seagoing education that under ordinary peacetime conditions would have taken years. Some of the seamen of NY 119 would not survive the passage. Others who lost their ships but lived were to be dumped on the wharves of an English port, where, because of confusion on the part of Port Command, they were reduced to the status of penniless beggars. This followed days of thirst, hunger, violent seasickness, and stark terror.

The naval escort crews that were to nursemaid and herd this motley bunch were, for the most part, pretty green themselves. Of the officers there were a few, such as Lieutenant "Vic" Mauldin, C.O. of the O'TOOLE, who wore the Naval Academy ring. Others like Lieutenant (JG) Larry Phipps, Lind's towing specialist, were up from the ranks. A handful of officers with Merchant Marine origins could be found, and the senior USNR's had experienced the hard knocks of the sea before. But by and large, many of the naval officers of TG 27.5 were as new to the sea as were the civilians of the Army craft. The great difference, though, was the discipline, excellent training, and esprit de corps to be found among the Navy's destroyer force. The DEs also had the benefit of a cadre of seasoned senior petty officers.

The destroyer escorts were themselves, like many of their junior officers, recently commissioned, but again, there was a marked difference between them and the Army ships. The DEs had undergone shake down and some operational duty with the crews that now manned them. The Army tugs and Ys had, in most instances, just come from the builders' yards, often with different crews than were to sail them overseas.

The fact that NY 119 survived is mute testimony to the skills, discipline, and dedication of the U.S. Navy and to many of the men of the Army's cockleshell fleet which, after 30 days and 3 hours, finally arrived, exhausted, in Falmouth, England. Once there, they were to find that the rushed urgency of their passage was not appreciated locally. Many of them would be ordered to leave the shelter of harbor within hours of entry to help salvage the flotsam of their passage—a move that was to cause Lind great agitation.

NY 119 was a product of the conditions of 1944. It was a victim of the violence of the sea. It is a mixed story of incompetency, high professionalism, dereliction and dedication, cowardness and valor.

* * * * * * *

Commander Lind, unaware of future events to follow but apprehensive of the worst, began a complete study of SECRET reports concerning earlier 1944 Convoys NY 118 and its predecessor, NY 78. Both of them had been composed of small craft. NY 78 also had had a large number of towed barges arranged in "pick-a-back" style. This was a method whereby a compartmented steel barge (BCF) was dry docked, then flooded, whereupon another barge, wooden (BCL) or perhaps a steel unit, was floated atop and secured. Next, the lower barge was pumped out and thence the whole unit floated, making a double-tiered single barge.

Commander Task Group 27.5 (CTG 27.5) not having a full knowledge of Merchant Marine crewing practices or vessel designations, may have been unaware of crewing differences in that the earlier NY 78 had been partly composed of War Shipping Administration (WSA) tugs crewed by licensed Merchant Marine officers and certificated seamen, thus differing from his assignment. Also the WSA tugs were far more powerful and better built than the Army tugs of NY 119 with which he must deal. Additionally, within NY 78 were quite a few Navy tugs, equal in power and efficiency to the WSA vessels, and both with experienced and well disciplined crews. The tows of NY 78 were in better condition at the onset than Lind's. Further, the weather it encountered was of a generally moderate nature and not worse than normally to be expected in the Atlantic. This Convoy, during the period of its transit from March 25 to April 19, 1944, had lost one vessel, a Navy tug, the ATR 98. She had collided with another Navy tug, the ABNAKI, a vessel soon to be included within NY 119. During that voyage, four vessels, three Navy and one WSA, had parted their tow lines. According to the Commander Task Group of NY 78, these breakages may have been caused by the vessels not properly carrying out towing procedure orders. This failure of obeying instructions was to become a continuous thorn in the side of Lind.

NY 78, although spared by the weather, did pick up an enemy sound contact two days before the Convoy reached England. After an attack by screening vessels, contact faded. CTG reported a probable kill.[4]

Of particular interest in the report of NY 78 was the comment concerning lack of preparations to receive the Convoy by the Army port authorities at Falmouth, England. Harbor conditions were such that the ships and tows were forced to lie outside in the outer harbor being thus vulnerable to enemy E boat attack. It was not until four days later that this situation was corrected and the vessels safely sheltered. The officer in charge at Falmouth was Captain Hurst, T.C., U.S. Army. This was the same officer that Lind was to deal with five months later.

The report of NY 118 by Commander C.R. Simmers, USN (later a Captain) was more relevant to Lind's purpose. Simmers' Convoy had left New York on July 23, 1944, arriving in Falmouth on August 17. This convoy had traveled the same routing now planned for NY 119. The vessels were similar, having been composed of LTs (Army large tugs, ranging from wooden 113 footers to steel 149 footers); Y Army boats (self-propelled tanker barges) varying in length, but averaging around 180 feet overall; and STs (Army small tugs, 85 footers, designed for harbor towing and push service).

The crews were also alike. They were not, in the true sense of the word, members of the Merchant Marine, but rather civilian personnel employed by the War Department. A proportion of them serving as officers held Merchant Marine licenses as Masters, Mates, or Engineers. Most of those serving in licensed capacities did so on large Army transports and hospital ships. A few, though, had elected the small craft on which they were generally signed on in a capacity senior to their licensed ratings. It was not unusual, for instance, to find officers with Third Mates licenses holding down a Master's job on an LT or a Y boat. Neither was it difficult to meet LT Chief Officers whose sole professional document was an Able Bodied Seaman's certificate. A few of the small craft officers, mainly Masters, held foreign licenses: Scandinavian, Panamanian, or Greek. Others of the Army small craft were officered by graduates from the New Orleans and St. Petersburg Mates and Engineer's Schools—cram course establishments run by the War Shipping Administration under contract to the Army, which turned out a total of 2,588 junior marine officers to man the Army's fleets. The personnel that served as deck hands or as "black gang" were a motley and diversified group. Some were no longer on good terms with their maritime unions or men who, because of shore leave termination, joined to prevent a call-up by Selective Service.[5] Others were foreign seamen, without American papers, many of whom had jumped foreign ships. Others were youngsters of pre-draft age, who, dissatisfied with school and lured by adventure, had signed up with A.T.S. or the Maritime Service. The training of these green hands varied. The Maritime Service training, considering the heavy demands for seamen, was the most thorough and included usually two months of instruction with a smattering of discipline thrown in. The A.T.S. program, if one wants to call it a program, consisted of either putting a youngster on a harbor-based tug for "on the job training" or assigning him to the local training ship. The author's own experience in October of 1944 at Charleston, S.C., could be considered somewhat typical. After signing obligatory papers and taking a perfunctory physical, he was assigned to a docked freighter of World War I vintage, THE M/S WINANS, upon which the "training" consisted of standing security watches and listening to "sailor tales." Two weeks later, blissfully ignorant, even of knot-tying or how to abandon ship, he was assigned as a deck hand to an LT which five days later began its maiden trans-Atlantic voyage to the United Kingdom (later Convoy CK 4). Thus were ATS small craft manned. A sort of no questions asked, "Foreign Legion of the Sea."

Simmers' NY 118 report, by his own admission, could not be considered highly informative concerning difficult weather, in that the prevailing conditions during that trip were exceptionally good. Only for brief intervals did his group experience winds or seas of any consequence. How a barge convoy or its personnel would react under gale conditions was unanswerable by Simmers.[6] The pick-a-back barges, like those of NY 78, were serviceable and of recent vintage and created little trouble, except for an occasional pumping. Routine procedure was the norm except for a change in convoy routing west of the Azores to avoid contact with a U boat reported by CINCLANT.

Abeam of Corvo in the Azores, the Y tankers of NY 118—Y 74, Y76, Y 77, and Y 79—were detached with one escorting destroyer. After a one-day layover in Horta, Azores, a move Simmers later felt was unnecessary, the five ships left for Oran, Africa. The departure from Horta involved some diplomatic parley on the part of the escort skipper. It seems three crew members from Y 79 had left the vessel without a formal "OK." Their return, just before sailing, was under the escort of local police followed shortly by a screaming delegation of "ladies of the night," who, presumably were incensed by lack of promised dollars. Some of the "salts" from Y 77 must have also slipped away for a brief shoreside interlude since a few days later the medical officer from the escort transferred over to delouse them. Lind, reading this, wrote off Horta as a possible liberty port.

Entry at Falmouth for Convoy NY 118 went smoothly except for the towed STs, who loosed themselves "by the simple expedient of unshackling their 800 foot 1 1/8 inch diameter wire hawsers which were allowed to sink unbuoyed." (Materials of this nature were not too easily come by in the steel-short war years.) Simmers reported this to Army authorities upon landing, with the suggestion that disciplinary action be taken against the offenders. He was politely told it was an Army affair. Before leaving Falmouth, Commander Simmers requested Captain Hurst to retrieve Navy radios from the Army ships. This was done, but all the expensive and hard-to-come-by coaxial cable attached to the sets was ruined by careless removal.

In concluding his report, Simmers warned of some of the deficiencies of the Army craft:

1. The electric steering gear in the Y boats was of poor design and poorly located.[7]
2. STs had poor water carrying arrangements that should be corrected prior to departure. (It is assumed he meant the poorly-sealed filler plates which were located at weather deck level.)
3. All Army craft were woefully deficient in machinery instruction books and blueprints. Nameplates on electrical units were missing

and, apparently, had never existed. Spare parts were difficult to obtain and insufficient in number.

4. Wooden LT tugs were dangerously unsafe, having no water tight compartments. Deck equipment on all tug craft was in need of changes and additions.

5. It was recommended that the Army should be more careful in approving vessels before delivery. Also that a more liberal use of Navy inspectors from The Office of the Supervisor of Shipbuilding were needed.

It seemed the Army had a great deal to learn about ships, but time to learn was not an available commodity before the sailing of NY 119.

Chapter I

PREPARATIONS

After Commander Lind (CTG 27.5) and his Towing Specialist, Lt. (JG) Lawrence Phipps, had completed their thorough review of the two earlier convoys' reports, CTG called a meeting on August 22 at his temporary office at Commander Eastern Sea Frontier (CESF). It was at this meeting that Lind first outlined the Convoy plan which included a combination and spacing of units in each tow.[1] He stressed the need to Army authorities for 13 large tugs instead of the 10 as specified in the original orders of August 14. Phipps had prepared a list of miscellaneous hardware needed, such as extra bridles and other assorted towing gear. This was read to the Army people who held the responsibility for assembling equipment. The list was agreed upon. The justification for the three extra large tugs was thoroughly discussed, and at this meeting the Army people stated that the extra vessels would be provided. Captain Bror E. Torning, a former Master Mariner and now a civilian official at the Army's New York Port of Embarkation (NYPOE), explained that a snafu had developed which had resulted in a number of barges and tugs being late for arrival in New York; therefore, they would not be ready for scheduled departure. By mutual agreement and after a phone call to the office of Commander in Chief Atlantic (Navy), the sailing date was postponed until September 12.

Once the meeting was adjourned and the junior officers attending had dispersed, Lind was privately briefed on the importance of the Convoy he was charged to deliver.

The car floats, equipped with parallel tracking running fore and aft, were required to transport railroad rolling stock from the depots near Southampton, England, to the French shore. Originally, Transportation Corps planners had envisioned transshipping this stockpiled rolling stock as deck cargo aboard freighters. However, the almost complete demolition of rail car unloading piers equipped with heavy cranes in Cherbourg and LeHarve now made this impossible. The advantage of the car floats was that they were adaptable to being maneuvered up to small wharves or quays laid with track, thus alleviating what had developed into a serious supply shortage.[2]

The wooden barges now being pick-a-backed atop the car floats had an equally important mission. An Army Colonel, recently returned from France, elaborated on the condition of the damaged French harbors and explained that existing facilities in those ports could not turn over enough shipping to keep up with the gargantuan logistical requirements of the troops ashore. The supplies had been routed overseas and were there in the hulls of merchant ships, but upwards of 150 ships were awaiting unloading. This situation had been anticipated, and many were being discharged onto lighters in mid-stream, using the merchant ships' own cargo booms and winches. The Army, looking futuristically toward such a need had inaugurated a barge (lighter) construction program at Falmouth, England, in early 1944, but the supply of these barges was not keeping pace with the demand for them—thus the importance of Lind's pick-a-backed lighters. Apparent to everyone was the usage for the STs—that of towing lighters from mid-stream shipping to the wharves and other push and tow harbor duties on the far shore. Previously to NY 118, the STs sent across had been transported as deck cargo.[3] Now with the accelerated demands for tanks and wheeled vehicles to equip our invasion forces battling toward the German frontier, deck space was at a premium. The Y boats to be included within NY 119 were in the main earmarked for shuttle duty between the petroleum tank farms on the Isle of Wight (England) and France, where their small size would allow discharge at minor harbors, thus easing the congestion on the major ports. Later, these Y boats would be put to even more valuable service once the barge canal system in Belgium came under Allied control. The LTs were scheduled for return to New York, except for a few which were to remain in the European Theater of Operations (ETO).

To emphasize the critical need for the wooden barges (lighters), the Colonel told Lind that before the Cherbourg Peninsula breakout, Army artillery batteries had been rationed to 25 rounds per gun, per day. He went on to say that the situation was improving but was still critical—not because the ammunition was not there in the ports, but because they simply couldn't unload it fast enough.[4]

Lind, now personally convinced that his improbable armada was expediently necessary but still apprehensive as to its chances for survival in the Atlantic in October, questioned the Colonel, "You, of course, realize that we will probably have losses?" The Colonel responded that this was expected and that the Army had accepted a planned risk factor of 25% materiel loss with the realization that the exigency exceeded the hazard.[5]

The meeting breaking up, a few of the officers, including Commander Lind and Major C.F. Monninger, Army Transportation Corps, reassembled in Monniger's office for some less formal shop talk. Monninger, years later, recalled this casual get together over a bottle of Scotch as more productive in ironing out details than the scheduled meeting. The relaxed atmosphere laid the ground work for a rapport between parties that later paid dividends in the hectic days remaining before the Convoy sailed.

* * * * * * *

The following day CTG called a meeting of his staff and the skippers of his destroyer escorts. At that time he stressed that the standardized operational orders used for most convoys did not appear to suit the needs of NY 119. The factor of its projected slow travel and the inexperience of the ATS ships' crews precluded the usual planning. Staff officers would take this into account and would coordinate closely with CTG and Lt. Phipps as they prepared their operational appendices.

Lt. (JG) Sabin Sanger, Anti-Submarine Warfare Officer, was told that the wide convoy front would require a longer than usual screening arc for each escort vessel. Lt. (JG) Edward H. Glucker, Staff Communications Officer, was given the task of insuring that the Army vessels were thoroughly briefed in the use of radio telephone equipment and its maintenance in addition to the preparation of a detailed operational order.

CTG brought forth a few chuckles when he asked Glucker to give the escort vessels liquor names for call signs, with CTG to be "Grand Dad" and the Convoy as a group to be spoken of as "Bar Flies."

Lt. (JG) Leroy H. Clem, Lind's Weather Officer, reported tropical disturbances were suspected in the Caribbean area and might bear watching. CTG told Clem to keep an eye on them and report any storm making up that might endanger the sailing of the Convoy.

Lind concluded by stating that he and Phipps would make continual inspections of the ATS craft to determine progress on that end as the sailing date grew closer.

* * * * * * *

While Lind, his staff, and the Army authorities at NYPOE were engaged in "big picture" planning for NY 119, lesser bit players were having their own strategy conferences.

Two young Navy Signalmen 3rd Class, who, having been deposited along with their sea bags on a pier head within the Brooklyn Army Base, were engaged in subdued conversation.

Both men had been briefed that morning at the Armed Guard Center in that they were to be assigned to Army tugs ST 719 and ST 511 and were told to report aboard and to hold themselves in readiness for radio-telephone and signaling procedure instructions from a Naval officer off the Convoy's flag ship. Their verbal instructions had further stated that the tugs were going "somewhere in Europe." Upon arrival overseas they were to report to the flag ship, whereupon her Communications Officer would place them under orders for return passage to the United States. Following the briefing, the two were driven in a Navy station wagon to the pier upon which they were now seated atop their sea bags.

Clarence V. Harding, who had been assigned to ST 719 turned to the other boy who had drawn ST 511, "Mac, I sure don't think a tiny tub like that over there will ever make it—maybe our best bet is to throw our gear into the drink, turn ourselves in and go to the brig." "Christ! If we do that it'll mean six months and maybe even a Bad Conduct Discharge." The two batted the subject back and forth, arriving at a decision wise for Harding of the ST 719 but unfortunate for his companion, since he and the ST 511 were destined to terminate the voyage long before reaching the English coast. Finally deciding to report aboard, they reluctantly shouldered their gear and headed down pier to their individual assignments.

Reaching a point high above the deck of the ST 719, Harding, remembering his recent boot camp training, sang out, "Permission to come aboard." Two heads, belonging to Able Bodied Seaman (AB) Ridgeway C. Leonard and AB Jack Thebus, ATS, thrust out from the ST's mess room; both looked up. Thebus, indicating a lack of the niceties of naval etiquette, answered the request with, "Suits us; toss down your gear." Once on deck, Harding was invited to join the two who were finishing a late lunch. The ST's cook, Tom Janos, a Greek national, filled a plate for him. Harding, more out of a sense of courtesy than hunger, began to eat. Between mouthfuls he inquired about the rest of the crew and what those present knew about the trip they were to make. Leonard, who had been aboard longer than anyone, answered Harding in a round about way, describing how he had become a crew member. Returning from a 30-day leave at home, he had reported to the National Maritime Union in downtown Manhattan, only to find that a temporary surplus of seamen prevented his signing up for a ship that day. Aware that the situation in which he found himself meant a possible call-up from his draft board, he reasoned that he must take some other route if he were to remain a civilian. Leonard had gone through the Maritime Administration's Training Camp at Sheepshead Bay in May, 1943, and had no wish for a repeat performance at a Navy boot camp, or worse than that, Army basic training. Joining a group of other seamen who, it turned out, had the same problem, the possibility of signing on with a non-union outfit was discussed. One man mentioned that he had seen a notice on the Union bulletin board that jobs were open for deck and engine ratings with the Army Transport Service. Walking over to the board, Leonard read the notice which stated the place of hiring as the Brooklyn Army Base. Leaving the others, who were still undecided, he picked up his possessions at the locker room and hopped a subway.

Arriving in Brooklyn, there followed a 6-block walk from the 59th Street and Fourth Avenue subway station to the hiring hall just outside the

Army Base. After an hour, unpleasantly seated next to an old-timer who obviously was sleeping off a drunk, Leonard was beckoned into an interview cubicle whereupon he produced his seaman's papers and asked if any ships were signing on crews. Before answering, the interviewer asked Leonard if he had any background in small craft. The young AB stated that he was brought up in a fishing and oystering community on the Maryland coast and had spent his life around the water and small boats. This appeared to please the hiring clerk since it was explained that crews were needed to man harbor tugs which were to be shipped to Europe on the decks of freighters with the tugs' crews traveling aboard as passengers. Leonard was told that the usual ship's articles would not be drawn but that each man was to be given a one-year contract. The contract was produced with instructions to read it over in the outer office and to return it to the cubicle for signature, at which time he would be issued a pass to the pier at which the tug was docked. "That's how I got here, but I think I got 'shilled'—we just heard that we're getting towed over." Thebus laughed, "So what, Leonard, it's better than the Army, isn't it?" "I guess so. Anyway, you'd be surprised how a little thing like this can take rough seas. It isn't the size, it's the way they design them, I guess." Harding, not reassured, went on to inquire as to where the skipper and the rest of the crew were. Thebus told him that a Master had not yet been assigned, but that they expected one any day, probably coming from the training program presently being conducted at the Base Terminal Building. There was an Assistant Engineer and a Mate aboard, both ashore doing some shopping. The other crew members had not arrived; but when they did, there would be twelve men in all, Harding included.

The Signalman, now worrying over the possibility of having an untried Master, almost wished he had thrown his gear in the harbor. He wondered aloud what would happen if the tug broke its tow line and they had to make it alone in mid-ocean. Thebus, laughing again, told him that word was out that a sea-going delivery captain was going to be put aboard for the ocean trip.

The conversation broke up with the arrival of an older man who Leonard and Thebus introduced as William L. Malone, the ST 719's Mate. Malone shooed the two AB's on deck with instructions to paint over the red lead on the life boat davits. Pouring Harding and himself a cup of coffee and referring to the Signalman as "Flags," he asked him how he liked the Navy. Harding answered, "OK, up to now, but I never thought I'd have to cross the ocean in a little tug like this." "Don't worry, kid, when I was in the Navy as a 'swabby' in the first War, I sailed on a 'PC'—she was bigger than this, but she pitched around a hell-uv-a-lot more than this one will. This trip will give you something to tell your kids about. I keep telling myself that when I was an AB on tankers in the 'Carib' in early '43, we had more to worry about than just a little rough weather—at least the subs have quieted down since then." "I suppose you're right, Mate. Where do I find the signal gear?" Malone, pointing toward the overhead, said, "You'll find signal flags in a box next to the machine gun on the flying bridge—the blinker light is ashore being repaired, and they'll bring the radio-telephone aboard in the next couple of days." "Thanks, I'll look around." Malone grunted a reply and unfolded a newspaper to the sports page.

* * * * * * *

Across the harbor at Bayonne, New Jersey, a commercial tug was headed to Brooklyn with two rust-streaked Pennsylvania Railroad Company car floats in tow. The tug's crew was oblivious to the fact that their floating cargo was soon to be en route to a continent over 3,000 miles to the east.

August 26

On August 26, Commander Lind was informed by the Army that they, The War Shipping Board, and the Navy Department had reaffirmed the original decision to supply only ten tugs. CTG, as it now developed, was not one to accept lying down what both he and Phipps knew to be a dangerous omission. Again, dragging out the NY 118 report, both men began a careful analysis of the difference in tows—tug horsepower ratings and service tug ratios between the two convoys. Their arithmetic matched their foreboding in that there was no doubt that NY 119 had been assigned an excess load over the earlier convoy.

Armed with this indisputable data, Lind visited the Operations Officer, Commander in Chief Atlantic (CinClant) who, after reviewing Lind's figures, arranged an audience with Vice Admiral Jonas Ingram, CinClant.

CTG, not at first completely at ease in the presence of flag rank, but game, reiterated his concern over the shortage of service tugs. He confessed that the abilities of the Army LT's and their crews was an unknown factor to him. He went on to say that even if he could get the Army to supply the three service tugs he needed, his peace of mind would be increased if the Admiral could provide him with one powerful Navy tug for assignment to the Task Group. Lind requested from the Admiral authorization for a supply of inflatable rubber rafts. He described their use as invaluable in transferring men and equipment, not to mention their essentialness for rescue operations should it come to that.[6] Ingram, no desk-bound Admiral and being fully aware of the red tape types that CTG had been dealing with said, "Mr. Lind,

I want you to know that if there is anything you want, come to me, and I will see that you get it." Relieved, Lind listened as the Admiral phoned Washington. Upon hanging up, Ingram said, "you've got them, the tug and the rafts."

After leaving Admiral Ingram's office, Lind thought—"At last, maybe, just maybe, I'm going to be given the tools I need to do this job." Had he known then that the tug promised was to be the USS ABNAKI, Lt. Dewey Walley, USN, commanding, his morale would have soared. The ABNAKI had been with NY 118. Her skipper and crew, as CTG was to discover, was one of the best the Navy could provide.

When Lind returned to his temporary office, Larry Phipps was waiting. "What happened, Sir?" CTG broke the good news, whereupon Phipps added to it by announcing that the fleet oiler assigned to TG 27.5 was to be the USS MAUMEE. The MAUMEE, according to Phipps, had a top notch crew which was well-versed in convoy refueling. Phipps had apparently assembled quite a dossier, since he was able to give Lind a run-down. The MAUMEE was originally built for the Navy during World War I and at the time of construction was one of the first diesel ships the Navy had. Continuing, Phipps told CTG that her first Engineering Officer had been Admiral Chester Nimitz (then a Lt. JG). The oiler had been laid up after the War, until 1942 when she was recommissioned after being fitted with new diesels, guns, and a modern deck house—"And get this, Commander, she has a complete machine shop, soup to nuts." Lind, after telling Phipps he should have been in Naval Intelligence, asked, "What about her Skipper?" "I don't think you've got any worry there, Sir; I'm told he's an ROTC graduate from some college in Georgia. (Georgia Tech '35—Author's Note) He's been on her since she was recommissioned and has held every job from Gunnery Officer to Executive Officer until he took over as Skipper this June." "Fine, what is his name?" "Ballard—Lt. Commander Hollis C. Ballard." "O.K., Larry, we've got ourselves an oiler; let's get those LT's we need. I want you to prepare a letter to the Commanding General, NYPOE. Make it a comparative analysis of the towing load of our convoy and Simmers'. We figured it out already for CinClant, so it shouldn't be difficult to write it up. After you've got it down on paper, give it to me, and I'll incorporate it with what we found out yesterday over at the Army Base."

September 1

On September 1, Lind, armed with the letter as transcribed below, appeared for a pre-arranged meeting at the offices of Eastern Sea Frontier, 90 Church Street, Manhattan.[7]

CCD SD

Serial 02

CONFIDENTIAL

30 August 1944

From: Commander Task Group 27.5
To: The Commanding General, Port of Embarkation, 58th Street,
          Brooklyn, New York

UNITED STATES ATLANTIC FLEET,
Commander Task Group 27.5,
U.S.S. O.Toole (DE 527), Flagship,
Fleet Post Office
New York, New York

Subject: Task Group 27.5 Barge Convoy, Disposition of.

References: (a) CTG 27.4 Dispatch 171255.
             (b) CTG 27.5 Dispatch 241100.
             (c) CTG 67 Report 00645 of 10 May 1944.

1. After a careful study of the above references and the recommendation contained therein, pertaining to the subject convoy now in the process of being assembled, the Commander Task Group 27.5 has arrived at the conclusion that this Task Group has been assigned the responsibility of delivering at their destination, expeditiously and in serviceable condition, vessels and material far in excess of the capacity of the Towing and Service vessels assigned to accomplish the task.

2. This Task Group has been assigned the following Army equipment:

14 CARFLOATS, length 200 to 250 feet, gross tonnage about 650 T.
12 BARGES, DPE & BCL Type - as deck loads for above.
 1 60-TON LIFT CRANE, on barge - gross about 1500 tons.
15 ST TUGS (85 Feet) to be towed astern of carfloats.
16 "Y" OILERS, SELF-PROPELLED, 633 ton, 700 H.P.
10 LT TUGS, are provided to tow and service the above.

3. Task Group 27.4 known as N.Y. Special 118, was assigned and delivered the following equipment with almost perfect weather:

12 CARFLOATS, 250 to 360 ft., 650 to 1100 Ton.
 2 CARFLOATS, smaller size, carried as deck loads.
 7 FLOATS, all wood, carried as deck loads.
 1 100-TON LIFT CRANE, on barge.
 1 70-TON LIFT CRANE, on barge.
11 ST TUGS (85 foot) towed astern carfloats.
12 "Y" OILERS, self-propelled.
12 LT TUGS, were provided to tow and service the above.

30 August 1944,

Subject: Task Group 27.5 Barge Convoy, Disposition of.
- -

    4. It is apparent, from the above, that Task Group 27.5 has been assigned at least a twenty-five percent greater load per Towing and Service tug than was carried by T.G. 27.4 in perfect weather.

    5. Reviewing the pertinent recommendations of CTG 27.4 as contained in references (a) and (b) above:

        (a) "That there be no lowering of material standards in succeeding similar convoys".

        (b) "That service tugs should number at least one-third of towing tugs and should have more power".

        (c) In reference (b) after safe arrival through almost perfect sea and weather conditions: "That Autumn similar convoys tow but one piggy-backed carfloat with one ST Tug in tandem".

    6. Attention is invited to the following logical conclusions derived from the above:

        (a) Increasing the load twenty-five percent per towing and service tug, and its associated equipment, is in fact lowering the material standards and the possibility of successful delivery by exactly twenty-five percent.

        (b) That similar good sea and weather conditions will not exist during this voyage as existed during the passage of Task Group 27.4. Increased bad weather adds a tremendous load in direct ratio to the length and weight of the tows and again indirectly reduces the material standards.

    7. On Monday, 28 August, 1944, the Task Group Commander, in company with Lt. (jg) Lawrence Phipps, U.S.N., Task Group 27.5 Towing Officer, visited the Army Port of Embarkation and inspected the vessels and the material assembled. We also interviewed the Army Officers and personnel engaged in the assembly, equipping and inspection of the Army equipment involved in this movement. The following conclusions were formulated:

        (a) The material for towing meets the standards of Task Group 27.4.

        (b) The progress of assembling and conditioning for sea of the vessels of the convoy is behind schedule and will cause a delay in departure of at least seven days.

        (c) The carfloats provided are far below the material standards of those previously acquired.

        (d) Three of the "Y" tankers scheduled for this movement are of the same type as the one that was returned to New York shortly after departure of T.G. 27.4. The failure of this type is apparently due to the lack of sufficient freeboard forward and the consequent shipping of heavy seas in even relatively calm weather. The army proposes to remedy this shortcoming by a much lighter load of bunker fuel and a trim by the stern. The Task Group Commander is dubious of the results.

        (e) In T.G. 27.4 the "Y" Tankers added greatly to the load of the Service Tugs in that four out of the twelve in convoy required towing services fifty percent of the distance to destination.

30 August 1944,

Subject: Task Group 27.5 Barge Convoy, Disposition of.
- -

 (f) The LT Tug towing the 100-Ton lift crane mounted on a barge with one ST in tandem had a 62% slippage indicating that she was towing about 25% in excess of her maximum load.

 (g) Although the information (Ship Characteristics) requested, regarding the Towing Tugs and their equipment, had not been furnished CTG 27.5, it was ascertained that at least two of the LT's would be steam and that four would be Diesel Electric (similar in construction to Navy ATR's with a HHP of 1900 and displacement of 198 gross ton.

 8. On Tuesday, 29 August, 1944 the Task Group Commander visited the Operations Officer, CinClant and after reviewing the above facts it was determined that the following minimum requirements would be insisted upon in order to insure them success of the task assigned:

 (a) One unencumbered Service Tug for each three Towing Tugs and/or fraction thereof.

 (b) One LT Tug of 1900 HHP for each tow of two carfloats and one ST Tug in tandem.

 (c) One LT Tug of 1200 HP or better for each tow of one carfloat and one ST Tug in tandem.

 (d) That should the Army be unable to furnish the above towing and service tugs in the ratio indicated, carfloats and other towed craft in excess of that amount would of necessity have to await the arrival of suitable towing equipment.

 (e) That each added days delay in departure caused by the unreadiness for sea of vessels to be towed increases the probability of unfavorable weather and that every effort must be made to have the convoy ready for sea at the earliest practicable time.

 9. This letter is not written in criticism of any personnel connected with this movement as the Task Group Commander has received excellent cooperation from all hands; but it is the intention of the CTG 27.5, upon whom the responsibility of safe convoy rests, to point out the apparent defects in the plan while there is still time to correct them.

A. L. Lind,
Commander, U.S.N.R.
Commander Task Group 27.5
and ComCortDiv 80.

CC:
 CominCh
 CinClant
 10 Flt CAR
 CESF
 FAO NY

After a moment's reflection, Commodore Moran USNR (the peacetime owner of The Moran Towing Company) put some questions to CTG regarding his presentation. Commodore Kurtz, of Navy's Eastern Sea Frontier (ESF) inquired as to the condition of the barges. Captain Shoemaker, also of ESF, then turned to Colonel Fiestal and Major Monninger with the request for comment as to the Army's opinion of the argument CTG had presented. Since it soon became apparent that all parties were in agreement, Commodore Moran and Colonel Fiestal each phoned the Office of the Chief of Transportation in Washington. The phone calls completed, CTG was told that come what may he would have his two extra service tugs.

Lind, feeling like a small boy at Christmastime, knew that the worst barriers had been overcome. Yet one major piece of business still remained— that of putting into effect an inspection and instruction procedure for the Convoy's Army vessels. Lind's concept for this had been taken from the closing remarks of Simmers' report on NY 118.

To effect the inspections, Lind assigned to each ship within his Task Group the responsibility of providing teams which would visit each of the Army craft including the barges. Each team leader, in addition to inspecting, was to answer all questions directed to him by the ATS crewmen, provided they were in context with the mission each ship was to perform. Team leaders were instructed not to give any orders to the ATS personnel but to report to Lind's office with a list of deficiencies, whereupon CTG would coordinate with Army's Monninger and Torning to insure that corrections were made whenever possible.

The teams were to find much amiss: it was discovered that none of the Army craft had a semblance of damage-control equipment; that fire fighting gear was inadequate; tools for making the simplest repairs were missing; spare parts, as in the case of Simmers' investigations, were again sadly lacking; crews were only partly assembled, and those that were present appeared to have little knowledge of the machinery, equipment, or presence of spare parts aboard their vessels.

At Major Monninger's end, once he was appraised of the shortages by CTG, everything possible was done to correct the situation. Many of the parts found missing were unobtainable. A few could be requisitioned; some he successfully scrounged. Coordinating with Monninger on crew matters was Captain Torning who had his problems, too. Not only did he have difficulty in filling crew slots, but as sailing time approached, many of the civilian seamen began to have second thoughts as to the attractiveness of an ocean voyage aboard such lilliputian craft. This somewhat understandable concern on the part of a few of the ATS crews was to keep Torning hopping up to, and through, the day of sailing.

* * * * * * *

Major Monninger, sitting down at his desk to begin what he thought would be a relatively routine day, was apprised of a complaint that had just come down through channels. NYPOE, it appeared, had precipitated some ill feeling with an Allied government. The Norwegian Consulate in New York was alarmed at the recruiting efforts then being conducted by Captain Torning and company. The higher pay rates offered by those endeavoring to fill the ships' officers' berths on the tugs and Y boats of NY 119, was creating a shortage in the ranks of licensed Norwegian officers normally used to crew that nation's ships then using New York as their home port.

Monninger phoned the Norwegian Consul and arranged a luncheon date with him at the Lawyers' Club in Manhattan. Over lunch he was able to successfully placate that gentleman with the explanation of the essentialness of the barge convoy and the information that it now appeared that most of the vacancies had been filled. The Consul, at rest in the knowledge that the ATS raids seemed to be over, departed satisfied. Monninger returned to the relative security of the Army Base which did not normally deal in international relations.

* * * * * * *

Lt. (JG) Sabin Sanger, taking time off from Anti-Submarine Warfare (ASW) preparations, had attached himself to an inspection team off one of the escorts.

The team leader, an engineering officer, accompanied by Sanger and two petty officers, was walking down one of the piers to which a group of Army tugs was moored. The engineer pointed toward a line of nested STs. "There they are, Sabin." "You're joking! They're really going with us?" "I'm afraid so. We'll go aboard one of them later so you can take a look, but right now I've got a couple of the larger tugs and a Y boat to check out."

The first tug to be checked was the LT 63. On boarding, the two naval officers were met by Paul Monsen, the tug's Master. Monsen, a 38-year-old Norwegian, invited them into the mess room for coffee. Before entering the lower deck house where the galley and mess room were located, Monsen directed his 2nd Mate to show the Navy petty officers to whatever they asked to see.

Making small talk, Sanger asked the Norwegian if the LT 63 was his first tug. Monsen explained that he had been with ATS small craft since October of 1943, and "No!" his assignment before this had been a tug, also. Previously, he had sailed Norwegian freighters. Monsen, turning the conversation to the present order of business, asked what he could do for them. The escort engineer told him that his men were checking out the deck and bosun's stores. The engine room was the inspecting officer's immediate concern. "Could you introduce us to the Chief Engineer?" Monsen, answering affirmatively, led the naval officers through a doorway adjoining the mess room and down a ladder into the engine spaces.

Back on the pier and on their way to the Base Cafeteria for lunch, the engineer told Sanger that this had been his third inspection. In all cases he had found the ATS engineers lacking in both a knowledge of their power plants and in any attempts to have organized their engine departments.

Over lunch, the escort officer related how the day before he had met the delivery master of the ST 751. The man was a Spaniard by the name of Pascual Ruiz, who, under questioning, had turned out to be a former Spanish naval officer who had served as the Executive Officer on one of Spain's heavy cruisers. That was back in 1939. Through some unexplained avenue, the man had left the Spanish Navy and had become a Master on foreign merchant ships until the past month when he had signed on with ATS. Sanger was told that very few of the tugs or Y boats had American skippers aboard. Most were Scandinavian, but the engineer had met a Filipino who was assigned to the ST 742. This man had told a story of being a deck officer with a Phillipine steamship company until the Japanese had overrun his homeland.

Sanger's luncheon companion seemed to be full of anecdotes concerning the ATS crews. He told of another team of officers off the BERMINGHAM. The team under Lt. Robinson McIlvaine had inspected a number of Y boats. They found that some of the little oilers had only enough food and water for a few days, no one in the crew having taken the initiative or responsibility to inquire if any more was to be provided. McIlvaine had said, "The crews appeared to have been swept up from 'Skid Row'." One of them, again according to McIlvaine, was a cook, "Who took the position that he should have the rank of Chief Purser and accordingly went out and bought himself a cap with scrambled eggs on the visor and three-stripe epaulets. Thus decked out, he had refused to dirty his hands with cooking."[8]

Sanger, fascinated, but with more work to do back at his office, left the engineer to his afternoon chores.

* * * * * * *

Aboard the Y boats, the Task Group inspectors had discovered one common problem. The Y's steering gear, all alike, had inherent imperfections in manufacture and installation. Electric contact points tended to corrode quickly. Also, the electric steering control panels appeared to be too light. The Y boat crews reported that the clearances in the electrical circuits caused contacts to burn out frequently, with resulting steering casualties. CTG, through Monninger, brought this to the attention of the Army, but the report came back with the notation that alterations were not possible. CTG then issued a memo to the escort engineers that the Y boat personnel were to be instructed in preventive maintenance in order to circumvent corrosion whenever possible.[9]

Early September

During the first week in September, the USS MATOLE,[10] a Navy oiler which was not part of the Task Group, cleared the outer harbor for a fueling exercise with four of the LT tugs. The Masters and Chief Engineers of six other tugs which were in the shipyard for repairs, were aboard the oiler as observers.

Shortly after this, the MAUMEE, TG 27.5's oiler, took another group out to sea, whereupon additional fueling exercises were conducted. Some of the STs and more "sidewalk supervisors" went with this bunch.

The practice fueling operations were by the astern method—later to be revised by the MAUMEE's CO, Lt. Commander Ballard. The ATS crews appeared to get the hang of things while certain equipment deficiencies were noted. These were to be provided before the Convoy's departure date.

While this was taking place, Captain Torning and his staff made dry runs with some of the LTs and car floats to insure that the towing hook-ups would perform satisfactorily in a seaway. One run in particular has remained clearly in the mind of Torning's assistant, Bill Nelson: The scene was a wild night, rainy and windy. Shortly after streaming the tow which consisted of two car floats, Nelson saw a dark object resembling a mine dead-ahead of the tug. A "hard right" was executed, and the object, now definitely identified as a mine, was cleared.[11] Everyone held their breath for a considerable period since the probability of one of the barges or their umbilical cables hitting it remained high. Finally, after what seemed an eternity, the mine was safely astern. The latter miss was as good as a mile; tragedy was to occur a couple of nights later.

Nelson was supervising the mooring of two of the car floats against stakes (pilings) specially driven in front of the 69th Street Pier for that purpose. An LT was maneuvering alongside and had just put a young deck hand on board one of the floats to assist Nelson's gang. The boy was warned to be careful afoot since the float had a cut-under bow in its center section and no guard railings. The boy accepted the warning cheerfully enough, but he obviously did not take it seriously enough. A minute or two later he was seen toppling backwards and falling into the water. The tug's screws were turning over at half throttle, creating a turbulence difficult for a swimmer.

Being night, the LT turned on her search light and swept the area for a period of time long after rescue seemed probable. Apparently, the youngster had been immediately swept into the pier, his body becoming lodged under some cross ties. Two weeks later it was found floating in the same general area. The night of her husband's drowning, the deck hand's wife was in the hospital delivering their first baby.

* * * * * * *

Lind's staff had by now completed their detailed Operational Orders which were reviewed, altered, and added to by him. One of the major changes he made was a re-organization of the Task Group's repair unit. Originally it had been planned to house the entire unit aboard the MAUMEE and to transfer them as needed by service tug around the Convoy. CTG's change specified splitting the group into three parts, with a unit to be placed aboard each of the three ATS service tugs. It was agreed that this would be more efficient and would prevent the necessity of one service tug having to steam through the Convoy to the MAUMEE everytime a repair party was needed and back through it again to deliver the party.[12] The fact that repair units would be billeted on each of the service tugs would furthermore cut the 'tween ship transfers in half, thus alleviating 50% of the dangers.

* * * * * * *

A further delay was necessitated when word came in of the late arrival of the last two steel car floats. CTG figured that once they arrived at the Base at least two days were needed to dry dock them, float on their wooden pick-a-backs, and lash them down. Lind again put ahead the sailing date—this time from the 12th to the 14th.

* * * * * * *

Clem, the meteorologist, had been keeping his weather eye on the situation building to the southward. On the morning of the 10th, he knocked on CTG's door and reported that the U.S. Weather Bureau was plotting a severe hurricane located 300 miles north of Puerto Rico and heading northwest. Clem had explained that the storm had taken the classic course pattern of the famous 1938 hurricane (the one that had so devastatingly plowed through New England). Weather patterns indicated a probability that New York might be hit. Lind queried the meteorologist as to what his guess might be as to the time of the storm's arrival. "I think, Sir, that we can give it around four or five days. If it's going to veer off into the

Atlantic, we may know sooner how it's going to affect us." "Keep your eye on it; the last thing I want to do is head this conglomeration into heavy weather at the start." "Yes, Sir, I'll have the Weather Bureau put me on their alert schedule."

Lind, picking up the phone, put a call through to Admiral Ingram, whereupon the Admiral told him to use his judgment and not to jeopardize the Convoy by sailing into anything that might endanger it. The phone, back in its cradle, CTG decided to leave the departure date temporarily as it had been set. This was done on the theory that even if he had to delay it to later—an event that now appeared likely—he did not want to relax the crescendo of preparation that was taking place in the harbor.

* * * * * * *

Valentine B. Swartwout, a former New York City mounted policeman, hired by ATS as an Engineer, stepped aboard his first and last floating command, the ST 719. The day prior he had been told that all engineering berths had been filled but that a Master's job on an ST was open. This last minute switch was not entirely out of order since his background with the U.S. Power Squadron, (a civilian yachtsman training organization) had qualified Swartwout for a pre-war commission as an Ensign (temporary) in the U.S. Coast Guard Reserve.

Three months before his stepping on the deck of the ST 719, Swartwout had had every indication of becoming an Army 1st Lieutenant in the Amphibious Engineers. A notification of acceptance had arrived from the War Department. Simultaneously, a freeze order from Washington arrived stating that no longer would New York City policemen be appointed or enlisted in the Armed Forces. Mayor LaGuardia, faced with a shrinking Police Department, had sealed off Swartwout from the War—or so it appeared. The mounted cop had other plans. Having heard of the ATS small craft program, he journeyed to Brooklyn for some firsthand information. Briefed by ATS as to the "good overseas prospects," he returned to Police Headquarters to request an audience with Police Commissioner Valentine, before whom he stated flatly, "I want out." Valentine told him that in view of the freeze order, it was beyond the Commissioner's power to grant permission; however, if upon Swartwout's return from the Wars, he (Valentine) was still in office, he would make sure Swartwout got his job back. With a "Thank you, Commissioner," the now ex-cop handed in his gun and badge and began a new career.

After settling in his gear on the ST 719, the former policeman was told by "Mate" Malone that his arrival marked the completion of a full crew. The delivery Master had reported aboard the day before, but in the words of

Malone, "needed an interpreter." It seemed that the gentleman was a Greek with very little English lingual ability.

Swartwout was next informed that the Army would deliver frozen food and dry ice the next day. It was to be stored in a thinly insulated box now being made fast on the life boat deck. The Mate, continuing his news commentary, said that a Navy petty officer had come aboard to inspect the tug and left a list of shortages which included a number of spare engine parts—none of which had yet been produced by anyone ashore. "Anything else?" "Yeah, we're supposed to take her out in the harbor tomorrow for some practice maneuvering—the Greek is supposed to run her, I guess." "By the way, where is he now?" Malone shrugged, "I think he's up at the Harbor Master's Office."

The next morning, having met the delivery Master whose name was Christos Papliolios, Swartwout knew that the Mate had not under-estimated the Greek's command of English. "It's going to be tough getting across to him, or for that matter, vice versa," he thought. Later that day his worries were compounded. The practice run had been an embarrassing disaster. Papliolios coming close to a set of pilings, with the intent, or so the crew assumed, of simulating a docking maneuver, had reversed the engines at too high a speed causing the tug to swing with the current. The ST 719 came hard against a floating stagework and damaged her rudder shaft and steering gear housing. Fortunately, dry docking facilities were immediately available, and repairs were started as soon as the ST was out of the water. The ST 719 was high and ignobly dry; her crew was thankful that the fiasco had gone relatively unwitnessed by their colleagues from the other tugs.

During the ST 719's stay upon the ways, Swartwout was given the opportunity to get to know and evaluate the crew:

In addition to Papliolios, the 48-year-old delivery Master, there was Bill Malone, Navy veteran of World War I, who had returned to sea when he joined the Merchant Marine in 1943. These two, in addition to himself, constituted the deck watch officer force. The Able Bodied Seamen who would stand the wheel and lookout watches with them were Ridgeway C. Leonard, who the reader has met; John A. Thebus, 19-year-old graduate of the Maritime Administration's boot program; Bastian Van Der Linden, a 37-year-old Dutchman who had sailed since the War's outbreak; and Thomas M. Scott, an 18-year-old who was about to make his first trip, his previous experience having been on harbor-bound dredges. The engine room staff was headed by John A. Dorwart, a 21-year-old from Newark, Delaware, who had dropped out of the U.S. Merchant Marine Academy in January, 1943, after a 3-month academic career. After leaving the Academy, he had sailed on merchant ships filling varied black gang jobs. As his seaman's certificate indicated, his experience included one trip as an acting Junior 3rd Engineer on a waiver.[13] Dorwart's back-up man as First Assistant was Paul R. Williams, 22 years old and a Maritime Academy dropout. Williams had also served on a waiver as a Junior Engineer and held ships' discharges dating from November 1942. Acting as Oiler under Dorwart and Williams was Arthur J. Moran, a 24-year-old former employee of Todds Shipyard—another first-tripper. The ST's cook, Thomas Janos, 38 years old, was an experienced cook, having served on large merchantmen for over two years. Harding, the Signalman, was not, in fact, an assigned crew member but had been attached by the Navy.

Swartwout knew that good relationships with all hands were essential if the long voyage was going to be bearable. At first appraisal, he was pleased and grateful that his bunch was not the scrapings such as he had seen on a number of the other tugs. Williams had particularly impressed him, the young Engineer having, on his own initiative, raised no little Hell around the Army Base in an attempt to have the ST's fuel pump repaired—unfortunately with no luck.

September 12

The forenoon of September 12th, the first pre-planned date of sailing, (later postponed to the 14th) brought confirmation of Lind's apprehension as to the approaching storm and another postponement. The storm center at 7 a.m. that morning had been reported due east of Miami, Florida, heading, it seemed, right for the Eastern Seaboard. The Weather Bureau had already christened it "The Great Atlantic Hurricane", an apt name since an Army reconnaissance plane had recorded the winds at 140 miles per hour. The pilot had reported turbulence so great that with himself and the co-pilot on the controls it was all they could do to prevent the plane from crashing. Upon return to base, it was discovered that 150 rivets had been sheared off one wing alone.[14]

By 7 a.m. on the 14th, the storm was reported east of Cape Hatteras heading directly for New York.

Accelerating, the storm center crossed the eastern shore of Long Island at 10 p.m., traveling at 40 miles per hour. The whole of New York Harbor became a wind-whipped cauldron; tides were six to seven feet above normal, and the steady winds were clocked at 78 miles per hour. One gust made it to 96 miles per hour. Within the Army Base, on Pier 4, things became very lively. A Liberty Ship which was moored to the pier broke some of her hawsers and threatened to hole the small craft tied to the opposite pier. Only the efforts of all of those that could be mustered, including Base troops, prevented serious damage. The entire Base dockage area was flooded.

The manned vessels of NY 119 were nursemaided by their crews. The pick-a-back floats moored to pilings were left to fend for themselves and took the worst beating, grinding and heaving against their companion floats.

The ST 720, first docked at Staten Island, had the day before been shifted to the Army Base. Her present berth was directly ahead of the recently dry docked but now repaired ST 719 which lay on the windward side of Pier 2.

Signalman 2nd Class Charles H. Buswell, assigned to the ST 720, had "turned to" with the tug's deck force to put out extra lines. Additionally, port personnel passed steel cables from the pier outboard as many of the tugs were nested together. The ST 720's Skipper, Edward Wallace, figuring the cables were not enough, had signaled his Engineer, Jim Scrivener, to give him "slow ahead" in order to ease the strain on the lines. At this point, Wallace noticed that Buswell was turning green. In answer to a question from Wallace, the Signalman said he doubted his condition was caused by the little tug's pitching but rather by the smell of the rubberized rain gear he was wearing. Wallace, busy with his ship, yelled over his shoulder that maybe it was both, and that "Flags" might be more comfortable on the dock. Buswell, embarrassed but relieved, climbed up on the dock and rode out the Convoy's first storm ashore.

September 15

On the morning of the 15th, all hands appraised the damage—slight, except for the possibility that some of the car floats had sprung leaks. The latter was difficult to assess since many of the floats had not been tight-bilged at delivery. This, although not considered desirable, was nevertheless expected because of the age of many of them. At any rate, each float was equipped with a gasoline billy pump; given any luck, seas would be moderate enough to allow boarding the floats when the Convoy was underway to periodically start the "billies."

September 17

On the 17th, Commander Lind held final briefings for the Masters and escort vessel commanders. All was ready or as ready as it would ever be. Convoy NY 119 was scheduled for sortie starting the morning of the 19th.

* * * * * * *

The storm had delayed the rigging of the late car float arrivals, whose pick-a-backed barges had to be expertly lashed down. This undertaking was not to be accomplished by a few "boy scout" half hitches but rather required a large gang of stevedores equipped with heavy cable and chain gear. Also, the towing cables and bridles had to be spliced, shackled, and carefully flaked down for paying out.

Bill Nelson spoke to Torning and expressed the opinion that if the floats were going to be readied on time he would need to work his stevedore crews all night and feed and coffee them on the floats. Agreeing, Torning set things up. Nelson met the deadline with only minutes to spare.

The Convoy prepared to sortie the morning of September 19.

Commander Alfred L. Lind taken before NY 119. (Courtesy of A.L. Lind).

143 Ft. Army LT class tug. (U.S. Army).

Army Y class tanker. (U.S. Army)

Tank cars shown on carfloat at anchor; probably in roadstead off Southampton, England. (U.S. Army).

U.S. Army ST class harbor tug. Same class ST vessel as accompanied NY 119 although the tug is not one of those which did. (U.S. Army).

USS POWERS, DE 528. (Courtesy of Sabin Sanger).

Crew members of the USS POWERS having last look at New York Harbor underway with NY 119. (Courtesy of K.C. Valentine).

Lt. Commander W.M. Blackford, USNR, shown with black enlisted men on deck of the USS MASON following commissioning ceremonies. (Courtesy U.S. Navy)

Chapter II

SORTIE

P rior to Convoy departure time, Commander Lind, along with a Navy repair unit and accompanied by Colonel Fiestel and Major Monninger, boarded an Army picket boat to make a last-minute check on the ATS vessels now at anchor off the Army Base awaiting sortie.[1]

More problems: The Y 82's cook was missing; the Y 80's engineering force was lacking an Assistant Engineer who had failed to report; the ST 751's Chief Engineer had disappeared.

On the ST 676 a donnybrook had broken out between Captain Holm and his Chief Engineer over the subject of conserving water. CTG asked Monninger to arbitrate. The Major, passing the buck back to Lind, commented that the Convoy was now under Navy control and CTG had become the law. This remark was broadcast in loud volume in front of the contestants. Lind first got tough, but he followed with the philosophy that peace seemed to be advisable as the time between shore leaves was going to be long indeed. He suggested the opponents shake hands and cooperate with each other. The lecture must have bore results since "no homicides were reported from the ST 676 during passage."

Continuing to travel among the anchored vessels, it was discovered that Y 48's fire pump was inoperative and needed repair; Y 17 was short a battery needed to start one of her auxiliary motors.

Monninger had called out another Army picket launch, and her operator was kept busy shuttling to Pier 2 with written orders to fill the deficiencies, all of which were remedied, including the missing crew members.

Shortly before the completion of their inspection tour, the three officers were informed by ship-to-shore radio that the LT 643 had discovered a malfunction in her towing engine. The trouble had developed while she was picking up her two car floats at the 69th Street "stakes."

The picket launch full throttled to the scene, whereupon the Navy repair unit boarded. They found the trouble was a fault in an electric unit. An Army repair team simultaneously arriving, took a look-see and gave forth the opinion that there was evidence of recent tampering. They claimed that everything had been in working order a few days before when tow tests were conducted. Apparently a person or persons intended to remain in New York Harbor.

A Lt. Colonel, in charge of the Army mechanics, informed Lind that he was going to substitute one of the service tugs: "The LT 643 could be repaired underway," Lind disagreed and insisted that either the Army repair the towing engine on the spot or the whole unit, tug and floats, would be left behind. This brought a swift reaction from the Army officer who replied that he considered CTG's insistence "unreasonable." Lind impatiently retorted that the LT 643 was not capable of performing as a service tug since her horsepower rating was not high enough. Also her general design for service duty was not on a par with established standards for that use. Furthermore, he was damned if he was going to be faced with a tow transfer at sea when there was an alternative. The Lt. Colonel, now cognizant that the Commander Task Group meant what he said, dispatched his launch to round up the best repair men the Base could provide.

Completing the tour, Lind bade goodbye to Fiestel and Monninger and boarded the destroyer escort, the USS O'TOOLE, his Task Group flagship. The O'TOOLE was commanded by Lt. Commander Victor Mauldin, USN, a cousin of the well-known GI cartoonist. Lind, as Commander Task Group, was to use the O'TOOLE as his floating command post; the command of the vessel rested with her Captain. This arrangement gave CTG a free rein to handle the overall responsibility of the Convoy.

Climbing to the bridge, Lind ordered the escorts of his group to weigh anchor and move to a point just inside the harbor ASW nets where they were to check over the Convoy's ships as they passed through the gates.

Once Lind had boarded the O'TOOLE, the departure of the ATS craft and the forming of their tows came under the supervision of Captain Torning and his staff.

Outbound through the Narrows steamed the LTs with their floats tight cinched astern. The service tugs and the ABNAKI were next, ready to lend a hand where needed.

Following came the STs, at this point under their own power.

Next went the Y boats and two British naval net tenders with tickets to join the Convoy.

Bringing up the rear, to be passed through the nets last, were the MAUMEE and a tramp steamer called the SS SUERTE which flew Panamanian colors and carried an all Greek crew. The SUERTE had been assigned at the last minute since it was felt her slow speed was insufficient for the regularly scheduled New York to United Kingdom mercantile convoys. Eastern Sea Frontier had conferred with Lind, and it was agreed that she would be compatible with Lind's convoy—a decision later to be regretted.

Arriving at Gedney Buoy, the ATS tugs with floats had their STs hooked up by a gang of stevedores specially sent out to assist in the operation. Hooking up completed, the barges and STs were streamed to "sea tow" intervals.

Following this operation, projected as troublesome, but going off without a hitch, the Ys and the other unencumbered craft set predetermined courses to an area of rendezvous east of Gedney Buoy. This part of the operation created some problem since a heavy fog was overlying the area and none of the Army craft were equipped with radar.

Shrinking in the flanks and highly active was the SC 1294, a Navy patrol boat temporarily loaned to Lind to perform this function. Aided by 27.5's escorts, it was not long before the columns were roughly formed and proceeding.

By 3 o'clock that afternoon, the fog having cleared, things were well in order and in a near semblance to a correct formation. By sundown the spacing was even and CTG messaged, "Thank you" to the SC 1294 and told her she could return to base.

Convoy NY 119, covering an area of the ocean 10,000 yards wide and 2,200 yards long, had become the sole responsibility of the United States Navy, represented by Commander Task Group 27.5.

September 20

The next morning at daybreak, Lind surveyed his domain.

A gentle ground swell was running, an aftermath of the recent hurricane. There was a complete absence of wind, and the sky had hardly any cloud cover. At first appraisal, the columns looked in reasonably good order.

CTG joined Mauldin in a cup of coffee, watching as that officer supervised his ship's General Quarters drill, a procedure often conducted at first light aboard all warships in waters frequented by enemy submarines. Following the securing from GQ, Lind asked Mauldin to tour the Convoy front so he could see on the ground what his Operation Order had produced:

Column 1 was headed up by the LT 63 towing one car float and two STs. Following were the Y 80 and one of the British net tenders. The service tug LT 581 brought up the rear.

Column 2 was led by the LT 643 which had joined the Convoy during the night, her towing gear now in good repair. She towed one float and two STs. Following were the Y 17 and Y 126.

Column 3 was led by the LT 536 with a tow of two floats and the ST 748. Following were the Y 34 and the Y 127.

Column 4 had at its head the LT 653 towing two floats and the ST 747.

Following were the Y 84 and the Y 86. The powerful Navy fleet tug, USS ABNAKI, brought up the rear.

Column 5 was led by the USS MAUMEE, the Convoy's oiler. Her skipper, Lt. Commander Ballard, wore two hats, also serving as the Convoy Commodore under CTG. The Commodore's ship acted as Convoy "guide-on", thus having the function of setting the pace for the other ships within the formation. Column leaders to her port and starboard also dressed on her, or at least this is how the Operational Order had put it. Behind the MAUMEE at a 500-yard interval came the SUERTE.

Directly to starboard of the MAUMEE, the 6th column was headed by the LT 784 under the command of the ATS Master, Clarke. Her tow consisted of two floats and the ST 510. Following were the Y 81 and the Y 83. Bringing up the rear of the column was the service tug LT 537 under the command of Waaler with Lt. Phipps, the Task Group's Towing Officer aboard.

Column 7 was headed by the LT 651 with a tow of two floats and the ST 511. Following were the Y 82 and the Y 104.

Column 8 was headed up by the LT 580 with her tow consisting of two floats and the ST 501. Following came the Y 48 and the Y 128.

Column 9 was led by the LT 538 towing two floats and the ST 720. Following were the Y 49 and the Y 106.

Column 10, the starboard column of the Convoy, was headed by the LT 492, to be unofficially nicknamed by the Convoy's inhabitants as the "Mama Duck" because of her tow, which consisted of four of the little ST harbor tugs. Strung out in line behind the LT 492 were: ST 719, ST 718, ST 742, and ST 752. Behind the "four little ducklings" followed the Y 105 and HMS PRETEXT, the other one of the two Royal Navy net tenders. Bringing up the column's stern was the LT 579, the third of the ATS service tugs.

As Lind inspected the Convoy's front, he noticed the established intervals were being maintained—1,000 yards port and starboard of lead vessels, the exception being each side of the MAUMEE where a 1,500 yard interval had been stipulated.

CTG next requested Mauldin to steam through the length of the Convoy. The O'TOOLE heeled to port and ran down the length of column 7, close enough to make out faces on the bridges of the ATS craft. Lind noticed that the two floats astern of the LT 651 seemed to trail well at the end of their 1,200 foot steel cables, as did the little ST trailing on an 800 foot cable astern of the second float. Checking by eye, he estimated that the ordered 200 yard intervals between the two Y boats appeared to be maintained.

The O'TOOLE swung to starboard after passing the Y 104 and cut around the rear of the Convoy to its port flank, whereupon Lind was able to examine the lineup from that vantage point. Here he could see some indications of potential straggling. Some of the Ys would never stand a "pass in review."

Pressing the transmission button on the TBS set, he voiced some acid remarks to "Bar Flies."[2] "Straggling will not be tolerated!"

* * * * * * *

A cardinal rule, practiced by any competent sheep drover when starting a drive, is to have his dogs reacting well at the onset. Without the "shepherd's helpers" nervously working, the sheep will stray. Lind, although not experienced in the mutton business, put the same theory to work on his escorts.

Woe be it, that first day out, if an escort was off station; if she was, CTG's comments to her skipper were not versed in the politest of terms.

* * * * * * *

Following this initial sharpening up of his shepherds, Lind turned his attention to what appeared to be a maverick among the sheep. The SUERTE, or rather her Greek skipper, persisted in running ahead of the MAUMEE; this happened despite the fact that he had been ordered back once by Ballard. The Greek's wanderings were not only a breach of Convoy discipline, but as the SUERTE elbowed ahead of the MAUMEE, she began to interfere with the screening escort vessels.

Lind messaged the SUERTE to take station. The U.S. Navy Signalman assigned aboard her "Rogered," but it soon became apparent that her Master had no intentions of obeying. Lind followed with another transmission, "Do you understand my orders?" The Signalman blinked back, "Yes, he understands, but you can't argue with a Greek." CTG, getting irritated dictated the following. "The Commander Task Group orders you to take Convoy station assigned immediately." Not waiting for a reply, Lind had Mauldin head directly for the miscreant. The Greek, finally waking up to the fact that the fellow on the DE meant business, dropped back into position.

* * * * * * *

On the MAUMEE, Ballard soon discovered one mistake that Lind had made in setting up the Convoy Order. The MAUMEE, being of a far larger bulk than the average of the vessels in the Convoy, was not suitable for a "guide-on" role. Her size caused her to be much more subject to sea-drift.

Furthermore, since she was twin screw it was necessary to run on one shaft if she was to maintain a speed adequately slow enough for the rest of the Convoy; this aggravated the situation. Ballard, over TBS, brought this to Lind's attention, with the request that one of the lead LTs in either column 4 or column 6 be assigned the "guide-on" function. Lind, after discussing Ballard's reasoning, responded with a negative. Ballard, still sure that he was correct, but not one to disobey, continued as before.

* * * * * * *

The first three days at sea were relatively routine. CTG cracked his whip; the Convoy, particularly the escorts, reacted in quick time. Some winced at the sting of it, yet NY 119 began to be forged into a workable entity.

September 22

The fourth day out, in the nick of time, two of the ABs on the ST 719 prevented the cook from jumping overboard. The cook had long ago attuned himself to the normal sea motion on larger ships, but the exaggerated roll of an ST was something else. Consequently, he had become violently seasick almost immediately upon leaving New York. After four days of it, which resulted in the vomiting of blood, he had decided to end his life.[3]

From left to right: Commander Alfred L. Lind; Lt. J. Bryant; Lt. Commander Victor Mauldin on phone. Taken on the bridge of the USS O'TOOLE during convoy's transit. (Courtesy of E.A. Adams).

Lt. Robinson McIlvaine shown during convoy's transit. McIlvaine entered diplomatic service with the U.S. State Department following the war, becoming an Ambassador to several African nations. (Courtesy of H.H. Hannaman).

Lt. (jg) Kendall C. Valentine checking relative position of USS POWERS and other convoy vessels. Ensign Arthur McCarthy with dark glasses. (Courtesy of K.C. Valentine).

Signalman Charles H. Buswell; survivor of the ST 720. (Courtesy of C.H. Buswell).

The "four ducklings" — LT 492 towing STs 719, 718, 742, 752. Photo probably taken on the first or second day out of New York. (Courtesy of K. Truelsen).

ST tugs as seen in a moderate ground swell from the deck of the USS O'TOOLE. (Courtesy of Sabin Sanger).

*Y Tanker in moderate sea. Note the submerged well deck.
(Courtesy of Sabin Sanger).*

*One of the British net tenders, probably HMS ASTRAVAL;
taken from fantail of the USS MAUMEE, again probably on
the 30th of September. (Courtesy of J. Dodson).*

The Army steel tug LT 784 shown taking on fuel from the USS MAUMEE. Note the LT's two carfloats and trailing ST in tow. (Courtesy of J. Dodson).

Two ST tugs in tow behind a BCF unit as seen from a 20 mm gun tub on the USS POWERS. (Courtesy of K.C. Valentine).

Section of convoy underway in smooth sea west of Azores. To the right is a carfloat with picka-back atop — note the sea breaking against the fairing between the top and bottom unit. At the center is one of the British net tenders and to the left is a Y Boat. (Courtesy of H.H. Hannaman).

Beam view of USS MAUMEE during refueling operations. (Courtesy of H.H. Hannaman).

USS CHASE (DE 16) alongside the USS MAUMEE. (Courtesy of R.V. Bradley).

*Unidentified LT with carfloat in tow. Vessel in background is "low bow" type Y boat.
(Courtesy of Sabin Sanger).*

LT 63 alongside USS MAUMEE. Note the BCF unit and ST in tow upper left hand corner. (Courtesy of J. Dodson).

The ST 676 shown when alongside the USS O'TOOLE on October 6th. The ST was in the process of having water transferred from the DE's tanks. (Courtesy of Sabin Sanger).

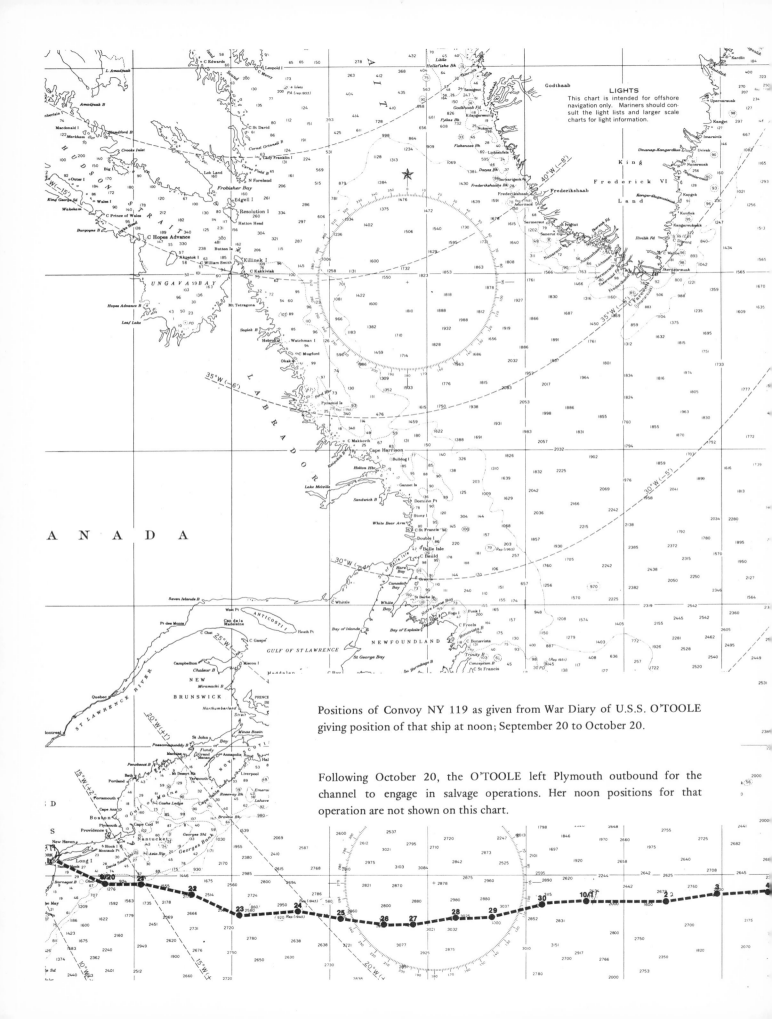

Positions of Convoy NY 119 as given from War Diary of U.S.S. O'TOOLE giving position of that ship at noon; September 20 to October 20.

Following October 20, the O'TOOLE left Plymouth outbound for the channel to engage in salvage operations. Her noon positions for that operation are not shown on this chart.

LIGHTS
This chart is intended for offshore navigation only. Mariners should consult the light lists and larger scale charts for light information.

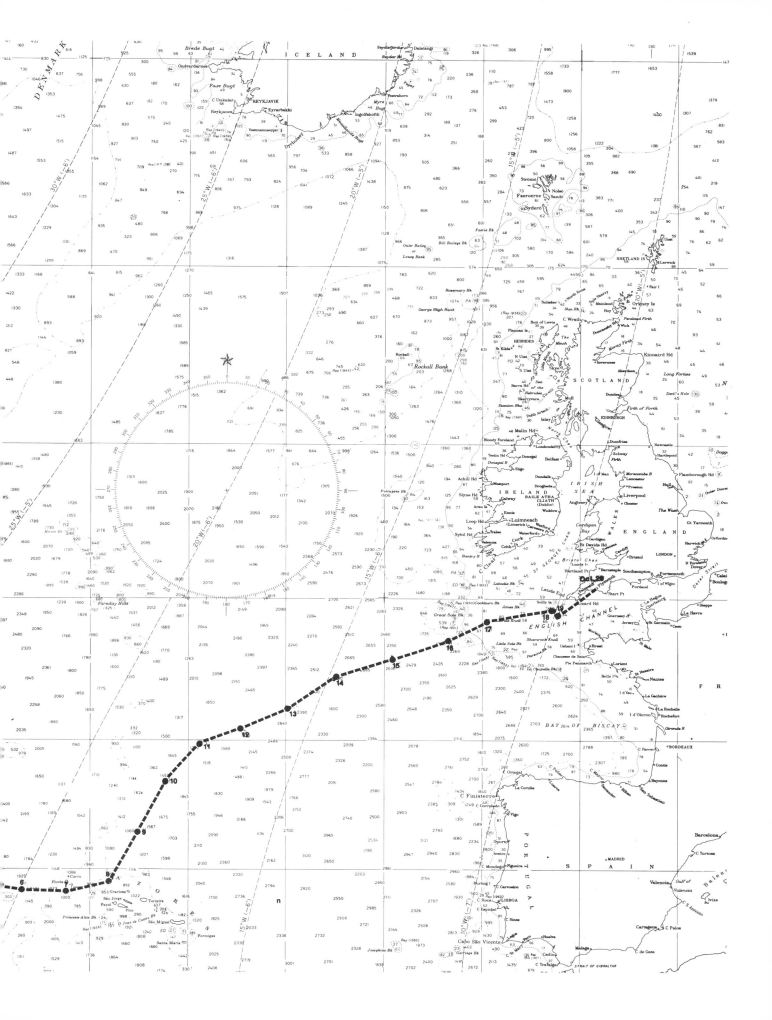

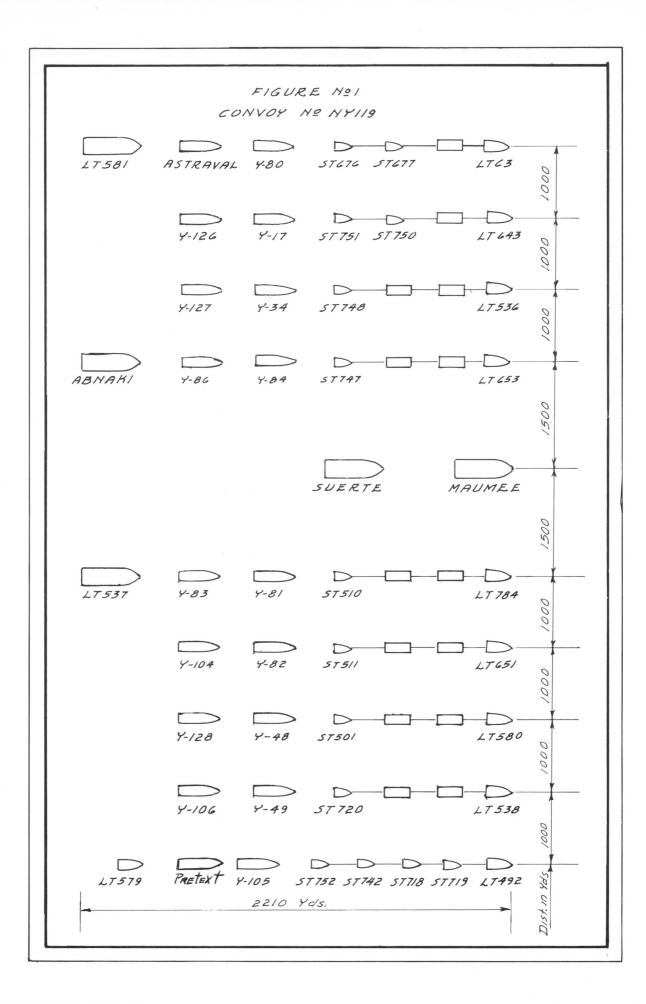

FIGURE No 1
CONVOY No NY119

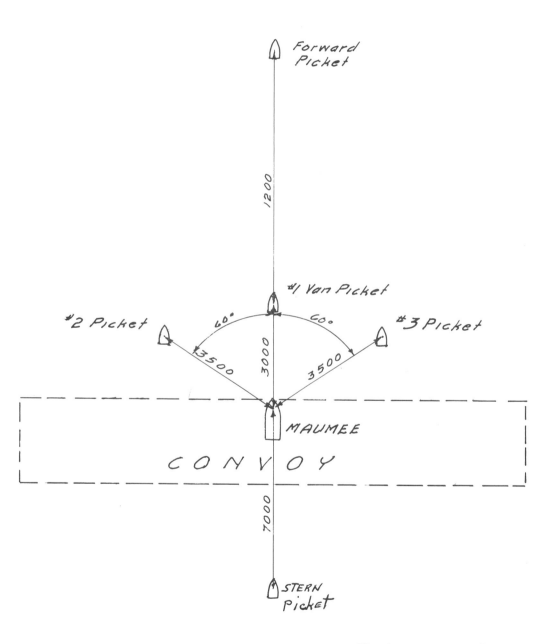

FIGURE No 2
ESCORT SCREEN
TG 27.5

Chapter III

ON THE EDGE OF THE SARGASSO

At 0629, the morning of the 23rd, the USS MASON (DE 529) began her dawn sweep off the Convoy's port van. On her bridge stood Lt. (JG) John C. Phillips who had the watch and the DE's skipper, Lt. Commander William M. Blackford, USNR. Both officers were white-skinned, in marked contrast to the enlisted men standing at station near them.

The MASON was an experiment for the Navy; she was the first ship to have a complete crew of black enlisted men. The officers, though, were white as were the majority of the Chief Petty Officers. Later, in the MASON's career, additional black CPOs were to be added, and it was planned to place black officers aboard as soon as they became available.

In general terms, it could be said that the DE 529 was a happy ship.[1] Some unusual problems had to be overcome. One of them had already been undertaken by Phillips who was also the ship's communication officer. It was to drill those of the men who had pronounced southern Negro dialects in the use of better enunciation over the ship's intercom system. A few cases of animosity had occurred between the white CPOs and their men, but these were rare and of a frequency rate not unusual aboard the average ship. The officers and white CPOs were all volunteers, and none appeared outwardly sorry for having requested the assignment.

By 0730 the dawn patrol sweep was over, and the MASON was off the Convoy's stern checking up on the foremost of two straggling groups.[2] The first to be visited was the Y 127 and the LT 579 which had taken the Y under tow. This tow job for the LT 579 followed closely one which she had carried since the second day of the Convoy's departure from New York when another Y boat, the Y 128, had lost power on both engines, requiring her to be towed for 35 hours while she was undergoing repairs.

Speaking over a bull horn to the LT 579, Blackford was told by her skipper that despite his towed burden, he had been gaining on the Convoy since dawn; and he reckoned that he should have the Y back in her position in column 3 by noon.

Satisfied, Blackford headed the MASON further on the back track toward the last group of stragglers composed of the LT 536 with her two barges and the ST 748 astern. Standing alongside them was the ABNAKI. On inquiry he was told that the group, now a good fourteen miles in the rear of the main body, would be underway as soon as the LT had corrected her difficulties, earlier discovered to be badly clogged fuel filters. Blackford then consulted Lt. Walley on the ABNAKI. It was determined that the wisest course would be for the ABNAKI to take the LT and her string in tow—lest further ground be lost. This done, the DE ranged out in a circular patrol screen.

Morning chores completed, the officers on the bridge of the MASON had time for coffee and some conversation. The talk centered around the chances of submarine attack. The skipper felt,[3] as did Leonard Barton, the Gunnery Officer, that a sub contact in the waters where they were now was unlikely. Firstly, Naval Intelligence back in New York had reported an apparent absence in the western Atlantic of German activity. Secondly, the sighting of a USN "Hunter-Killer Group" two days past, was reassuring in that the area must have already been well screened. To add to their safety, the Convoy would be in range of Bermuda-based aircraft patrols for at least the next four days. The dangers, Blackford reasoned, would probably begin eastward of the Azores. When they reached that point, the greatest jeopardy would be placed against the escorts and the MAUMEE. ASW people back at Eastern Sea Frontier had agreed that the majority of the Army craft were too shallow draft for a torpedo hit—unless, of course, a proximity type torpedo was used. The officers were all of the opinion that the escorts would make ideal targets due to the exaggerated patrol tracks which they were forced to set because of the Convoy's slow speed. Blackford concluded by stating that these same wide tracks would expose the escorts, once they struck bad weather, to a variety of sea headings guaranteed to effect their crews in a way that would resemble the contents of a washing machine in high gear.

By noon, the straggling group was gaining on the main Convoy; by 1400 hours the LT 536 was under the power of her own engines, and no longer under tow. The ABNAKI returned to her astern position in column 4, and the MASON went to her regular patrol area off the northeast corner of the Convoy.

* * * * * * *

While the MASON, the ABNAKI, and the LT 579 had been busy with the straggler problem, another of the service tugs, the LT 581, had placed its Navy repair crew aboard the ST 719 to attempt repairs on both of the ST's generators. The team shortly passed their diagnosis to the Convoy Commodore over TBS. "The leakage of salt water into the tug's fuel tanks had caused a freezing up of the injection pumps on both of ST 719's auxiliary generators." Although not related to any mechanical failure, the tug's permanent skipper threw in a word or two concerning the ship's fresh water supply; this was also badly contaminated by salt water. Both conditions had been brought on by the ill-fitting bunker plates which Simmers' NY 118 Report had urged should be corrected.

The repair crew removed both of the pumps intending to take them to the MAUMEE for repair or, if that was not possible duplication.[4] Before the Navy men left, Swartwout called aside their senior petty officer. "Son, come up on the boat deck with me, and I'll show you something I expect you won't see on a Navy ship." Upon arrival on the upper deck, the ex-cop pointed to a coffin-like box. "See that? It's our refrigerator. Now let me show you what's inside it." Lifting the lid, an unpleasant odor wafted upward. Swartwout explained that the last of the dry ice by which the meats were refrigerated had evaporated that morning. "All fifty lousy pounds of it. I figure tonight's meal is the last we can risk, or someone will end up with food poisoning." The Navy man, sympathetic, asked what the crew was going to eat for the rest of the trip. "We've got enough canned goods to get by on if we have to. I suppose the other STs must be in the same fix since all of them have the same set up."

The young PO, glad he wasn't scheduled to stay for dinner, signaled in the LT to take his party off.

After the repair team had left, Leonard and Thebus began throwing overboard what they later estimated to be close to 900 pounds of fresh poultry, eggs, and beef. They found some chicken still relatively cold and saved it for the evening meal. It was Leonard's turn to do the cooking; the regular cook, days beyond this chore, was now lying in his bunk in a state of semi-consciousness.

After supper, during which remarks were made that the chicken tasted half rotten,[5] the crew began to discuss what appeared to be on everyone's mind, "Would the ship capsize?" The ST's starboard list, which had not been corrected in New York, had become accentuated by the towing cables which led fore and aft from her hull. Everytime she took a roll, she would heave further to starboard because of the list. The tow cables, which at times were as taut as a bow string, tended to prevent a normal return motion. The day before they had passed through a series of squall lines which had raised seas to a point where the hesitancy of the little tug to return to port had alarmed all hands. Should the weather make-up, it was felt that prospects were not good since even now with winds at only 12 knots and seas about four feet high, the starboard weather deck was continually awash. The crew, which had given up any faith they may have ever had in Papaliolios, were taking all their orders from Swartwout,[6] so naturally they turned to him now for reassurance.

"Look, boys, this whole thing is new to me. I'll go along with you that things don't look good; but if we're lucky enough not to have any really bad weather, we'll make it O.K. As soon as we get our pumps back we'll have the power to transfer water and fuel to the port tanks which ought to help the list. First off, we'll have to drain them some, to make room." Dorwart remarked that the tanks could be part drained while they were awaiting the return of the pumps. "Better not, we'll just have the stuff sloshing around in the bilges since we can't pump them out until we get the auxiliaries running." Dorwart agreed.

Malone and Thebus, not due on watch until 2000, decided to leave the others talking and go get a little rest in their bunks which were located forward in the starboard fo'c'sle. Entering the compartment was a challenge since it was practically impossible to get into it without getting soaked. Timing the seas and the tug's roll, they rushed to un-dog the steel door; but just as they got it open, the ST rolled hard to starboard, wetting both men halfway to the waist. Cursing, Malone pushed the younger man inside and swung the door shut behind them. Stripping off their wet clothing, the men dropped into their bunks only to discover that the bedding was as damp as the clothing they had just removed. It didn't take long to find out that sleep was going to be impossible.

After a few moments of morose silence, Thebus asked the Mate what he thought their chances would be if they had to swim for it:[7] Were there sharks to worry about, and what were the odds on being picked up? Malone seemed to want to talk. Both men yarned of the sea and those things within it. Thebus was particularly impressed by the other man's description of the Portuguese Man-o-War, a type of jelly fish that the crew had seen in profusion over the last two days. From the surface they had the appearance of transparent floating membranes, mostly whitish in color with purplish red fringing; below the surface they trailed a score or more of filamentous tentacles. Malone told how he had been stung by one a few years before while swimming off a southern beach. He described the pain, an experience caused by coming in contact with just one or two of the tentacles. The Mate's opinion was that a full contact would probably so shock a man that drowning would soon follow. "Sharks? Well, kid, we ain't seen any yet, but you can bet your ass they're around."

* * * * * * *

Aboard the MAUMEE the machinists had given up on the ST 719's fuel pumps. They were so badly damaged that duplication was impossible since accurate measurements could not be taken. Ballard informed Lind of the situation over TBS. A survey of the other STs was made, and the ST 677 offered one on loan for a pattern. Lind decided that picking it up had better wait until the morrow. It was getting dark, and the sea was making up.

September 24

The morning of the 24th was rainy, the wind had swung to the northeast and clocked around 17 knots; the air temperature stood at 78°.

Following out the orders of CTG, the LT 581 pulled alongside the ST 677 to take aboard the promised fuel pump; but now, despite her Master's offer of the night before to loan it, the pump was not forthcoming. The LT dropped astern to the ST 676 whose Engineer obligingly agreed to remove one of his. The LT then ran it over to the MAUMEE whereupon it was discovered to be beyond usage for a pattern. Returning to the ST 677, the dilemma was explained and the request for the loan of the pump was repeated. Again, it was refused. The LT 581's Master suggested that the skipper of the ST would be on better ground if he was to report his refusal directly to CTG rather than have the news of it come from another source. The ST's skipper saw some wisdom to this advice and TBS'd Lind, stating that it was impossible to remove either of his pumps; he couldn't get to them. Lind, knowing better, but not wishing to create a verbal scene over the Convoy's radio circuit, had Mauldin bring the O'TOOLE directly alongside the ST, whereupon her skipper again pleaded several excuses as to the impossibility of removing them, concluding with a flat statement that he couldn't spare either of them.

"Captain," bellowed Lind, "you have exactly twenty minutes to remove that pump and deliver it to the LT 581, or an armed guard from this ship will board yours and place you and your Chief Engineer under military arrest." This appeared to produce an immediate change of policy aboard the ST. Her skipper spent the next eighteen minutes assuring CTG of his full cooperation—at which time the pump was handed over with two minutes left to deadline.[8]

* * * * * * *

The day was not to be a restful one for the LT 579. From the MAUMEE, Lt. Commander Ballard messaged her to proceed astern of column 8 and "render aid to the Y 128." Upon arrival on the scene, Jacob Fredenborg, Master of the LT 579, found his charge of two days past without power and drifting helplessly. The LT's stern was placed within a few yards of the Y's bow while the little oiler's crew again heaved aboard the tug's heavy steel cable, preparatory to being taken under tow.

Close in to the noon hour, it was Fredenborg's turn to call on Ballard, "My ship has lost power on the port engine. Can you give me assistance?" The Commodore responded by sending the now unoccupied LT 581 to lend a hand. Since his own Navy repair team was aboard the Y 128, Fredenborg requested the transfer of the LT 581's team over to help out his engineers who were busy at work below. Thorstnes of the LT 581 agreed to the transfer; a short, wet ride in a rubber boat effected the shift in personnel.

* * * * * * *

While the MAUMEE's machinists were fabricating new fuel pumps for the ST 719, the LT 581 and the LT 579 were busied at the rear of the Convoy. The third service tug, the LT 537, was intent on proving that life can be beautiful, even in a barge convoy. She was passing out ice cream which had been donated, courtesy of the USS POWERS, to the Army Craft.[9]

Following the ice cream run, news was received that the LT 538 had broken down. The ice cream vender hooked on, thus managing to keep the LT 538 and her tows of column 9 reasonably closed up on station.

September 25

September 25th was another rainy day; winds had increased to 28 knots.

Aboard the MAUMEE, Ballard was having an increasingly difficult time in performing his "guide-on" function which Lind had been so emphatic in insisting that he continue.

By mid-day, Ballard had reached a personal decision. He decided to circumvent Commander Lind's orders as discreetly as possible and transfer the "guide-on" function to the LT next to him in column 6.[10]

Conning his ship to starboard, he brought the MAUMEE to within bull horn distance of the LT 784, Emery S. Clarke, commanding. Ballard explained the problem he was having in maintaining station because of the tanker's high superstructure which gave it a tendency to drift to windward at a greater rate than the Army craft; this was abetted by having to operate his ship on only one engine so that her speed would correspond with the turtle crawl of the rest of the Convoy. "Would you take over the guide-role?" The ATS Master readily accepted the responsibility in the best "down east" spirit of cooperation. The Commodore had picked out the right man for the job. Clarke, a native of Machiasport, Maine, held an unlimited license as a Chief Mate in the Merchant Marine. He had been sailing on ships' bridges since 1927 and knew the business.

After delegating this authority, life became more manageable for Ballard. He could now concentrate on his major task of Convoy Commodore and the responsibility of supervising his ship's role as repair vessel, not to mention its additional duty of refueling the DEs and the tugs. The Ys were to bunker themselves via their own cargo tanks, thus removing this chore from the MAUMEE.

* * * * * * *

The Y 127, it seemed, needed her mother. Again, she lost power, and this time help came from the LT 581 which took her under tow.

* * * * * * *

At 1535 the ST 719's pumps were returned. Dorwart and Williams started to assemble them.

It was not all peaches and cream aboard the ST 719. The cook now had company in his seasick misery; Harding, the Signalman, had become ill the day before. He attributed his condition not to the sea but to the half spoiled chicken that Leonard had prepared. Others in the crew were not exactly in the peak of condition either, but so far the only two on their backs were Harding and Janos.

Malone and Thebus had spent the night of the 24th and 25th, while off watch, on the pilot house deck. They, like most of the others, were reluctant to restrict themselves to within the coffin-like confinement of their fo'c'sles lest the tug turn over. Crowded as it had been in the pilot house, sleep had not been easy to come by. Tonight, Malone and Thebus had decided to sleep in their bunks—this on the theory, "That if she hadn't gone over yet, she probably wouldn't." Dorwart and Williams, their own quarters flooded, had moved their mattresses into the galley which was now unusable for its normal cooking function due to the lack of stove fuel which couldn't be pumped topside because of the inoperative auxiliaries.

* * * * * * *

By the latter part of the afternoon, all the ATS service tugs and also the ABNAKI were occupied with tows. Lind knew that his insistence of being supplied with extra service tugs and the ABNAKI was more than justified. He only wished now that he had a couple more available.

* * * * * * *

When the sun went down that night, NY 119 did not resemble the orderliness of CTG's convoy chart, what with stragglers astern and a tendency of many of the tows to veer out of their columns. The wind was still fairly strong at 30 knots. The waves were white-tipped and beginning to curl. The monotony of the seascape was broken by huge mats of floating seaweed. The weed was a species known as Sargasso. The Convoy was now on the northern edge of the huge tideless vacuum of the central Atlantic known as the Sargasso Sea.

Chapter IV

A DUCKLING DROWNS

During the early hours of the night of the 25th to 26th, most of the crew members aboard the ST 719 were vocal in their opinion that the ship's starboard list had increased. Williams estimated that it was close to 15°; however, no one could account for the reason. The lube-oil drums which had been carried in reserve and lashed atop the boat deck were now empty, having been punctured and drained on Papaliolios' orders. The ice box carried topside was also empty, its contents jettisoned.

Both Williams and Dorwart, assisted by Swartwout, had worked until 2100 on the fuel pumps, hoping to get them running so that part of the contents of the starboard fuel tank could be transferred to port, thereby helping to stabilize the vessel. Despite their best efforts, the pumps just would not work; probably an error in the attempt to refabricate them. The bilges were still relatively dry with only four or five inches of water in them, so this couldn't be the cause of the increased list.[1] It had to be external. Most of the men thought it was brought on by the increasingly bad sea conditions which were whipped up by a wind which was taking on more violence as the night wore on. The sky was heavily overcast with intermittent rain, yet there was enough phosphorus in the water to light up the wakes of the vessels forward and behind them. From this, those on the ST's bridge were able to gain a relative prospective of the position of the LT 492 ahead and the ST 718 trailing astern. They noticed that as the steel towing cables fore and aft would slacken, a noticeable yawing of their little ship would take place, causing the ST 719 to swing to the port of the LT 492's stern; at times it was as much as fifty yards out of alignment. While this was happening, the ST astern of them would still trail on the ST 719's previous track, or even slightly to the starboard of the track of the LT 492. When the tow cable connecting the LT and the ST 719 would jerk tight, the little tug would swing sideways, back to the right (starboard), causing her to heel in that direction as she sliced slantingly on a return track through the sea. The extent of the list appeared to vary, depending on how far she would yaw between the intermittent tightenings of the forward tow cable. At times it would be unnoticeable; at others, the effect was bladder constricting in the fear the experience produced among those aboard the listing tug.

* * * * * * *

The post-midnight watch of that night, September 26, was already as active as any daylight stint aboard the USS JOHN J. POWERS (DE 528).[2]

At the onset of the watch, activities were conducted by Ensign Arthur J. McCarthy, USN. McCarthy, a junior in rank to the other watch officers, was highly respected for his knowledge and competence. He was a "Mustang," having come up through the enlisted ranks from Chief Quartermaster.

Lt. Commander E. Allen Loew, USNR, the POWERS skipper, had retired to his cabin during the last watch, but shortly before 0100, he entered the ship's Combat Information Center (CIC) for a fast look at the radar in order to get the perspective of the Convoy's organization.

At 0100, McCarthy swung the POWERS from her assigned station at the rear and traveled up the outboard side of column 10, to a position roughly off the beam of the LT 492's last tow. There, at about 9000 yards out, she came upon the LT 581, steaming way out of assigned position with the disabled Y 127 in tow. The LT 581, like the rest of the Army craft, was not equipped with radar. In the darkness of the night her captain was unknowing of his ship's position and of the fact that he was on a converging course toward the main body of the Convoy. McCarthy instructed Thorstnes, the skipper of LT 581, to bring down his speed and come in by the left behind the Convoy, with the purpose in mind of later regaining the Y 127's proper station under radar con from the POWERS.

Rerouting his ship back to astern of the main body, McCarthy brought the POWERS around behind the last tow of the LT 538 which was being assisted by the service tug LT 537. This group, despite the heavy load on the service tug, had been able to keep up and was just behind their assigned alignment in column 9—their present position being 3000 yards directly astern of where they should have been had things been entirely normal.

* * * * * * *

At 0201, the POWERS was cruising at 15 knots on stern screen about six miles back from and slightly to port of column 10. That column consisted of the LT 492 and her "four little ducklings," the STs. McCarthy had just propped himself against the coaming of the starboard bridge wing when he saw a flashing light to starboard—dead abeam. Flipping up the sight vanes on the gyro repeater, he took a fast bearing—85° true; the light read as a series of inarticulate SOSs.

McCarthy immediately reported what he had seen to Loew. The skipper then took over the con, operating from CIC so as to direct his ship through the maze of Y boats and tows which were between him and the light. As soon as the POWERS responded to her new heading, Loew voice-radioed CTG to report his action. CTG replied that the light had just been bracketed by the O'TOOLE and the MAUMEE, and it was assumed to have come from the forward part of column 10's string of tows. Lind, now awake and in CIC aboard the O'TOOLE, personally took over.[3] His first order was to direct Loew to continue as he was toward the light. Next, Lind plugged into the MAUMEE to inquire as to what service tugs were available. Ballard told him that all three of the tugs and also the ABNAKI had tows. "Which one can you spare?" Ballard came back with the information that the Y boat under tow of the ABNAKI had one engine going and could make four knots unaided. "OK, have Walley cast off the Y and run in to assist." Lind then ordered the USS BERMINGHAM, on screen off the Convoy's starboard quarter at station No. 3, to leave position and proceed to the scene of what was now definitely assumed to be a disaster. The MASON, on van picket, was ordered to swing right to replace the BERMINGHAM at station No. 3 (see figure 2 of text).

While CTG was readjusting his escorts and sending in the rescuers, radio traffic began to increase over TBS. Many of the Army craft had also seen the distress signals, and they wanted to know "What the hell is going on?" Immediately, Lind ordered the circuit cleared for emergencies only. In order to insure uninterrupted transmission, he then switched to VHF voice radio as added insurance of being able to communicate. The use of VHF radio, in addition to his ordering that the TBS circuit be cleared, had the advantage that while CTG was transmitting through VHF to the escorts, the Commodore on the MAUMEE could, in turn, use TBS to handle the necessary ATS traffic which was now, thankfully, reduced from the hysterical babble of a few minutes before.

The situation, administratively, at least, appeared to be in hand.

* * * * * * *

Aboard the ST 719 and back tracking in time to shortly after the change of watch at midnight, the situation could be described as follows:[4]

She was still yawing wildly, perhaps more so, since at times the wind was gusting upwards of 50 knots in squall lines.

On the little tug's bridge and peering into the darkness, stood Swartwout. Papaliolios had retired earlier to his quarters in the cabin aft of the wheel house. Ridgeway Leonard stood at the wheel. Sprawled out on the deck in the congested space was the sleeping form of Paul Williams. Directly below the wheel house, off the weather deck, were Malone and Thebus in the forward starboard fo'c'sle. In the opposite port compartment were AB Scott, Janos the cook, and "Flags" (Harding). Midship, on the galley deck, lay Dorwart. Back in the after cabin were Van der Linden and his roommate Moran.

On or about 0135,[5] Papaliolios was thrown from his bed to the steel deck. Awakened, but dazed, he could nevertheless see that the cabin was oddly tilted. Someone shouted, "She's gone over!" Papaliolios, crawling on his hands and knees, entered the wheel house whence it became apparent that the ship was lying on her starboard side and still under tow. The electricity was still operative, and so the four men present could clearly see white water cascading against the wheel house windows. For an instant they were all hypnotized by the sight of it, but the spell was broken when one of the windows explosively shattered and the sea began to fill the compartment. The only escape was through the port doorway, which, as the ship was now on her starboard side, was no longer accessible but lay at a 70° angle above their heads. The compartment was flooding fast; the lights went out. "Grab a lantern!" Someone remembered that there was one attached to the bulkhead, and he reached over to wrench it loose. Snapping the light on, a near panic was averted as the men could now see the door above them coming closer as they floated upward with the incoming torrent. "Open it!" Williams reached for the latch and shoved; the door swung open and back against the bridge house. One after the other, the men scrambled out to the relative safety of the tilted deck and pulled themselves along a guard rail to a point against the smoke stack. Swartwout, seeing Harding, shouted, "Give 'Flags' the light!" Leonard handed it over, and Harding began blinking out the series of SOSs which initially had alerted McCarthy on the bridge of the POWERS.

Meanwhile, the occupants of the after cabin had also made their escape. Van der Linden[6] had squeezed himself through a porthole and once outside had opened the fo'c'sle door and pulled Moran to safety. The two men then clung to the side of the deck house, at first unaware that there were others alive until they saw the beam of a lantern emerging from the wheel house doorway.

In the galley, Dorwart's first realization that the ship had capsized came when he awakened to the sound of breaking glass and a sensation of riding a toboggan as he and his mattress slid along the deck, finally coming to rest against the starboard bulkhead amidst the assorted debris that had been flung there. Struggling upright, his bare feet were cut by glass, but in the excitement he hardly felt any pain. Reaching for the door leading to the starboard weather deck, he un-dogged it and pushed. It wouldn't budge! Then it hit him as to why it wouldn't open; he was shoving against solid water. Refastening the dogs, he tried to climb up the slanting deck, slipping backwards two feet for each foot that he progressed. Finally reaching the handle of the port door, he couldn't get the leverage to open it. He then began to scream for help.[7]

Scott, Janos, and Harding had made their escape from the port fo'c'sle and were clustered next to the smoke stack before the pilot house group had made theirs.

56

The experience of Mate Malone and AB John Thebus can best be related in Thebus' own words, which come from his memory, vivid and accurate, despite the passage of twenty-six years.[8]

"This was to be a night of horror, because this was the night that the ST 719 took the last starboard roll and didn't come back up to even keel. I remember my feet getting wet and trying to get them back into the bunk, then First Mate Malone saying (not in a shout, but loudly enough to wake me), 'Better hurry, Johnny, she's over this time.' Wide awake, I began to move the cases of cigarettes which were covering the porthole, under water, and our only means of escape. The forward porthole had a blackout screen in it, but the side porthole didn't. It was dogged down, so had to open it, raise it, and hook it up, leaving about a 15'' opening to get out. By the time this was done, I was under water, as the cabin was filling rapidly. I came up for breath and First Mate Malone went down for his first attempt at escape. He got stuck in the porthole, and I helped pull him back up for air so I could make my first attempt to get out.

"I must describe an unusual experience at this point. Anyone that has been to sea will recall that on a dark night you notice a weird greenish phosphoresence, particularly at the stern of the ship as the bubbles break the surface. In the cabin, and because of the black-out screen being in the forward porthole, water was churned into the cabin showing around the opened porthole. We couldn't open the door, as the ST 719 was still being towed, and we couldn't force it open against the pressure of the water passing by.

"On my first attempt out, I became stuck also, and Mate Malone helped me get back up for air. He made his second, and I will assume last unsuccessful attempt, came back up and said, 'Good luck, Johnny, this is about the last try.' I put my nose to the top which was the wall of the forcastle, took a deep breath, and with all my might pushed as hard as I could, down and out of the porthole. I got my hips out, largely due to the current of water passing by, pulling me out, scraping my sides, etc. Out of the porthole and under water, I grabbed hold of what was the railing to the pilot house and let myself slide backward, kicking my feet to try and find the life boat davits. My feet touched them, (life boat still securely fastened, as it was on the starboard side and under water also). Using this as a brace, I reached up above to get hold of the railing which went around the top of the pilot house and pulled myself upward until my head broke surface. Lungs nearly bursting at this point, I briefly rested, got my bearings as to where I was, and at this point saw other members of the crew of the ST 719 sitting on the gunnel and the side. I moved down the stack and joined them on the side."

Swartwout, bracing himself against the smoke stack, began an informal roll call, trying to count noses in the dark. "1 - 2 - 3 - 4 - 5 — where's the cook?" "Back aft, I think." Then another man accounted for and another, and an eighth, "Is the Mate here?" Thebus, shouting against the wind, said that he thought Malone must have drowned. Another man was located, then, "Where is the Chief?" Moran said that he had last seen Dorwart in the galley. Swartwout asked for a volunteer to help him search for the missing Chief Engineer.[9] Williams and another man went with him, and the three of them crawled forward and down to the galley door. As they neared it, they could hear shouts and thudding. Dorwart, by this time near total exhaustion, was holding on with one hand to the door handle and pounding with his other. Swartwout and Williams got it open, but in so doing, they dislodged the Engineer's grip. The trapped man skidded across the slanting deck but caught up halfway down, one foot braced against the galley range. Mustering his strength, he heaved himself up to within the reach of Williams' outstretched hands. With Swartwout's aid, the two men pulled him clear. Taking a few seconds to catch their breath, they groped their way back to the others. Now there were eleven.

The tug was still being towed through the water. The LT 492, "Thank God," had seen them for certain. The huddled survivors could see frantic activity taking place on the LT's fantail under the illumination of deck lights. "Are they cutting loose the cable?"[10] It was hard to tell at that distance, but when they turned and looked astern toward the ST 718, they could definitely make out the glow of a cutting torch as that crew tried burning through the steel hawser that connected the two STs.

Ten, or maybe fifteen, minutes went by.

It was hard to tell at first, but by noting the curtailment of the phosphorescent wake, it became apparent that they were no longer making headway. Within seconds thereafter, the ST 719 began a slow roll back to an upright position. She stopped revolving, but as she did, the deck began to pitch toward the stern. She was filling up and going down. As the hull took on more water, it became less buoyant, and the seas washed over with increasing force. It took all their strength for the men to hold on as each successive wave broke over them. The hiss of the approaching combers gave a little warning of the punch they carried. Eight of the men, in mass, were hurled off the starboard side of the sinking hulk. Still left clinging, but not for long, were Papaliolios, Van der Linden, and Williams. They hung there for another minute or two, at which time the ST 719 went out from under them, leaving nothing to mark the place of her submergence save the floating crewmen.

Mate Malone, entrapped and probably already dead, accompanied her to the bottom.

When the ST 719 went down, the three men left aboard her feared that they would be pulled with it by the suction of the sinking ship. To their relief, there was little suction (although Williams was dragged down a short distance), maybe because the breaking seas had pushed them clear of it. A few large bubbles were seen and a gurgling noise was heard, but this was difficult to distinguish above the sound of the wind and the waves.[11]

In the few minutes between when the first group had been washed overboard and the ship had gone out from under Papaliolios, Williams, and Van der Linden, there was just enough of a time interval to place the latter three directly in the path of the ST 718. The trailing tug was clearly visible to the men in the water as she had switched on her deck lights and was sweeping the area with a searchlight. The three swimmers were immediately seen by those on the deck of the ST 718, and before ten minutes had elapsed, Papaliolios was pulled aboard as were Van der Linden and Williams, in that order.[12] After Van der Linden had climbed safely to the deck, he still had enough reserve energy to rush forward and help his hosts unshackle the cable attaching them to the now-invisible ST 719. The acetylene torch (seen earlier from the ST 719's hull) had failed to function properly and had sputtered out before the cable could be burnt through. Now the men were trying to manually loosen it. Although everyone seemed to be getting in everyone else's way in their haste to cast off, the ST 718 was finally freed.

In retrospect, it is a miracle that the sunken tug did not pull the other one down with it. If this had happened, there would have followed in sequence, the sinking of not only ST 718, but most likely the ST 742 and the ST 752, all four being shackled in line as they were. What apparently had happened was that the ST 719 had, in fact, not completely sunk but was buoyant a short distance under the surface. The entrapped air within her may have shifted and thus temporarily increased her buoyancy before she made her final dive to the bottom. If this assumption is correct, it might have accounted for the lack of suction that the survivors reported. At any rate, whatever the cause, it prevented the sinking of the entire string of "little ducklings."

When the excitement over casting loose the cable had receded, Wallace S. Olivey, Master of the ST 718, yelled down the news to those on deck as to what he had just heard over TBS. "The LT 492 was also free, her towing cable having parted some minutes past."

In summarizing the events, it is the author's opinion that at the time the LT's cable broke the ST 719 lost her headway and began to sink.

* * * * * *

The eight men that were washed overboard together off the ST 719's hull, were no longer grouped.

A careful reconstruction of what followed after the eight were catapulted into the sea, concludes that Swartwout, Leonard, Thebus, Harding, and Dorwart were in close proximity of each other at the beginning. Other than seeing Janos on the hull shortly before the wave struck, no one had seen him beyond that point. It may be reasonably assumed that in his weakened condition and without a life preserver, he drowned immediately. The group initially attempted to stay together by "ringing up" and holding hands, but the force of the seas kept tearing them apart. While in the water, one of the men said he heard Moran and Scott call out, but no one else did. The ST 718 soon passed them by as did another ship searching too far to windward.

Slowly, the group broke up; Swartwout first and then Dorwart drifted out of sight into the pitch blackness of the rain-streaked night. Leonard, Thebus,[13] and Harding were still together, but they no longer tried to hold hands. Of the three, Harding was the only one with a life preserver. Still thinking that the three of them should stay close together, the two ABs treaded water in order to hold a position nearby the Signalman. Harding, beginning to give into the first stages of hysteria, became obsessed that the other two were going to grab hold of him for support, and he panicked whenever they swam too close. Before long, the two life preserverless seamen lost sight of Harding but knew he was near as they could clearly hear his screams for help.

Minutes passed, or as it seemed to the swimmers, hours. Thebus began to think back on Malone's sea tales of sharks and jelly fish. Seas broke over the men's heads, ducking them under for five or six seconds at a time. The noise of the sea was awesome; the phosphorescence, frightening. "What was that streak of light?" Sea weed brushed against their faces, compounding their fear of the unknown. Once, Thebus was swept under by a breaking wave and came up directly beneath a mat of Sargasso weed. He came close to panic, thinking it to be one of the Portuguese Men-O-War Malone had told him about. Leonard, speaking reassuredly, calmed his friend down.

Soon, the half-drowned twosome spotted a searchlight coming closer by the minute. Sweeping, then stabbing through the night, it finally picked them out. Screaming over and over for help, the men waited in fear that the ship wouldn't stop. The rescuing vessel was the POWERS, and she bull-horned the survivors, "Save your voices, we see you; we will pick you up." Unimpressed, having been passed up already by the ST 718 and the other ship (the BERMINGHAM), the two ABs and Harding paid little heed and continued to scream. Loew on the POWERS was having a hard time of it trying to maneuver in the high winds, but he finally worked to windward of the swimmers and stopped engines while his crew threw out life rings. Thebus and Leonard each managed to grab one, and they were pulled in toward the point where a landing net had been strung from the ship's waist. Aided by members of the crew, the men half climbed and were half dragged onto the DE's deck.

Harding, further to leeward than the ABs and toward the POWERS' stern, appeared to be wildly hysterical, and he failed to grasp or even see the life rings thrown toward him.[14] Loew, his ship now too close for comfort to the oncoming BERMINGHAM, knew that the man in the water could stay afloat until the ABNAKI arrived from astern, so he swung his ship clear, intending to spotlight the area from a safer vantage point.

What will now be related is difficult to describe, yet in a time of war and other disasters, it is not uncommon. Call it what you will: A psychic phenomenon? A true religious experience? Or perhaps it could be as simple as the aftermath of a period of great stress compounded by hysteria. Who knows? This author will not be so presumptuous as to attempt to explain a reason. What is pertinent, is that Clarence Vernon Harding, alone and afloat in a hostile environment, experienced something that September night in 1944 that was very real and very religious and has remained so for him over the years.[15]

When the POWERS had swung off to avoid the BERMINGHAM, Harding realized that neither ship was going to pick him up, and his terror began mounting to a crescendo. Then, quite suddenly, a peacefulness began to settle over him, and he heard a resonant voice speaking slowly and with great authority, "YOU'LL BE ALL RIGHT, SON."

Whether or not what Harding heard was real or imaginary, it did have the effect of calming him, and it convinced him that he would be rescued. The ABNAKI had earlier scooped up Scott and Moran, and it was this vessel which picked up Harding ten minutes or so after he had heard the "voice."

* * * * * * *

After Swartwout had become separated from the rest, his first reaction was a sense of desolation. Whenever he rose on the crests of a wave, he could make out searchlights and the silhouettes of some of the rescuing vessels reflected in the rain by their deck lights. They seemed so far away. It had been over an hour since he had lost voice contact with the other survivors, and despair began creeping into his mind. Reconciling himself to death, he prayed that the end wouldn't come knifing up from beneath to cut him in two. The water was around 80°, and he knew that this temperature was perfect for sharks. The phosphorescence, creating fiery streaks and pockets of light with each breaking wave had reacted on Swartwout as it had on the others. It did little to allay his fear of what sea creatures might be around.

Swartwout was wearing a life preserver, so unlike Thebus and Leonard who had none, he was riding with the crests of the waves and down into their valleys; thus he escaped the complete submergence that the latter two were experiencing. Nevertheless, the same life preserver that gave him this floatation caused his upper body to be subjected to a battering that the other men had escaped. Instead of being ducked under by the seas, he was receiving the full breaking force of their plumes, and consequently, he involuntarily breathed in a considerable amount of salt water which produced a gagging reaction in his efforts to expel it. His throat was becoming cracked from the salt water and the gagging. Before long, he began to retch up blood.

More minutes passed—seeming like an eternity to Swartwout as he was twisted and pummeled by the waves. It was then that he saw it. A ship with her running lights on and her searchlights stabbing, was heading directly toward him. Ripping off the one-cell flashlight that was pinned to his life jacket, he held it upright and began waving it at arm's length. The ship kept coming closer; he could see the white curl of its bow wave, but it was difficult to gauge the distance as it came on. The ship, appearing to be 100 to 200 yards off, was all of a sudden almost on top of him. As the knife edge of her bow loomed high above him, the bow wave subsided, yet he could tell that she hadn't stopped. Flinging out his arms and legs, he spread-eagled himself across the bow point of the ship and clung desperately. The barnacles clustered on her hull gave him something to hold on to; their sharp shells produced not pain but exhilaration that he had something to adhere to. The ship rose and fell with the sea as Swartwout dug his fingers deep into the barnacles, knowing that if he lost his grip he might be sucked under and ground to pieces by the propellers. "Why didn't she stop?" The clinging man knew that he couldn't hang on much longer as the lunging bow as submerging him every time it came down from the crest of a wave. Then he could feel her stopping; the pressure of movement no longer pressed against his back. He then began losing his grip. Hearing voices above, he looked up to see faces peering down at him. They lowered a rope which he grabbed and double wrapped around his arms. He pulled, but there was no response; they weren't trying to hoist him up. Instead, the "faces" began to lead the tethered survivor back toward the stern of the vessel. Swartwout's body slammed against the ship's side near a rope netting, and he began to lose consciousness. Before blacking out, he saw men climbing down toward him.

Two hours later, the former permanent Master of the ST 719 woke up in the Sick Bay of the POWERS. He was being massaged by two anxious Navy Corpsmen who were trying to bring circulation back to what had almost been a dead man.

There was a sound reason as to why the POWERS had run down Swartwout. The day following his rescue, he was told by Lt. Commander Loew what had happened: After the POWERS arrived at the scene of the sinking, she sighted Thebus, Leonard, and Harding on her first search sweep. A few minutes following and after maneuvering to avoid the BERMING-HAM, Dorwart had been spotted and was pulled aboard. Loew then began a criss-cross search pattern, whereupon the LT 537 with the LT 538 and her column 9 string of tows came steaming up from their laggards position astern of the Convoy. On the POWERS' bridge, Loew had just spotted Swartwout's life jacket light close ahead; at the same instant, the ship's CIC informed him that radar indicated that they were directly between the LT 537 and the LT 538. In other words, the heavy steel towing hawser which connected the two tugs was under the POWERS' keel. Reacting instantly, Loew barked out orders that the man in the water was to be picked up on the run, since to risk stopping the DE before he was clear of the line of tows would seriously endanger his ship. The tolerance of passing the vessel close enough to insure that the survivor would be reached and not actually running him down was slight and meant but half an inch either way on the helmsman's turn of the wheel. That half an inch turn was not made and so Swartwout and the POWERS' bow had met head on. Loew had reduced his speed considerably before the impact; and, in fact, the ship was probably doing no more than three knots at the moment of meeting. But to the man in the water, it must have felt like twenty. Just as soon as the POWERS had cleared the track of the towing hawser, Loew rung his engines to "Stop", and it was then that Swartwout was led back to the boarding net.[16]

* * * * * * *

After Swartwout had been picked up, it remained uncertain to those crowded into the CIC room aboard the O'TOOLE, as to how many men had actually composed the sunken ST's crew. The survivors were punch drunk from their experience, and the reports coming in from the rescuing vessels were conflicting. "Had there been twelve men aboard, or was it thirteen?" "Had Janos been picked up?" "Was he alive or dead?" Lind ordered the O'TOOLE and the BERMINGHAM to keep searching the probable drift path.

At 0952, the following morning, Loew radioed CTG that the entire area had been covered with a fine tooth comb. "Further search appears fruitless." Lind then ordered the DEs to head eastward back toward the Convoy.[17]

* * * * * * *

One small tug had been lost, along with two members of her crew—not really serious from an operational standpoint—but a disaster to the morale of the crews aboard the other STs.

Chapter V

WEST OF THE ATLANTIC RIDGE

The morning of September 28th dawned with conditions much improved over those of the past four days. The wind was out of the northeast with a marked reduction of velocity down to 5 knots. The clouds were higher than the low scudding cumulus and thunderheads which the Convoy had almost grown used to. There were still rain showers around, but they were intermittent; the air temperature was still sub-tropical at 70°. The mats of Sargasso were becoming less frequent; and when the weed was seen, it was in small patches.

Flying Fish were a constant sight, and each morning some would be found on the weather decks of the Ys and tugs upon which they had unexpectedly ended their graceful flights from wave to wave. An enterprising deck hand on the ST 720, noting this abundance of fish life, reasoned that where there were little ones, there should be big ones. Putting his theory to the test, he liberated a fishing rig from among the survival gear in the tug's lifeboat and rigged it to trail astern. Trolling conditions were just what a charter boat skipper would have ordered. That noon the ST's crew enjoyed their first fresh meat since they had jettisoned the contents of their deck refrigerator four days out of New York.[1] The 3-foot fish the deck hand had pulled aboard was a Dolphin (not to be confused with a Porpoise) which abounds wherever Flying Fish are seen.

* * * * * * *

The day had started out well with every ship in her proper position; and for the first time since the morning of the 20th, every one of the service tugs and the ABNAKI were traveling free, unencumbered by tows. There was some difference, though, in the landscape. Changes were made in the Convoy's organization after the break-up of the LT 492's string and the sinking of ST 719. The LT 492 had lost her tow cable when the dead weight of the capsized and half-flooded ST had stripped it all out. In the process, her towing engine had been totally disabled. Without cable or towing engine, she had been prevented from picking up her tow consisting of the three remaining STs.

At first light, the ABNAKI outfitted the ST 718 with a new towing bridle and cable, her previous ones having gone to the bottom with the

ST 719. She then helped her hook up to the HMS PRETEXT, one of the British net tenders which had taken passage with NY 119 and was now going to pay the conductor.[2] Next, the ABNAKI passed a new bridle to the ST 742 to replace the one she had cut as a precautionary measure the night before. Following this, the ABNAKI took both the ST 742 and the ST 752 in tow and then, pacing the LT 492, sent over a repair crew to assist that vessel in repairing her towing engine. The damage was too serious to patch; Ballard ordered the LT over to the MAUMEE for the removal of the towing engine to his ship for major surgery. After daylight, repairs were completed, and the unit was placed back aboard the LT. The ABNAKI then cast off the two STs which proceeded under their own power. Next she put her stern near the LT's and paid out a new towing cable to the former. When this task was completed, the rejuvenated LT 492 took back her "two ducklings." Damage-control work completed, the Navy tug with the LT and her two STs, along with the BERMINGHAM, which had been screening them, steamed forward to their regularly assigned Convoy stations.

Commander Lind, Lt. Walley of the ABNAKI, and Lt. Phipps, the Convoy's towing specialist, all agreed that the new arrangement (whereby the LT 492 was only trailing two STs astern instead of four) would cut down the whip-lash effect that in all probability had been the cause of the ST 719's sinking. On the 28th, when Lind steamed the O'TOOLE close aboard the LT 492, he noted with satisfaction an elimination of the yawing that had been so apparent before the catastrophe.

Since the 28th was the first day in a week that the weather would allow it, CTG ordered off boarding parties from the service tugs to pump out the bilges of BCF car floats No. 3203, No. 3204, and No. 3205, all three of which had shown noticeable lists since the storm of the 25th and 26th. BCF No. 3203 was in tow of the LT 63 in column 1 while BCFs No. 3204 and No. 3205 were pulled by the LT 538 heading column 9. The three barges had been requisitioned from the Philadelphia and Reading Railroad Company and were of the oldest vintage of any of the Convoy's car floats, having been built in 1928.[3] The repair parties were able to start the gasoline billy pumps on all of them, and their bilges were sucked dry within an hour. Upon returning, the repair crews submitted pessimistic reports that all three BCFs were still taking on water and would have to be repumped whenever the weather again permitted boarding.

Later in the day, another P&R car float, BCF No. 3211, (the lead tow of the LT 580 in column 8) was noticed to be down by the head. A repair party was put aboard; they reported that she, like the other BCFs, would require repumping within a matter of a day or two. To Lind, this news meant only one thing; the Convoy would be slowed down. Each time a car float needed boarding, the tug towing her had to move at a crawl. In turn, the main body of the Convoy, so as not to outpace the stragglers, would need to reduce speed in order that the stragglers could rejoin. Another side liability was that everytime a tug with her barge dropped astern for pumping, an escort would have to shepherd the unit, thus weakening the already-stretched ASW screen.

At 1600, CTG thought that things were beginning to go his way. The day was passing without a mechanical breakdown. Yet, before the watch struck its first bell, he was to be disillusioned; the Y 49, whose steering gear had been giving her trouble since New York, dropped out of her column; same old problem persisted. By dusk, the crew had made repairs, and she was back in line. At least the Convoy viewed the sunset as it had greeted the dawn—as one unit.

September 29

By dawn on the 29th, the bad weather was back with winds at 20 knots.[4] Fearing even worse conditions coming, CTG ordered the refueling of the escorts.

At 0857, the POWERS was brought alongside the MAUMEE to begin drinking in her estimated need of 24,000 gallons of diesel fuel. At 0905, and still alongside, a sea flung her stern in toward the oiler resulting in the two colliding. The collision opened a 3-foot hole in the POWERS' hull. Before an hour was up, her damage control party had everything in order, and the DE, again seaworthy, took van picket station, No. 1. The escort she relieved came in next to nurse from the mother oiler.[5]

By 1615, all the escorts had been refueled and were back on regular picket station with the exception of the BERMINGHAM which was screening the LT 492 which was having minor engine troubles and straggling two miles astern.

September 30

The wind had dropped to a workable velocity by 0800 the morning of the 30th, and the better weather conditions prompted Ballard to request that CTG allow him to begin refueling the LTs. Permission granted, the MAUMEE turned over her role as "Guide"—this time officially—to the LT 784 and dropped astern. Bearing to port, she began the refueling of the LTs of columns 4, 3, 2, and 1. When she had dropped out of regular station, the USS CHASE (DE 16), Lt. Commander Russell V. Bradley, USNR, commanding, hustled close into the oiler as her personal bodyguard. Without the MAUMEE, the Convoy would stop in its tracks.

Later in the afternoon, the MAUMEE, then back in position,[6] invited the second of the two British net tenders, HMS ASTRAVAL, to come up for provisioning and refueling. Alongside, the ASTRAVAL began transferring stores. Everything went well until the bottom fell out of a box of lemons while it was in transit between the two ships. When this happened, much to the amazement of the Americans on the MAUMEE, the Britisher swung his ship off, and members of the crew began leaping over the side to retrieve the citrus fruit—jewels to an Englishman after five years of war deprivation. After the lemons were rescued, the net tender came back alongside to take on fuel, and her skipper invited Ballard and his Executive Officer, Lt. Bruce Beagly, USNR, to come aboard. Curious as to what life was like aboard a "limey," the officers transferred over by breeches buoy. Ushered into the wardroom, the Americans discovered that the Royal Navy was superior, in at least one respect, to their own; it wasn't "dry." Toasts of dark rum were drunk to the success of the Convoy; the Americans' return trip to their ship was probably far less hair raising than the one going over had been.

At 2306, Task Group 27.5 picked up its first sonar contact of the voyage. Foxer gear was streamed; all engines cut in; General Quarters sounded. At 2345, the sonar target faded and dispersed, proving the contact false. All vessels secured from GQ.

October 1

The first day of October was ushered in with more severe weather when a tropical storm crossed the Convoy's path bringing with it steady winds of 33 knots which swung from northeast to northwest and back again. Straggling now became a real problem as the Convoy proceeded blindly in heavy rains which lasted well past midnight into the morning of the third. The weather was accompanied by a rash of breakdowns beginning the first and lasting until the fifth when the wind began to moderate.

* * * * * * *

To illustrate the heavy work load which was placed on the service tugs, one needs only to examine the work log of the LT 581 for the 3rd of October, a day in which although not burdened by a tow, her crew was subjected to a schedule which would convince any "iron man of the days of sail" that this was no steam-powered pleasure cruise. The log for the 3rd of October reads as follows:

0300 — Call from "Applejack" to inspect barge in Column 1 and report condition and stand by. Reported condition about the same.

0815 — Picked up parts from the MAUMEE for the Y 127.

0855 — Delivered same.

1035 — Gave ST 742 six 5-gallon cans of fresh water.

1215 — Picked up Navy man from the ST 676.

1230 — Picked up electric motor from the LT 643.

1340 — Picked up parts and supplies from the MAUMEE and delivered electric motor.

1455 — Picked up generator part from the ST 747.

1555 — Delivered cheese cloth to the ST 751.

1805 — Picked up water hose and gave parts from the ST 747 to the MAUMEE.

The last entry of this report, which was made at 1805, is significant in that when the LT 581 picked up the water hose she had taken on a new function for herself as water-tender. By this time, the STs had all reported that their fresh water tanks had been contaminated by sea water which had seeped into them through the poorly sealed filler plates. There was little that anyone could do to correct the situation as when their crews tried to remove the covers for resealing, more salt water would slosh in. Up to October 3, those of the tugs which were in the worst need had been provided for with 5-gallon cans of drinking water passed to them by the service tugs and the escorts. By the third, the condition of the STs' tanks had become so universally bad that Ballard concluded that a more efficient and faster method of resupply should be instituted. The LT 581 had therefore been selected to transfer drinking water to them directly from her tanks by the use of hoses. This was not considered any hardship on the LT, since the production of her evaporators could amply supply her own tanks plus the estimated requirements of the STs'.

* * * * * * *

The day before, on the second, the Convoy had crossed the 43rd Meridian and was now traveling that part of the central Atlantic where submarine attack was considered to be more likely than it had been to the westward. Due to the increased risk, the MASON stepped up her watch complements.[7]

This precaution, which had been duplicated on the other escorts, soon seemed appropriate. At 1659, on the third, while the MASON was 15,000 yards ahead of the Convoy on forward picket screen, she picked up a sound contact with strong traces. Closing on it, Lt. Commander Blackford rang General Quarters at 1706 and changed course to say with the contact. Suddenly the pings faded. A minute later, a seaman standing at his station next to the stern depth charge racks misunderstood an order and rolled over one of the depth charges. This put the MASON's sound man out of business momentarily, yet long enough so that he was unable to relocate the contact. At 1744, the O'TOOLE,[8] patrolling on inner screen at station No. 3, picked it up 1,000 yards out and off to the starboard wing of the Convoy. This was too close for comfort, and the O'TOOLE leaped forward to evaluate. At 1750, both Lind and Mauldin agreed that this might be the real thing. Eleven charges were dropped with a scattered pattern in order to embarrass and force the target, should it be a sub, to move away from the Convoy.[9] A smoke float was then put over to mark the last contact. The O'TOOLE thrashed over the narrowing area between her patrol position and the Convoy, but no further contact was made.

CTG immediately alerted the POWERS on stern picket to come forward and screen over the point of last contact with her sonar. The POWERS thoroughly searched the area. This was acoustically difficult since the main body of ships was almost upon it. Nothing further was picked up.

Post evaluation led those on the O'TOOLE to believe that the contact had most probably been a concentration of fish. The rapid movement of the mass and the erraticness of range, which did not appear to hold a relative rate, pointed to that conclusion.

October 5

On October 5, the base course of NY 119 was changed to 100° true in order to make good a side slip, estimated at 10° to 12° left of course line. The wind was southwest at 12 knots; the sky was overcast with showers.

Shortly after the midnight change of watch, Ballard received word that the ST 718 had broken loose from the PRETEXT. The cable connecting the two had parted at the nip on the PRETEXT's stern. The Commodore TBS'd the LT 581[10] to swing over and investigate. When she arrived, she found the ST laying dead in the water, her skipper fearing that if his engines were turned over, the result might be the fouling of the tow cable around the screw.

Ringing the MAUMEE, Thorstnes of the LT 581 conferred with Ballard. The conference produced the decision that Thorstnes should retrieve the cable which was now dangling straight down into the depths from the ST's bow. The plan was to wait until daylight before retrieving it and reuniting the ST 718 with the PRETEXT. The crew of the LT 581 found that it was no small task to drag in the 800 foot cable plus bridle, yet by improving on "Knight's Seamanship," the job of flaking down the hard-to-manage steel hawser on the service tug's deck was completed by 0300.

By dawn, the two tugs had rejoined the Convoy whereupon it was decided by Ballard that since the ST 718 was running free under her own power, she might as well take advantage of the opportunity afforded and refurbish her supplies and the contents of her contaminated water tanks. On Ballard's orders, the ST ran up alongside the MAUMEE from whence all good things were to come. Her skipper, Olivey, not overly experienced with the sucking-in effect that a large ship can have on a smaller one, made too close an approach and rammed the tanker. This opened up a hole in the ST's fore peak tank. The hull casualty was not too serious, but it did produce a gash 3" by 12" which was luckily above the water line.[11] The puncture was in the ST's port side, so Ballard directed Olivey to drop astern and come in on the ST's starboard side. This placed him on the port side of the MAUMEE. The tug was lashed in tow alongside. A damage control team immediately boarded and welding was commenced to close up the hole. While this was going on, the ST's engineers drained dry their water tanks, pumping the residue overboard. A complete refill was taken aboard from the MAUMEE's reservoirs. As soon as the tanks were topped off, the Navy repairmen "water-tight" sealed the tank covers, thus giving the ST 718 the enviable distinction of becoming the only small tug in the Convoy to complete the voyage with a plentiful supply of palatable drinking water.

By 1215, the ST 718 was in better shape than when she had first come down the ways. Olivey had her cast off and headed back to a position rearward of column 10. Upon arrival, he and Lt. William Muirhead, RNR, the C.O. of the PRETEXT, heaved to their ships while the LT 581 passed over a heaving line to the ST 718. This was followed by a messenger line secured to the end of the under side of the flaked towing cable, whereupon the bridle and a short length of main cable was heaved aboard and secured to the ST's bridle pad-eyes. The ST then held her position close into the LT 581 while Muirhead maneuvered the PRETEXT and repeated the procedure with the other end of the cable. Thorstnes, instructing the net tender to ease out slowly, payed the cable free. The PRETEXT was steaming with the ST 718 in tow by 1525 hours.[12]

* * * * * * *

It was probably on this day or shortly thereafter, that the MAUMEE's

Medical Officer, Lt. Aaron Z. Oberdorfer, USNR, transferred by breeches buoy over to one of the service tugs to treat a seaman reportedly suffering from a fractured skull. The doctor, no trapeze artist by nature, gamely climbed into the breeches sling and was whisked in the usual erratic fashion across the space dividing the two vessels. When the seaman was examined, Oberdorfer decided little could be done for him other than rest, so the trip had been in vain.

Upon the doctor's return, Ballard, noting "Doc's" ashen features said, "I don't think I'll ask you to do that again," to which he got the reply, "I don't think I want to do it again, either." Ballard, amused and thinking a change of scene was what the doctor needed, invited him along as company on one of the periodic Captain's inspections of the security locker located in the tanker's dry cargo hold. Descending a stairwell, Ballard and Oberdorfer walked aft to a dogged doorway. It was unopenable, having been welded shut before the ship left New York. To the Captain's satisfaction, it was found that no one had tampered with the welds. Ballard's concern over the security of the sealed-off compartment was highly justified. The compartment held cases of Scotch whiskey, a re-import originating from the United Kingdom and now going back for distribution to American units. Ballard, when first apprised in New York of what his ship was to carry, had been worried lest some of his crew should decide to sample the cargo en route. He had hit on the idea of welding up the doorway to avoid problems.

Upon arrival in England, the welds were still uncracked and so, miraculously, were the Scotch bottles, except for three which had become casualties of the rough seas.

* * * * * * *

The Convoy was now approaching that geographical feature known as the Atlantic ridge—an underwater elevation running southward, longitudinally down the middle of the Atlantic from Iceland. The only part of it that rises above the sea is that known as the Azore Islands. They were expected over the horizon either the next day or early on the following.

Chapter VI

LAND-FALL ON FLORES

The 6th of October ushered in the beginning of three and a half days of moderate weather with clear skies. There were 15-foot ground swells from the southeast which were now beginning to level out. The gentle breeze of eight to ten knots provided little in the way of maintaining their momentum. At 0935, the O'TOOLE left picket station No. 1 to investigate the progress of a boarding party off the LT 581 that was engaged in efforts to pump our BCF No. 3203. This float, in tow of the LT 63, had now dropped astern.[1]

Lind, on the wing of the bridge of the O'TOOLE and upon arrival alongside the BCF, could see that the boarding party had started the gasoline billy pump. The result was a slow, steady stream of water ensuing from the discharge line. Lt. Edward P. Edmunds, USNR, the O'TOOLE's Engineering Officer, remarked that the discharge rate appeared inadequate, considering that the float was visibly down by the head. Lind nodded his agreement and replied that they might either have to supplement it with other pumps or abandon the unit. "I don't like the prospects of having to do that," commented Lind.

Further astern and trailing the car floats were the ST 677 and the ST 676 which Mauldin next checked out as he brought the O'TOOLE alongside them. Inquiring as to their welfare, the ST 677 reported life difficult but bearable; the report from the ST 676 differed. Her crew was practically destitute of any drinking water. By transfer line, the DE sent over ten gallons of water in cans, topped with a package of fresh meat.

* * * * * * *

Robert A. Linch, the cook of the ST 720 was in the process of being transferred to the MAUMEE. He was suffering from a badly infected hand which he had cut earlier on a galley knife. The day following the accident, Captain Wallace, the ST's permanent skipper, had TBS'd the MAUMEE to give a description of a progressive reddening of the wound site, accompanied by acute soreness. Dr. Oberdorfer had diagnosed erysipelas and prescribed soaking the hand in a solution of magnesium sulphate. The hand was soaked, but the next day there was no improvement; in fact, it looked worse. Wallace requested the transfer of the cook to the MAUMEE's Sick Bay. The cook's removal from the ST 720 in all probability saved his life—not from the infection but from the events that were to follow and affect the ST twelve days later.[2]

Since Linch's name will not reappear again in this narrative, it may be of interest to the reader to know something about the man. Linch's biography was quite unusual in that after completing four years of high school he attended two years of military school and followed this with two years at the University of California. "Why," the reader may ask, "would a man with this education select a galley of a harbor tug for a professional career?" One cannot answer this anymore than as to why the Mate of the ST 511, a Princeton graduate with three years of postgraduate work at Pennsylvania Law School[3] could answer why he had chosen employment as a First Officer on a tug.

* * * * * *

The cook's hand was not the only problem aboard the ST 720. An altercation had earlier developed between Navy Signalman Charles H. Buswell and one of the civilian AB seamen. The trouble had arisen during a transfer operation in which the ST was engaged in taking on water by cans from one of the service tugs. The work of pulling aboard the cans by use of a messenger line was not easy, and it appeared to have sapped the energy of the seaman. In protest, the AB remarked that he felt there was enough water aboard already and said, "The hell with it." Buswell, not agreeing, made some joking comments in an attempt to upgrade the man's spirits. The latter lunged at the Signalman, screaming, "I'll kill you, you bastard." The scuffle was broken up; but Captain Wallace, believing the situation had all the earmarks of a potential homicide, asked Buswell if he wanted to be transferred over to the MAUMEE. Buswell told him that he was not worried as he thought the fellow would cool off, but he promised to be careful so as not to cause another blow up. The episode over the water cans was the second outburst on the part of this AB. During the rescue operations which followed the sinking of the ST 719, the man had shown early evidence of paranoia. This arose out of an intercepted TBS message between one of the escorts and the MAUMEE. The radio conversation had related to the question of whether Harding, the Navy Signalman aboard the ST 719, had been picked up. To the obviously psychotic AB, this indicated a lack of concern by the Navy Task Group for the rest of the crew. Nothing could persuade him otherwise. The hours of unrewarding search which were conducted by the POWERS and the BERMINGHAM to find the ST 719's cook seemed to have escaped the seaman's thought processes. Since then, the man had become convinced that mutual hatred existed between the Navy and himself. Buswell, being the closest Navy representative, was the nearest target at which to strike.[4]

October 7

At mid-morning of the following day, Lind brought the O'TOOLE back alongside the BCF No. 3203. Everyone's fear of the day before that the car float was taking on a lot of water was confirmed. The float now had at least a 20° list and was well down by the head.

CTG had the lead tug, LT 63, reduce speed to steerage way so that a damage control party under the leadership of the O'TOOLE's Executive Officer, Lt. Lanson Ditto, USNR, and Lt. Edmunds, could board the float. They were assisted by six enlisted men who took along four gasoline billy pumps from the O'TOOLE's damage control equipment. They disembarked with a determination to "fix the damn thing, once and for all."

The LT 581 sent a repair team to join the 8-man team from the O'TOOLE. After an initial inspection had been made, it appeared to both teams that the job looked big if not impossible. To begin with, all but one of the float's starboard compartments were definitely flooded. The condition of the remaining one was questionable. The men had brought an inclinometer with them, and its reading showed that the barge had an actual list of 25° to starboard with a 4° pitch down by the head. Further inspection showed that a number of the cables which had secured the top mounted pick-a-back barge had been carried away. This had allowed the top barge to slip toward the front, shearing off one of the 2-inch tubes installed to enable the pumping out of the inner compartments from deck level. Since the float was down by the head with its starboard forward corner below water level, a steady 2-inch stream of water was pouring through the broken tube into that forward compartment.

Pumping was commenced. After a time it was noted that when three or more of the pumps were operative the water level within the float would drop. Yet to keep all the pumps running at the same time appeared impossible. The reason for the pumps quitting was that the car float had been constructed without air vents in the deck. The subsequent vacuum caused by the pumps' suctions caused them to over-heat and stop. Meanwhile, the water kept pouring in.

Ditto and Edmunds were of the self-punishing school in that they would never ask an enlisted man to do something they were not willing to do themselves. Both officers stripped to their underwear and lowered themselves through a manhole into the flooded compartments. Once inside, they dove to the submerged edge, where, with five feet of water overhead and under the illumination of an underwater light held by Ditto, Edmunds hammered a wooden plug into the end of the broken tube. After the officers had been hauled back up on the deck, the pumps were re-started, but they still continued to break down. So frequent were the breakdowns that the whole performance began to take on the atmosphere of a losing ball game. Calling over the bad news to the O'TOOLE, Ditto suggested that the only solution that he could think of would be to counter-flood one of the port compartments in the hope it might help stabilize the float. Lind granted permission, yet this, too, met with failure. The lack of air vents in the barge created a back pressure, making it as difficult to pump water in as it was to pump it out.[5]

* * * * * *

After the damage control party was first placed aboard the float, Mauldin dropped the O'TOOLE astern to effect the transfer by hose of fresh water to the ST 676. The decision to donate the water had been made the night before in the O'TOOLE's wardroom and had involved considerable debate between Mauldin and Edmunds. The latter officer was the ship's engineer; his argument was that to deprive the O'TOOLE's holding tanks might be an invitation to trouble since her evaporators were not in a state of reliability that could be depended upon. The argument was persuasive, but Mauldin, weighing it against the hardships that the ST's crew might face without the water, overruled.

Closing in to the tug, a fire hose was passed over, and the DE began to pump out what would amount to a thousand gallons of its precious fluid.

While the water transfer was taking place, the O'TOOLE was well out of bull horn range from the BCF. The ship's whale boat was kept busy dashing back and forth delivering Ditto's latest repair communiques addressed to Commander Lind. While the water transfer was taking place, there were many aboard the O'TOOLE who speculated as to how the ST's crew was going to keep sea water from entering the tank. The tug's deck appeared to be continually awash. Whenever inquiries concerning this were called over, the response always came back that everything was going fine and not to worry.

Edmunds, having reboarded the O'TOOLE via the whale boat, stood next to Mauldin and watched the transfer of an assorted package of foodstuffs to the tug. The ST's skipper megaphoned that his water tanks were full, but a minute later he added the delightful postscript, "I am awfully sorry, but we must have taken on too much salt water through the deck plates. My Engineer tells me the tanks are brackish; we'll have to pump it all overboard." Edmunds, the conservationist, was aghast. All he had left was 3,000 gallons to provide the 240 men that made up the O'TOOLE's crew. Turning to Mauldin, he pleaded, "Fun is fun!" Mauldin, this time agreeing, told the tug's captain that another request for water would be denied; they would have to get by on what they had, brackish or not.[6]

The DE pulled away from the disappointed ST 676 and back alongside the car float on which there was now an additional group from the ABNAKI. Walley had sent them over with a cutting torch, and the men were engaged in burning a hole in the high side of the barge. This was being done to relieve the vacuum effect which had been stalling out the pumps.

Lind, bull-horned Walley to ask what his opinions were on the chance of successful salvage. Walley replied that he felt that the barge would be lost unless it could be sheltered for a complete overhaul job, including refastening of the shifted pick-a-back. As the island of Flores was now clearly in view, he reckoned that the task could be performed, but only if he could take the float in behind that island's lee shore. Lind, knowing that the barge in its present condition could not continue with the Convoy, began putting into motion those housekeeping details necessary for breaking off a part of a convoy.

Calling Loew by TBS, CTG asked him to bring the POWERS alongside the O'TOOLE. There, the two of them could discuss the situation by bull-horn. The conference resulted in the following orders which were formalized within the message logs of both vessels and which are reproduced as follows:

"I MUST REJOIN THE CONVOY X CAPTAIN WALLEY BELIEVES HE CAN SALVAGE AND REPAIR BARGE IN THE LEE OF FLORES X IF HE CANNOT SAVE BOTTOM BARGE HE WILL ATTEMPT TO SAVE THE WOODEN ONE ON TOP X YOU WILL TAKE CHARGE AND STAND BY WITH HIM X IF NECESSARY SINK THE BARGE AND REJOIN WITH TUGS X TRY TO REJOIN NOT LATER THAN MONDAY X TAKE WHATEVER ACTION YOU DEEM NECESSARY X DO NOT, REPEAT, DO NOT PERMIT TUGS OR CREWS TO LAND AT AZORES X" (CTG 27.5)

The POWERS with the ABNAKI and the LT 63 with the car float and two STs in its tow peeled off to the southeast for Flores.[7]

* * * * * * *

CTG, following an inspection tour of the main Convoy body, put into affect an idea that had been kicking around in his head. It was to shift the LT 492's tow consisting of the ST 742 and the ST 752 over to a couple of the Y boats. Previously, the LT 492 had been forging ahead of position because of the lack of drag which the easy-pulling STs did not provide. This change by CTG would give the Convoy the added advantage of having an extra service tug available, a need created by the absence, although temporary, of that faithful work horse of all jobs, the ABNAKI. The weather was ideal to make a shift, and Lind felt the time was right to execute it. The Y 81 took behind her the ST 742; the ST 752 was shifted to the tow of the Y 34. Both of these Y boats had proved their reliability, and it was Lind's feeling that they could take care of their new loads without any problem. The LT 492 was then left unencumbered and awaited any duties that might arise.[8]

* * * * * * *

By 2300 that night, the POWERS' ATS group was lying with their anchors down in ten fathoms under the protection of the mountains of Flores. The POWERS was not resting at anchor; she patrolled on a half moon ASW screen to seaward of the tugs.

As soon as they had anchored, Walley put the ABNAKI's full resources into action with the project deadlined for completion by noon the following day. The work that took place can best be articulated through reproducing the salvage report of the ABNAKI:

"1. On the night of 7 October 1944, proceeded to the western side of Flores Island, Azores Group, where U.S. Army LT 63 with barge 3203 in tow was directed to anchor in ten (10) fathoms of water. After anchoring, this vessel went alongside barge 3203 and performed the following salvage operation:

   (a) After inspection of barge it was determined that all compartments (10), except the two after compartments, were flooded and the barge was listing at about 45° angle.

   (b) Two 3-inch pumps were transferred to the bow of barge where the two manhole covers were removed and pumping was commenced. After approximately two hours of pumping the two forward compartments were emptied of water, and inspection revealed that water was entering barge through open seams and around several rivets, one rivet being missing.

   (c) Pumps were transferred back to the ship, as they could not be further used to pump from barge due to excessive amount of hose required.

   (d) Men were sent between barges and opened manhole covers; then using the hose allowance of four pumps we were able to use one

3-inch pump from our deck. The 500 gallon per minute handy billy was next hooked up, but due to length of hose required, would not take suction.

(e) Ship's salvage hose (6") was too large and stiff to be of use between barges, as men working on their backs could not manage it. A reducer 6" x 4" was used to connect the 4-inch hose to ship's salvage pumps, which quickly picked up suction. Each compartment was then pumped down to about one foot, strainer depth. The small handy billy pump which belonged on barge was found to be broken, and was therefore taken on board ship and repaired. This pump plus ship's small handy billy pump was connected to suction lines on top of wooden barge, and continued pumping while manhole covers were being secured. All pumping was ceased at 1500, 8 October 1944, in order to make preparation for getting underway. . .

(f) The worst leaks in Nos. 1 and 2 compartments were welded. One missing rivet was replaced. Hole where suction line on starboard side was broken off was plugged, and hole which was burned the previous day was closed.

(g) There were several small leaks, rivets and seams which were impossible to make watertight within time available. Working conditions were difficult. Men working between barges had to lay on their backs or bellies. It is estimated that it would have taken 18 to 24 hours longer to have stopped all leaks. End ABNAKI Report. Enclosure "D" to CTG 27.5 Serial 002"

October 8

At 1630, the afternoon of the eighth, the minute task group departed the shelter of Flores Island. The tropical foliage of the island gave off a perfume that only seafaring men can appreciate as to the effect such a sensory experience can have on a ship's crew. While re-assembling the tows, the impact of it must have hit the minds of the tug's crew causing them to wistfully day dream of feminine delights, so near, yet so unobtainably far on the shores of the islands close aboard. The moments of absent-mindedness reflection came at the time that all hands should have been at a peak of alertness. During the streaming of the BCF's tow cables, the two trailing ST tugs became entangled in each other's hawsers. The snarl took all of an hour and a quarter to straighten out.[9] As the sun set over Flores, the group was finally underway to regain the Convoy, now some ninety miles ahead of them, on the southern edge of that maelstrom known as the North Atlantic.

Injured ATS seaman being transferred to deck of USS MAUMEE. (Courtesy of J. Dodson).

Navy Pharmacist's Mate being transferred from the USS BERMINGHAM to an LT. (Courtesy of H.H. Hannaman).

ATS officers and seamen along with Navy repair service detachment on the fantail of the LT 537. (Courtesy of J. Dodson).

Fantail deck of wooden type Army LT 492. The picture was taken from the deck of the USS MAUMEE on September the 28th following the sinking of the ST 719. The LT 492's towing engine was badly damaged during the sinking necessitating major repairs from the MAUMEE. (Courtesy of J. Dodson).

The ST 718 (Note numeral #18 painted on funnel for inter convoy identification purposes) lashed alongside and in tow of the USS MAUMEE. Picture was taken on October 5th minutes after the ST had collided with the oiler, causing a rupture of the ST's fore peak tank. The damage was repaired by MAUMEE's damage control personnel after the ST had been later warped to the MAUMEE's port side. (Courtesy of J. Dodson).

Probably the BCF 3203 with a boarding crew from the LT 581 which was attempting to pump it out on October 6th. (Courtesy of Sabin Sanger).

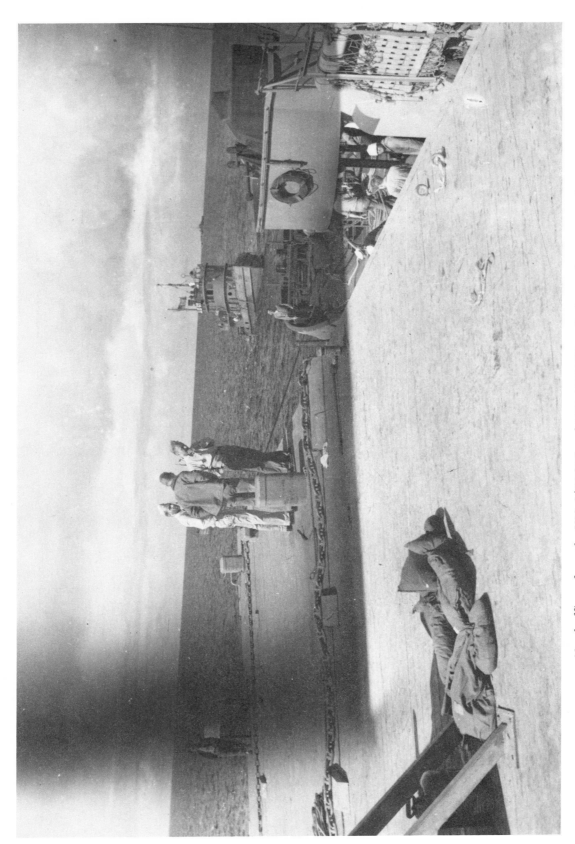

Naval officers from the USS O'TOOLE and USS ABNAKI conferring on damage control procedures atop the BCF 3203 unit on the morning of October 7th. The ABNAKI is lashed alongside, while astern and not under tow is the ST 677. One of the escorts can be seen on the horizon slightly to the right of the ST. (Courtesy of Sabin Sanger).

The ABNAKI laying alongside the BCF 3203 in the lee of the Azores on October 8th. (Courtesy of K.C. Valentine).

Flores Island, Azores: The fleet tug, USS ABNAKI alongside BCF 3203; the LT 63 is to the right. (Courtesy of K.C. Valentine).

The tow of the LT 63 shown after the carfloat had capsized and the picka-back barge had floated free. The carfloat is to the left. Photo was taken in the early afternoon of October the 13th. Note the overcast sky. (Courtesy of Sabin Sanger).

Salvage party shown aboard the BCF 3204 on October 15th. Men are located on the upside of the slanting deck from the box housing the gasoline "billy pump". Minutes after this picture was taken the float capsized throwing the men into the water. (Courtesy of K.C. Valentine).

Depth charge exploding alongside BCF 3204 while attempting to sink it on October 15th. ABNAKI is shown in the background to the left of the float. The "land" in the background is the result of a double exposure from an earlier exposure of the Azores; as the sinking of the BCF 3204 took place seven days after leaving the islands. (Courtesy of K.C. Valentine).

Probably the two units of BCF 3204 after capsizing; the towing tug can be seen in the distance to the right; taken from the deck of the USS POWERS, again probably, on October the 15th near the mid day watch change. (Courtesy of K.C. Valentine).

SPECIFICATIONS: USAT VESSELS MAKING UP CONVOY NY 119*

Number	Type	Lgth	Beam	Depth	Gross T.	Net T.	Type of Engine
LT 63	Steel Tug	122' 10"	30'	18'	394	268	Diesel
LT 536	"	143'	33'	14' 6"	505	333	Diesel Electric
LT 537	"	"	"	"	"	"	" "
LT 538	"	"	"	"	"	"	" "
LT 579	"	"	"	"	"	"	" "
LT 580	"	"	"	"	"	"	" "
LT 581	"	"	"	"	"	"	" "
LT 643	"	122' 10"	30'	18'	394	268	Diesel
LT 651	"	149'	33'	18' 9 5/8"	582	40	Steam Vert.
LT 653	"	"	"	"	"	"	"
LT 784	"	"	"	"	"	"	"
LT 492	Wood	126' 8"	28'	16'	335	290	Diesel

12 LTs (TOTAL)

Number	Type	Lgth	Beam	Depth	Gross T.	Net T.	Type of Engine
Y 17	Tanker	162'	27'	12' 9"	484	323	Diesel
Y 34	"	"	"	"	"	"	"
Y 48	"	182' 6"	30'	13' 6"	633	364	Twin Diesel
Y 49	"	"	"	"	"	"	" "
Y 80	"	"	"	"	"	"	" "
Y 81	"	"	"	"	"	"	" "
Y 82	"	"	"	"	"	"	" "
Y 83	"	"	"	"	"	"	" "
Y 84	"	"	"	"	"	"	" "
Y 86	"	"	"	"	"	"	" "
Y 104	"	178' 6"	"	12'	639.72	335	" "
Y 105	"	"	"	"	"	"	" "
Y 106	"	"	"	"	"	"	" "
Y 126	"	201' 7"	32'	11' 6"	548	321	Diesel Electric
Y 127	"	"	"	"	"	"	" "
Y 128	"	"	"	"	"	"	" "

16 Ys (TOTAL)

Number	Type	Lgth	Beam	Depth	Gross T.	Net T.	Type of Engine
14 STs	Steel Tug	85'	23'	9' 2"	143.77	49	Diesel

*Ships in Convoy Totaled: 5 USN Escorts; 2 USN Service Vessels; 2 RN Service Vessels; 42 USAT Manned Vessels; 1 Commercial Freighter—a total of 52 vessels not including the 14 unmanned barge units.

H.P.	Speed Max.	Speed Cr.	Fuel** Cap.	Water Cap. Potable	Cruising Radius Days	Aft	No. Of A.T.C. Crew*
1225	12 K	12 K	55978	36450	25	14'	19
1900	14 K	12.5 K	57674	26761	32	15'	26
,,	,,	,,	,,	,,	,,	,,	,,
,,	,,	,,	,,	,,	,,	,,	,,
,,	,,	,,	,,	,,	,,	,,	,,
,,	,,	,,	,,	,,	,,	,,	,,
,,	,,	,,	,,	,,	,,	,,	,,
1225	12 K	12 K	55978	36450	25	14'	19
1900	,,	11 K	82990	28600	18	15'	,,
,,	,,	,,	,,	,,	,,	,,	,,
,,	,,	,,	,,	,,	,,	,,	,,
1200	10 K	10 K	31785	3360	,,	13'	,,
400	10 K	7 K	9752	10005	24	11' 8"	15
,,	,,	,,	,,	,,	,,	,,	14
700	7 K	,,	12000	39630	22½	11'	19
,,	,,	,,	,,	,,	,,	,,	,,
,,	,,	,,	,,	,,	,,	,,	,,
,,	,,	,,	,,	,,	,,	,,	,,
,,	,,	,,	,,	,,	,,	,,	,,
,,	,,	,,	,,	,,	,,	,,	,,
,,	,,	,,	,,	,,	,,	,,	,,
460	,,	,,	,,	22500	,,	,,	,,
,,	,,	,,	,,	,,	,,	,,	,,
,,	,,	,,	,,	,,	,,	,,	,,
500	,,	6.5 K	7966	6390	30	,,	,,
,,	,,	,,	,,	,,	,,	,,	,,
,,	,,	,,	,,	,,	,,	,,	,,
650			19000				11

*Additionally, each USAT vessel of the LT and Y classes carried a Navy signalman and an Army radio operator. Some of the larger LTs may have carried 3 or 4 Navy gunners. STs carried a Navy signalman.
**Y Tankers were also capable of bunkering from their own cargo tanks, thus greatly increasing their cruising ranges.

Chapter VII

NORTH OF 40°

The morning of the ninth, the POWERS' group was still astern of the main Convoy. Loew, eager to comply with CTG's orders of the seventh, was doing his level best to catch up and rejoin. His problem: Where was the Convoy?

The watch within the POWERS' CIC at 1120 picked up a radar blip identified as aircraft and indicated through radar recognition as friendly. At 1138, Loew instructed his Signalman to contact the now visible aircraft by blinker and inquire as to the position of NY 119. No luck! The plane dropped a recognition flare but seemed to ignore the signals.

By noon, Loew decided to risk leaving his tug and barge group on its own and take the POWERS ahead to try to obtain a radar fix on the main body. An hour and a half later, he picked up a TBS message originating from the MAUMEE; fifteen minutes following this, he had established radio voice contact with the MASON which was on stern screen.

The Convoy located, Loew turned his ship back to rejoin his charges and was alongside them by 1600.[1]

October 10

By 0302 the morning of the tenth, the POWERS made a radar contact on the main Convoy, and by 0515, the group was in visual distance of the MASON. The tail was now back on the horse, and NY 119 had again become whole.

Although her return was welcomed by all, the POWERS was not allowed to loaf. After transferring an ill crewman and one of the ST 719 survivors to the MAUMEE, she was given the task of holding screen on the mother oiler. That vessel began her second round of refueling the escorts and LTs, an operation Lind considered advisable because of the strong possibility of heading into bad weather.

* * * * * * *

At mid-afternoon, the O'TOOLE, which was on van picket, sighted a floating object bobbing in the now building seas. Upon inspection, the object appeared to be about the size of a mine but resembled a buoy in its confirmation. Not taking any chances, Mauldin opened to 1500 yards and fired six rounds of 3-inch shells with no indication of a definite direct hit, or in any event, no explosion resulted. The distance was then closed, and the sharp-shooters among the ship's riflemen were allowed to get in a little practice. They hit it several times, but again, there was no detonation. Not much doubt remained that the object was non-mine. But for safety's sake, it was marked with smoke, and the Convoy was warned to steer clear.[2]

October 11

The 11th of October dawned a little chillier than mornings past; northwesterly seas were building up with the wind increasing out of the same direction.

Aboard the escorts, the crews had by now universally succumbed to that malady so common among destroyermen following long escort voyages in rough seas—a half sick and constant headachey feeling that only time on the beach can cure. Relatively speaking, though, the escorts' crews were living in environmental luxury compared to the poor devils on the STs.

When the seas worsened, it became increasingly hazardous for the ST tugs' crews to attempt moving from their bridge decks down to the galleys or sleeping quarters. Stanley Pasko, an AB on the ST 510, remembers this as the start of a period wherein the entire crew worked, slept, and ate either in the bridge house or on the flying bridge above it.[3] This would not end until the Convoy reached Falmouth. A few attempts were made to brave the awash regions of the weather deck, but these forays were only attempted when it was absolutely necessary to go down to the engine room or else to grab some canned goods from the galley to carry topside. Even if the weather decks had not been so dangerous to traverse, efforts to live in the fo'c'sles would have been fruitless; these areas were uninhabitable due to sea water which had leaked through ports and door jams to an extent whereby the sleeping quarters were completely water soaked.

Aboard the LTs and the Ys, life was miserable, but at least the quarters were comparatively dry when compared to the STs'. The LT crews were more fortunate as all their living and working compartments (except for the towing engine) could be reached from the vessels' interiors. On the Ys, the working space and living quarters were all contained within the after housing, a lucky thing since the weather decks separating the after house and the bow poops were continually awash. Observers from neighboring ships could see only the Ys' midship sections when the little oilers heaved upwards to cast off their burdens of green water. In the crew quarters of the Ys, most of the ports were leaking but not to the extent of intake that was being suffered on the harbor tugs.

* * * * * *

The Master of the SUERTE was again beginning to itch with a desire to leave the tortoise-paced Convoy behind him. This was his third time around with this compulsion, as he had the same urge west of the Bermudas and later on September 28. This time it looked like he was going ahead with it, as he had ranged forward of the MAUMEE and was almost abreast of the van picket, that position being well forward of the Convoy.

On the twenty-eighth, CTG had messaged the Greek by TBS asking what his excuse was for failing to keep his station. The answer had come back that the SUERTE was experiencing steering difficulties. Lind, although not a "Doubting Thomas," had by this time developed misgivings concerning the man's reliability and had sent a private blinker message to the Navy Signalman. The boy's reply was that there was nothing wrong with the steering gear that, "A well-directed shot across the freighter's bow wouldn't cure." Later that same day, the freighter complained of a shortage of water; her Master said that unless he could travel independently, his supply would run out before ten days had passed. To get authentication of that statement, Lind re-messaged the youngster at the freighter's blinker lamp. He was told that according to her Chief Engineer the SUERTE had a 50-day supply. This had settled it! The SUERTE's Master was told to maintain station; his request to leave the Convoy was adamantly refused. Apparently, the Greek did not feel that this was a time for confrontation with Lind, so all went well for the next hour or so. Later in the day, though, the Greek, deciding to test Lind's determination, again worked his ship out of station. This time in carefully selected prose, Task Group Flag issued the following ultimatum: "YOUR CONDUCT IS ENDANGERING THIS CONVOY X UNLESS YOU CARRY OUT INSTRUCTIONS IN MY OPERATIONS ORDER AND ORDERS YOU MAY RECEIVE FROM ME X I SHALL FILE AN OFFICIAL REPORT OF MISCONDUCT AGAINST YOU AND RECOMMEND THAT YOUR LICENSE AS A MASTER OR MATE BE FOREVER REVOKED BY ALL NATIONS X I DO NOT INTEND TO REPEAT ANOTHER ORDER TO YOU X MY GUNS WILL DO SO FOR ME SHOULD YOUR CONDUCT MAKE THIS ACTION NECESSARY X BT"

The SUERTE dropped back into position, her Master sobered by the threat of violence.

Now, twelve days later and in the home stretch, the Greek was again testing or rather calling the bluff of Commander Lind. Feeling that the use of further words was a waste of time, Lind called the poker hand. The O'TOOLE's forward gun was carefully trained, and a shell was sent whistling to land some few yards forward of the disobedient merchantmen's bow. Back came a message from the Signalman, "That's the only language the son-uv-a-bitch understands!" That statement proved correct since the SUERTE then became a model of good behavior, up and through the point where Lind officially released her from parental custody.[4]

It is interesting to speculate as to the unhappy situation of the young Signalman on the SUERTE. There he was, representing the might and majesty of the U.S. Navy aboard a tramp steamer, the Master of which was bound and determined that his supreme command at sea was not going to be subverted to the organizational control of a wartime convoy. To say the least, the Signalman's position must have been an awkward one.

* * * * * * *

The weather worsened, and with it developed continuous breakdowns and straggling on the parts of the Y 127 and the Y 128. Ballard, consulting with CTG, decided to put the Y 128 under the tow of the LT 492. The move was decided upon, not only because of the weather factor, but to a greater extent because of the Convoy's approach to the most hazardous area of its passage in terms of danger from submarine attack.[5] In such waters the escorts could ill afford to spread their screening capabilities to cover stragglers. Later, on the fourteenth, the Y 127 was to be hooked astern of the Y 128, thus giving LT 492 the responsibility of both of the troublesome vessels.

October 12

By the morning of the twelfth, the wind had moderated a little, but to the older salts it was clear that future good weather was not in the cards. The seas were now running twenty to twenty-five feet, the sky was leaden and the temperature had dropped into the low fifties. To the east of the Convoy was the Bay of Biscay; Iceland was due north.

Lind, on his morning pilgrimage to inspect the tows, took note that BCF No. 3203 had again taken on a list to starboard.

October 13

The following day, BCF No. 3203 was taking on its appearance of the week past. It again had a list of about 25° and was noticeably down by the head. The seas were still running high, and weather projections pointed to things getting worse instead of better.

It was Friday the 13th—not a day to take chances. Lind knew that to put men aboard the now awash car float would be the height of foolhardiness. His instructions to Monsen, skipper of the towing LT 63, were to keep the hulk hooked on, even if it upset. The theory was that the gamble of losing the LT's towing cable was worth it if there was a possibility of saving the float. Lind and Monsen agreed that as long as the wooden pick-a-back barge remained securely fastened, then the float could not sink. Monsen was ordered to have a team standing by on the stern with a cutting torch and orders to cut loose if the barge carried away.

Meanwhile, the ST 677 and the ST 676, which had been in tow behind the BCF, were cast off. Each had sufficient fuel aboard to continue with the Convoy under their own power to the English coast. This precluded the possibility of the STs being dragged down should the float sink.

At 1348 hours, an urgent TBS message came into CTG from the MASON: "The tow of LT 63 has turned over; we are standing by." Lind, flashing the LT 581 to report alongside the MASON, had the O'TOOLE close in on the source of trouble. On arrival, the scene before him disclosed the car float on her beam ends, with about five feet of its port side left bobbing above the waves. The LT 63's tow cable to the float was still attached; but the pick-a-back barge, lashed down atop the float, had broken loose and was trailing astern by a safety cable umbilically attached to the half-sunk float. A bull horn message from Monsen on the LT disclosed that he had full throttle on his engines, yet steerage way was minimal. He doubted whether even this could be kept up, as the towing engine was taking its maximum allowable strain before the cable on the drum would begin to strip. Figuring that the BCF was in no immediate danger of jeopardizing the LT by suddenly sinking, Lind instructed Monsen to reel in as much of his tow cable as he could; and when this was done, cut it free.

Once the LT 63 had cut free, the four vessels in attendance stood off to leeward to appraise the possibility of saving the wooden barge. Generally, opinion was that the immediate danger to the wooden barge was coming from the half sunk car float, which had by then floated parallel to the barge. Every breaking sea threatened to bring it closer. If the two collided, the seas would batter them apart in short order. No one disagreed that there was no alternative but to sink the car float.

Both the O'TOOLE's and the MASON's forward gun batteries were trained on the half sunken BCF's water line; whereupon firing commenced. After a number of hits, the car float disappeared beneath the waves. Now there was one less car float from the original fourteen which had cleared the New York narrows over two weeks past.[6]

During the shooting, the LT 537 had come back to join the spectators. That tug's skipper, Waaler, was then included in the conference which was to decide the fate of the wooden barge. No one was arguing Lind's point that to try to put men aboard it by rubber boat would be a physical impossibility. The reasons were clear. The barge rode a good ten feet above water, and there were no ladder rungs or other projections that men could use in climbing aboard it. Lt. Phipps, who at the time was not with Waaler's ship but on the MAUMEE, was auditing the conference over the radio. His opinion was that even if men were placed aboard, the whole thing would be an exercise in futility since the wooden bitts with which it was equipped were not structurally capable of standing the strain of a tow in any kind of rough sea. Again, no one argued the point. Since better weather seemed unlikely, Lind could ill afford leaving behind a retinue to await the improbable, as this would have meant sparing a tug with an escort to stand guard over it. The only sensible course was to sink it. To leave it floating free and unattended would be a menace to navigation.

What followed may not go down in the history of the sea as a gunnery engagement of magnitude, yet it certainly must have undermined confidence on the part of some regarding the destructive power of modern deck guns.[7]

The engagement began with the contestants squaring off:

On one side were the USS O'TOOLE and the USS MASON, both armed with main batteries of 3-inch naval guns along with 40 mm and 20 mm rapid fire cannons. The latest in technology had gone into the weapon design and the ammunition which was fired from them. The gun crews on both DEs had been trained to a fine edge, having had extensive target practice on towed screens and floats. Now at last they were going to show what they could dish out; a real target was before them. The proof of their destructive capabilities was about to be tested.

On the other side stood the wooden BCL barge, tough and defiant, yet unarmed. A cinch, one might think for defeat, considering there was no one aboard to fight her or anything with which to fight. This tough little barge, born and raised in the rough neighborhood of an east coast port city, was about to show the Navy that a New York harbor scow was no pushover.

The battle opened with the O'TOOLE and the MASON jockeying for advantage at a 2,000-yard range. Both vessels, steaming in line, (a formation reminiscent of Beatty at Jutland) opened fire. Away screamed a number of 3-inch shells, some of them on target, others a little over or short. The heat of battle was now warming the blood of the DE's gunners. Caution was thrown to the wind as the ships closed the enemy to 1,000 yards. Two more passes were made at this range, during which observers noticed that the firing was with precision. Still nothing happened; the brave little barge was not showing any lethal damage.

Aboard the MASON, all sorts of advice was freely offered to Leonard Barton, her Gunnery Officer. One by-stander suggested that since they were using armor-piercing shells, the rounds were probably going right through. This sounded logical, so the order was given to switch to explosive heads. Another pass was made. To Barton's satisfaction, a few explosions were recorded this time. The barge was reeling slightly but was still defiant and remained very much afloat.

Both DEs temporarily retired so that their gunners could lick the wounds of damaged egos. Things were not helped in the latter category, since titters and suppressed smiles were coming from among those who were not members of the gun crews. Barton, trying hard to remain cool and impassionate and showing the true spirit of a natural killer, commented to Blackford that since the O'TOOLE was equally unsuccessful, the only solution appeared to be a really close run—not really near enough to send away boarders, but around 100 yards. Blackford, just as frustrated but not yet ready to break out the cutlasses, agreed.

THE MASON, with every gun, including her machine guns, firing, barreled past the barge. The smoke of battle clearing, all hands peered aft expecting to see nothing but empty water—but, no there it was! The barge was still floating. A couple of fires were burning, but those were quickly quenched by the rains and breaking seas.

Sensing a major naval defeat, Barton suggested a different strategy which Blackford passed on to Mauldin in the O'TOOLE. Both skippers adopted Barton's concept which was activated. This began with the MASON making a run which straddled the barge with depth charges from her Y guns. Sweeping in close behind came the O'TOOLE which followed suit. The barge bucked and heaved, but still it did not sink. Once again the determined escorts charged in. This time a depth charge from the O'TOOLE was deposited directly on the barge's decking. Not daring to go in again, lest the charge should roll off in the path of one of the attackers, small arms were broken out and issued to the MASON's sharp shooters. The crack of Springfields was now added to the din of battle. Although a number of the riflemen—both officers and enlisted men, who claimed to be experts—declared hits, the depth charge still perched there unharmed. The O'TOOLE's crew had a better idea; her 3-inch gun commenced firing. The third round exploded the charge, but the force of it dissipated upwards and hardly rocked the barge.

Since fire power appeared useless, and the "enemy" could not be sunk, CTG, Blackford, and Mauldin decided that to retire seemed the better part of valor. Thus a retreat saved two U.S. ships of the line from the humiliation of striking their colors to a harbor scow. So ended the battle or so it appeared. (It was probably this barge—which was reported as a floating menace to navigation—that was to wrack vengence against the MASON some weeks later.)

Post battle inventory showed that on the O'TOOLE alone, a total of fifty-seven rounds of 3-inch shells and nine MK 8 depth charges were expended.[8] This does not include the 40 mm and 20 mm ammunition that was fired. A lesson was learned: a wooden barge is probably more difficult to destroy than the BISMARK.

* * * * * * *

It was also on this day that a most unusual event occurred that is unprecedented within research by this author in the accountings of World War II mercantile convoys. Upon request of a ship's Master, an entire engine room gang was replaced with naval personnel.

This incident, which occurred on October 13, was not the first regarding disciplinary difficulties that some of the ATS Masters were experiencing with their crews. Earlier in the Convoy, Lt. John Dodson, USN, had been temporarily transferred off the MAUMEE to the LT 581 where he was acting as an engineering trouble shooter. While in that capacity, he single-handedly had put down a near mutiny on one of the Y boats. The incident had been brought on when the Y's skipper ordered his crew forward to the ship's bow to attempt housing an anchor which had slipped out of its nest in the hawse pipe and was threatening to hole the forward plates. The crew, afraid of crossing the awash well decks, had refused the order. The Master, in desperation, informed Ballard who subsequently sent Dodson to go aboard the Y, whereupon he was to read the riot act. When the Naval officer arrived, he found a situation as akin to mutiny as things could ever get. To restore order he had gone as far as to threaten to throw the ring leader overboard. This cowed them, and the rabble then followed him forward to secure the anchor.[9]

The newest episode was not so much a refusal to obey an order as it was the accumulative effect of dereliction of duty and incompetence, compounded by an unwillingness to cooperate with the vessel's Master. On October 13, Johannes Waage, Master of the LT 536, who had captained his first ship at the age of 28 years, back in 1932, had come to the end of his patience with the amateurs that NYPOE crewing officials had given him for engineers. His pleas for a better job on their part had fallen on deaf ears, and there appeared to be a spirit of "go to Hell" emanating from the engine spaces. Waage, realizing the life of his ship and its crew depended on her engines performing, requested Ballard to replace the entire bunch with Navy men. The Commodore, aware that three major breakdowns, requiring seven days of towing, had already been visited upon the LT, agreed to the request. The service tug LT 581 transferred over to the LT 536 a total of seven Navy men and one officer from the MAUMEE and removed a like number of abashed civilians back to the Navy ship.[10]

SHOOTING — by (Torni?) of ST 510; Sept.-Oct. 1944.

"Chowtime in Heavy Weather" — by (Torni?) of ST 510; Sept.-Oct. 1944.

"Heavy Weather" — by (Torni?) of ST 510; Sept.-Oct. 1944.

"The ST 510 at Sea" — by (Torni?) of ST 510; Sept.-Oct. 1944.

'ST in Tow of LT'' — by (Torni?) of ST 510; Sept.-Oct. 1944.

"Safe at Falmouth" — by (Torni?) of ST 510; Sept.-Oct. 1944.

Chapter VIII

WITH THE POWERS

There were four ships which had missed the excitement surrounding the battle against the wooden barge and the relief of the engineers off the LT 536. They were the POWERS, the ABNAKI, the LT 538, and the ST 720. On the morning of the twelfth, the POWERS was fifty miles astern screening the straggling LT 538 with her three charges, the two leaking car floats, BCFs No. 3204 and No. 3205, and the ST 720. Traveling along with them to lend a hand where needed was the ABNAKI. The group had begun to get out of reliable voice radio range. Since Lind could no longer look upon it as a controllable command entity, he ordered the POWERS' skipper. Lt. Commander Loew, to consider himself on detached duty and independent until his group could regain the main Convoy.

October 13

At 0708 on the thirteenth, the LT 538's towing hawser broke, casting adrift both BCFs and the ST 720. Loew, viewing the situation from the bridge of the POWERS, handed the ball to Walley of the ABNAKI on the sound premise that he had the expertise to put the pieces back together again. Since the seas were running so high, Walley didn't have to think twice on the advisability of placing men on the barge to affect a re-hookup. Instead, he thought up a strategem of reversing the tow. To accomplish this, he had the ST pass her cable, then connected to the stern car float, over to the ABNAKI. In the process of reversing the line of tow, the ST 720 had been temporarily set free; she was then hooked up astern of the LT 538.

By 0100 hours, the group was back underway.[1]

October 14

The day of October 14 began poorly for the four vessels making up the POWERS' contingent. At 0720, Loew swung his ship past BCF No. 3204; it didn't look quite right. Coming in for a little closer look, he could see that the 2-inch planking which acted as a deflector between the upper wooden barge and the car float was badly shattered. (The deflectors had been constructed to prevent the force of the waves from breaking between the upper barges and the lower floats.) Since the boarding had partially broken away, a tremendous pressure was being exerted against the chain and cable lashings which held the two units together.[2] The wind was then at 20 knots, decreasing from a higher velocity since dawn, which led Loew and Walley to agree that a short wait before sending the men aboard the barge would be preferrable. By 1315, the breeze had dropped to 10 knots, and the sea conditions were acceptable to risk the trip. Ensign McCarthy and Signalman 1/C A.W. Christy dropped over the side of the POWERS into a rubber raft and were on their way over to the BCF. Once aboard, there was little the two men could do except start the billy pump and retighten, wherever possible, the cables securing the wooden barge. By 1829, they were back aboard the POWERS with a pessimistic report for Loew. "The float is leaking badly, and the top barge has shifted."

October 15

By dawn on the fifteenth, the car float 3204 was definitely not a sight for sore eyes. It lay at such a list that one side of it was completely under water while on the other side the bilges had been lifted clear. At 0920, Loew sent off another pumping party consisting of three Petty Officers: J. Klipp, H.E. Mitchell, and T.G. Lane. Again, there was nothing the men could really do except to restart the pump and tend it while the ABNAKI made as much headway as possible with the logy tow.

Despite one and a half hours of steady pumping, the list appeared to remain constant to the observers on the POWERS' bridge. At 1143, Loew, who was beginning to think at the time of recalling the men aboard the float, was horrified to see the barge up-end and capsize. When the three Petty Officers felt it begin to go, they clamored up to its high side; as it continued to roll over, they kept climbing until they had reached the float's bottom. Thus, they were saved from entrapment beneath it. The three men then swam to their raft which was still tethered on a long line to the barge. By the time they had climbed into the raft, the wooden pick-a-back broke loose from its lashings and floated clear.

Since the barge was free of the float, at least part of the unit was salvageable. It also made the destruction of the car float by the POWERS' guns a much simpler task. At 1313, the float sank from sight after absorbing the punishing effect of thirteen rounds of 3-inch shells, sixty rounds of 20 mm, and two depth charges. Lying almost totally submerged, it did not complete its dive immediately—sixteen minutes passed before the steel strands connecting it to BCF 3205 snapped. The float disappeared into the depths.

Fortunately, the sunken float had been astern of the BCF 3205, so the latter was still attached firmly to the ABNAKI. As previously related, it was also leaking badly so it was now made the recipient of another boarding party from the POWERS. Away in their rubber raft went McCarthy with his side kick Christy. Along with them were two other POs, W.J. Manulikow and W.R. Bergamini. Once on the float, they cast off the tow cable which attached it to the ABNAKI and hauled aboard the LT 538's cable. The ABNAKI was then free to take over the job of towing the loose wooden barge.

By 1402, the mini convoy was back under way. The wooden barge was behind the ABNAKI; the BCF 3205 was behind the LT 538. The ST 720 traveled independently with enough fuel in her bunkers to reach the coast of England should she have to continue without a hitch-hike.

At 1600, the LT 538 stopped to permit the pumping crew enough time to leave the float and return to the POWERS. At 1700, a heavy squall with winds rising to 40 knots in velocity caused more problems and a temporary laying-to so the LT could adjust and reset her towing cable. Half an hour later, the squall line had passed, and the winds had diminished to 25 knots.

By mid-watch of the 8 to 12 that night, the group was averaging an estimated 4.5 knots, and the possibility of regaining the main Convoy was reasonably realistic should the weather hold as it was.

October 16

Aboard the POWERS at 1000 hours, October 16: the swift, strong arm of Naval justice was in process as a Summary Court Martial convened with Lt. Robert B. Paddock, USNR, as its senior member. The case revolved around a dress blue uniform allegedly stolen by an enlisted man from one of his shipmates. The crime had been committed on September 29.[3]

At 1109, the LT 538 reported her car float, 3205, beginning to sink, an occurrence that promptly brought a swift adjournment to the trial. It was to reconvene at 1300. Two minutes following the sinking report, the wooden pick-a-back broke free of its bondings and drifted clear of the sinking car float. At almost the same time, the LT's cable either parted or was cut.

With no other alternative open to him, Loew ordered the destruction of this last remaining BCF. At 1143, 3205 was put to sleep with three rounds of 3-inchers and machine gun fire. The area now cleared, Lt. Walley transferred his wooden barge to the LT 538, preparatory to working in his ship to pick up the barge that had just floated free from the scuttled car float.

While the ABNAKI's crew was sizing up the method to be used in taking the drifting barge under tow, the LT 538 was just getting underway with its new load. Suddenly, her cable broke (probably at a point weakened minutes earlier when the BCF had sunk). The break occurred close on to the nip at the LT's stern; so despite the 30-knot winds, Loew was again forced to put his rubber boat to use. This time its passengers were: Lt. B. Cowan, USNR; Lt. (JG) Keefe, USNR; and BM 1/C J.W. Dusseault. Once on the barge, the men began the arduous task of hauling in by hand the loose cable dangling from the barge's bitts and then paying it back out again to the LT. The LT's crew had meanwhile thrown over a messenger line for that purpose.

Shortly before 1600, Cowan and his companions were back aboard the POWERS. Before hauling the rubber boat back aboard, Loew sent it drifting astern to the ST 720 for the purpose of transferring three cans of drinking water along with three cans of fuel oil for the ST's stove. A second drift back was accomplished when the tug indicated a further need for fifteen gallons of lubricating oil.

Darkness was settling in. Because of this and the high winds, the ABNAKI's efforts to pick up the barge had to be aborted. To attempt a try after dark was obviously impossible, so the plan for the night was "STAND-BY" to wait the coming dawn. The LT 538 with her barge in tow and the ST 720 in accompaniment were ordered to steam wide in a one-mile arc distance of the ABNAKI, which was lying to. Meanwhile, Loew kept his ship within a two and a half mile general patrol area, her sonar ears attuned for unwelcomed visitors.

The day ended with the Summary Court Martial still not reconvened—it was postponed indefinitely or until such a time had arrived when the ship was again a stablized platform—level enough for the accused to stand upright.

October 17

By 0935 the next morning, the ABNAKI successfully took the barge behind her, and the POWERS' group was back on a base course of 057° and making good a ground speed of 7 knots—fantastic when compared to the pace to which they had become accustomed, but this was not to last long. By the early hours of the evening, the smell of evil weather was in the air. The following day, the eighteenth, marked the entry into the maelstrom.

October 18

For the men within the POWERS' group there was a sensation of being on a "Nantucket sleigh ride." Their base course was 62°, with 40-knot winds dead astern of them. Forty to forty-five foot seas struck the ships just abaft their port beams. Although things were decidedly uncomfortable on the POWERS, the conditions aboard the LT and the ABNAKI were more than just uncomfortable. They bordered on the frightening. The light wooden barges which they were towing acted like bronchos on the end of a tether. For the ST 720 it was more like surf riding. The little tug handled uncontrollably as she tore down the slope of each mountain of water, broaching at a quarter turn before her helmsman could straighten her out to await the next on-rushing ride.

The wild yawing of its barge caused the LT 538's towing cable to chafe through at 0255. When it let go, its whip-like tension caused part of it to spring back and coil loosely on the LT's fantail before sliding back beneath the sea to aimlessly trail in the tug's wake.

Loew, who was now in voice radio contact with Lind, was told to heave to in the neighborhood of the adrift barge, near which the ABNAKI with her tow was standing by. The ST 720's Master, Edward Wallace, was instructed to hold into the sea, staying as close as he could to the ABNAKI. Meanwhile, steaming ahead with her back to the scene was the LT 538. Her voyage onward was quickly halted when CTG, who had been apprised of the situation, ordered her skipper, Bluckner, to return and stand-by with the ABNAKI.

It was not pre-determined that the three tugs and the POWERS were to remain together for long. Shortly after 0400, Wallace spoke to Loew over TBS to say that he couldn't hold his vessel into the sea; he would have to turn and run with it. Loew, conferring with Lind, a distant 70 miles away, was instructed to accompany the ST toward the Convoy. This left the ABNAKI in charge of the LT 538 and its drifting barge. The plan between Walley and Loew was that once the latter's ship had regained the stern most portion of the main Convoy and had come within sight of the BERMING-HAM (now on stern station) the POWERS was to turn over her charge to that vessel and head back southwesterly toward the ABNAKI group.

The ST's crew was not reacting at the highest plane of efficiency. Their bodies and minds had almost reached the limit of endurance. For ten days the diet aboard had been cold, canned hash and some fruit—meals that under normal circumstances might have been adequate. The conditions under which these men labored were far from normal. Their clothing was wet, sleep was difficult to come by, their bodies had taken a brutal beating from the pitching vessel, and the nervous strain under which they had existed since leaving New York was beginning to tell. To add to this misery, the drinking water was contaminated with fuel oil and had caused nausea among some members of the crew.

Signalman Buswell had been trying to sleep, curled in a corner of the cramped wheel house. When, at 0400, Wallace had turned to run with the sea, he suggested that the Signalman try to get some rest in one of the fo'c'sles below. The proposal had its practical aspects. With the seas coming in from behind, the ST's lower decks were not taking on the heavy green water that they had before when the little ship had been heading into the sea. Thus, the new heading provided more safety for those who wished to enter the lower deck house, and it also meant that less water was being taken into those compartments through the leaking ports and doors. With this in mind, Buswell, after checking out the TBS and reviewing Wallace on its operation, left the wheel house and went below to sprawl his fatigued body out on one of the wet bunks.[4]

A few minutes after Buswell left the bridge, at about 0405, the ST 720 broached at a wider angle than she had at any time before. Despite the frantic efforts of AB Michael O'Leary to wrestle her back on course line, she heeled over, to lay on her starboard side like so much flotsam. When she went over, the seas were breaking with such violence against the exposed port side that the men within the wheel house could do little else but cling to whatever they could grab hold of and pray. At some time during the estimated four minutes that she lay over on her side, with her propeller alternatively biting into the water and then thrashing madly at nothing but air, she drifted from broadside of the seas to a right angle with them. With the sea back on her stern, she righted herself.

Chief Engineer James E. Scrivener, 1st Assistant Frederick B. Lamude, and Oiler Robert L. Forbes were in the engine room. The men had decided earlier that there was no drier or warmer place aboard. When the tug had first lain over to the starboard, the three rushed for the port side escape hatch. Once there, they concluded that there was no chance of getting out against the force of the sea breaking against the hull. When she had righted, Lamude grabbed for the phone connecting with the bridge. "Shall we reduce speed?" The answer came back negative. On the bridge there were others with opposing sentiment. Both the Delivery Master, J. Thrasyvoulos, and the

1st Officer, Richard T. Croffman, pleaded with Wallace to reduce speed. The skipper, insisting that she wouldn't answer her helm if the revolutions were cut, said, "NO!" The argument raged while the tug uncontrollably tobogganed into the troughs of the huge seas.[5]

As soon as the tug had righted herself, Buswell lost no time in departing the confining space of the fo'c'sle where he had earlier gone to try to get some rest. Climbing back into the wheel house, he broke into the debate to ask whether anyone had gotten off a call to the POWERS. Wallace said that while she was on her side he had sent out a voice message, but he couldn't be sure it had been acknowledged. The Signalman, turning to the radio-telephone set, pressed its transmission button and began, "Come in Jameson —come in Jameson." No response. However, unknown to Wallace or Buswell, the first message that the captain had sent out had been received by the POWERS. When it came into the bridge, Lt. (JG) K.C. Valentine, then standing in front of the radio set, was unceremoniously pushed out of the way by Lt. Commander Loew who transmitted, "We're coming."[6] Undoubtedly, the heeled over angle of the ST with her radio aerial blocked by the barrier seas had prevented the message's reception.

With more of an angle of broach on her than any earlier, a sea caught the tug hard against the port side, and for the second time she capsized—not to recover equilibrium again.

* * * * * * *

Almost in the same breath with which Loew had acknowledged the ST's distress call, he sang out, "GENERAL QUARTERS," and headed for the radar blip which, to the relief of all, indicated that the tug was still afloat. By the time the POWERS had steadied on course, her CIC reported that the target blip was fading; then it was gone. Searchlights sweeping, the DE bore down on the last bearing; and it was then that Jack Thebus, survivor of the earlier sunk ST 719, now standing on the POWERS' flying bridge, was to see in the pre-dawn light what looked like "little dark pinheads on a large green pincushion sliding up and down." This was how the ST 720's crew appeared to one of those on the POWERS' deck as the men in the water fought for their lives.

Among those who recall the rescue, there is a clear remembrance that when they first sighted the floating survivors, two or three men were in a small raft while the others were loosely scattered—some with one-cell lights which, in the half light, made sighting easier.

Loew swung his ship to the windward of what was the largest group. With his engines countering each other, he attempted to hold his ship at a right angle to the seas so he could slowly drift down to the men in the water. The effect of a gale force sea on a DE held in this position will dry up the saliva in most men's mouths. To Thebus, who had already lost a ship in far lesser seas, the sight of the towering waves above him while he stood there on the flying bridge, had all the overtones of "Judgment Day."

* * * * * * *

On the ST 720 at the moment of her second and final capsizing, the Chief Engineer, 1st Assistant Lamude, and Forbes, the Oiler, made another dash for the engine room escape hatch. This time, with the tug laying at more of a right angle to the seas and therefore taking their breaking force further astern, the three felt escape was possible. Before heading for the ladder, Lamude shut down the fuel to the engine; so when the men struggled out through the hatch, all mechanical noise was absent. All that could be heard was the thunderous roar of the gale.

Buswell made his escape out of the wheel house and worked his way down the side to near the stack. There, the three engineers who had just emerged from the engine room hatch were busily unloosening the lashings of the life raft. By the time the raft was freed, AB McFarland had joined them. Then, in the words of Buswell:

Suddenly, the tug and I parted company. I was beneath turbulent water trying to swim in what seemed an upward direction, avoiding breathing or swallowing. Basically, it was still dark, but there must have been a little light. Somehow I got into, or was helped into, a small rectangular doughnut-like raft with a rope netting bottom. With or without reason, some of the life jackets or raft lights were turned on and waved. Then we saw a DE not too far away, pitching and rolling. Could it help us in such a sea? When first alongside, we couldn't hang on or tie on and were driven away. The DE came alongside again after a while, somewhat shielding us from the worst of the force of the waves, but rolling so that we seemed to see its bottom one moment and its deck the next.

For Lamude, his entry into the water was a deep one. By his own testimony, he was sucked down at least fifteen feet, all the while being bombarded with upcoming debris escaping from the sinking hull (probably a lot of this came out of the life boat still securely fastened to the tug). When he broke surface, he grabbed a wooden keg and held onto it until he spotted the life raft. At that point, he let go of the keg and scrambled into the raft.

It is fairly certain that Lamude was the first on the raft and that it was he who helped Buswell and Forbes aboard. The three made up the total population of the raft at the time that it drifted into the side of the POWERS.[7]

At what point Michael O'Leary made it out of the wheel house is uncertain, but it is fairly definite that he was not on the outer hull with Buswell or the three from the engine room when the tug sank. O'Leary never made the raft, but he did have on a life jacket, as apparently did McFarland, who, during O'Leary's stay in the water was reported later by him as having been in close proximity.

To Lt. (JG) Henry Wenzel, USNR, standing near the life nets at the POWERS' waist, the brutality of the conditions facing those in the water came to him forcefully. When a sea broke over the escort's deck, Wenzel remembers: "The water was so cold that when the waves struck me I was completely breathless from the constriction of my solar plexus." Aiding in the first attempt to recover the survivors, Wenzel later wrote, "As we drifted down on the men in the water, we threw them lines and life preservers; but those that struggled to them could no longer close their fingers to help themselves. Some men on a small floating object (probably Buswell, Forbes, and Lamude on the raft—Ed.) tried repeatedly but unsuccessfully to hold the lines in their arms, looking like bears trying awkwardly to clasp a small object."[8]

Before reaching the survivors, Loew had cut out his shafts so as to prevent the ship's propellers from sucking in and chopping up the swimmers. Without power, it was impossible to stay parallel to the sea for long, so a second drift down was made. When the POWERS next came toward the men in the water, Ensign McCarthy and BM 1/C Dusseault tied lines around their waists and went over the side and down the nets. Their bodies were completely submerged whenever the ship rolled toward them as they slantingly clung to the webbing. It was in this perilous position that they man-handled the four men who were eventually rescued—grabbing them, pulling them into the scrambler net, and then pushing them up to the eager hands waiting on the POWERS' deck.

When the POWERS drifted down on the first man, (who was probably McFarland) McCarthy grabbed his life jacket. To the horror of all, the man slipped out of it; the strings of the jacket had been left untied. Before Dusseault could grab him, the man was swept aft, just at a moment when the DE rolled hard away. This sucked the survivor under the hull. Some of those on deck, Wenzel among them, rushed aft, whereupon they saw the man's body, now apparently lifeless, surge out from under the opposite side of the hull to be washed astern.

Following this horrifying scene, the POWERS drifted down on the next bunch of survivors who were the occupants of the raft. Out of desperation, they mustered their last reserves of energy to assist McCarthy and Dusseault in getting the raft next to the nets. To Buswell the rescue was almost as bad as the sinking had been.

> This time we held the lines better and tried to help each other get into the cargo net. I managed to get into it, but got my legs caught in it at the knees, and I was left hanging head down, alternately dunking and draining. I tried to get my hands or arms into it to climb, but couldn't make it. A big Signalman came over the side to haul me up to the rail, then over the rail. I was laid on a 'head' deck briefly to drain, gasping for breath and feeling very cold. Then I was wrapped with bottles of hot water in blankets, on a bunk. I couldn't hold the drink the Pharmacist's Mate brought. I thought I'd never warm up or sleep comfortably again.

The three men from the raft were safely aboard; the POWERS readjusted her drift position to pick up the last remaining swimmer. And so it was that at 0540 O'Leary was dragged up to the safety of the deck. The rescue operation had taken forty minutes since the ST 720 went down.

The search patterns were continued for another thirty minutes, but all that was sighted were bits of wreckage. The remaining seven seamen out of the total crew of eleven were given up as lost. There was little else Loew could do. He turned his ship on a course toward the ABNAKI and the LT 538.

At 0825, the weather had become so severe that Loew ordered the sound dome for the sonar raised and the safety bars for the depth charge racks inserted.[9]

Heavy weather with a stern sea as seen from the bridge of the USS POWERS. (Courtesy of K.C. Valentine).

The onset of the "Great Storm". Taken from the deck of the USS POWERS. The tug in the background is either the LT 538 or the LT 536. (Courtesy of K.C. Valentine).

The "Great Storm" in the Western Approaches.

Falmouth   6682

Aerofilms Ltd London

Falmouth Harbor — Taken in peacetime.

LT 538 shown alongside carfloat — picka-back lighter combination; after arrival in England — probably taken at Falmouth. (U.S. Army).

Loading freight cars aboard carfloats; probably at Southampton, England, preparatory to cross channel tow to France. Late 1944 or early 1945. (U.S. Army).

Chapter IX

THE WESTERN APPROACHES

When this account related the activities of the POWERS' group in Chapter VIII, the reader left the main Convoy as darkness settled on the evening of October 13. We will now rejoin that main body of Convoy NY 119 as first light breaks the morning of October 14.

T he Convoy (less the POWERS' group) was relatively compact. The only stragglers were the Y 86, which had been experiencing steering gear difficulties, and the Y 81, which had the ST 742 under tow. The three vessels were lagging a mile behind under the MASON's guardianship.[1]

At 1310 hours, the main body of NY 119 came under the air cover of the British Biscay Bay Patrol; this was evidenced by the appearance of a Liberator which swooped in low and dropped recognition flares.

October 15

October 15 went by with things in fair order except for one breakdown. The Y 126 lost power to her steering engine; but it was repaired by the ship's own crew by noon, and she was soon back with the Convoy.

At 2200 that night, the MASON picked up on radar what was either a submarine or a whale. The incident related around a very clear radar pick-up—bearing ten miles distant off the starboard beam. It "stayed on the scope about four minutes and disappeared suddenly and completely. It showed practically no motion while on radar scope." Ten miles was beyond the escort patrol perimeter, so no follow-up investigation was made. If it was a sub, it apparently went elsewhere, as no sonar target was detected approaching or near the Convoy that night or the following morning.[2]

October 16

By early morning on the sixteenth, the weather was worsening as the main Convoy passed near a weather front. The group began taking increasing seas astern. (The effect of the winds and seas was greater by far than what was being experienced at the same time by the POWERS' group, then a hundred or more miles behind.) During the early morning watch, CTG discontinued wide patrol arcs, ordering the DEs to stay close in and shepherd.

At 0305, the LT 580's tow line parted close into the nip which cast adrift her two BCFs and the ST 501. A few minutes later the LT 643's cable also snapped, freeing her BCF and the ST 750 and ST 751 trailing behind it. The seas were by then twenty-five feet high. This prompted Lind to order the three STs which had by then cut loose and the LT 580 (the latter without cable and now useless) to proceed with the main group. Assignments to stand by the three car floats went to the LT 63, the LT 579, and the LT 581. The job of standing guard over them was given to Lt. Commander Morris Beerman, USNR, skipper of the BERMINGHAM. The LT 643, which still had part of her hawser intact, also remained with them.

When the sun came up, Convoy NY 119 was thus in three parts: the POWERS' group over one hundred miles to the southeast trying to catch up, the BERMINGHAM contingent wallowing in the troughs near the three floating barges, and the main Convoy ahead of them to the northeast and well over the horizon.

Beerman, on the BERMINGHAM and hoping for better weather, held his group in close all that day and into the next. At 0200, BCF 3211, the float which had earlier broken loose from the LT 580, filled with water and sank. As was the case with the BCFs which had sunk earlier, her wooden lighter broke loose and floated clear. Since little could be done in the dark, Beerman waited until daybreak. It was then that he would decide the fate of the two float units and the wooden lighter. Coded weather reports indicated a continuance of bad weather with a probability of heavy gales coming into the area.

As soon as it became light enough, Beerman ordered the tugs to put over rubber rafts to make a try at hooking up. With great effort the boat crews made it aboard the floats, but that was about all they could manage. Due to the high seas, the LTs could not maneuver close enough to maintain the weight of the tow cables, which was essential if the men on the barges were to haul them aboard. The heavy weights of the dipping steel hawsers were beyond the capacity of men to manhandle once more than a hundred and fifty feet was fed out. Finally, the boat crew off the LT 579, who, by this time, were near the point of exhaustion, managed to shackle up to the BCF 3211's lighter. The men from the LT 581 and LT 63 kept trying until it was obvious that it was hopeless. At that point, Beerman ordered them back to their tugs. With the wooden lighter under tow there were still two floats unrecovered, but there was little likelihood of picking them up. Beerman radioed the news to CTG and was told in return to keep the contingent nearby the unsalvaged units awaiting further orders.[3]

* * * * * *

At 1700 hours on the sixteenth, CTG, after conferring with his staff and Mauldin, messaged Lt. Commander Blackford of the MASON to consider himself on detached duty. He was advised to take the faster moving Ys (except for Y 127 and Y 128 which were in tow); the two British net tenders; the three free-traveling STs, ST 510, ST 676, and ST 677, and move them into a convoy formation with Lt. William Muirhead, RNR, of the HMS PRETEXT acting as Commodore. He was to work the group ahead, staying within five miles of the MAUMEE. This left CTG with the unwieldy remainder. By 1930, Blackford was conning his bunch ahead of the main Convoy and passing the order to prepare for heavy seas. Life lines were rigged, and all hands reconciled themselves to one final mighty bout with the elements before reaching the safety of an English port.[4]

When the MASON left, NY 119's main group was down to two escorts, the O'TOOLE and the CHASE. With the straggling that was going on, Commander Lind knew that he would be hard put to prevent an underseas attack if the enemy was about. He was thankfully aware that the Convoy was now within the patrol area of the Plymouth based British ASW force, so the risk of a U boat assault was measurably reduced over what it had been in the few days past. Yet the spread-out condition of the Convoy, as portrayed on the O'TOOLE's radar scope, presented a problem not encountered within the classrooms of Miami's Anti Submarine Warfare School. Lind fervently hoped that no German officer would risk exposing his position to attack the rag-tag assemblage.

October 17

At twenty minutes after midnight on the morning of the seventeenth, Lt. Mauldin brought the O'TOOLE close aboard what was a rare sight in any ocean during the years of World War II. A cluster of brightly lit vessels was square across the Convoy's path. It would be seven months before the lights went on all over Europe, but for the group of vessels ahead of them, the lights had never gone out. A challenge by blinker light brought no response, so Mauldin took his ship within bull horn range. Across the narrow space between the O'TOOLE and one of the vessels, a pigeonese form of English was exchanged. Conversation brought out that the cluster of lighted ships was a group of Portuguese neutrals engaged in net fishing. It was only after some parley that the fishing boats were persuaded to move out of the unmaneuverable Convoy's path. They were cleared to starboard by two hundred yards.

Dawn on the seventeenth brought to sight a sky completely covered with strato cumulus clouds. There had been a lessening of the winds just before sunset the night before. At dawn, the winds began increasing. By 0900, it was blowing steady from the west southwest at twenty-five knots, accompanied by steady rain. The sea water temperature was 57°, and the air temperature stood at 60°. An occasional airplane was detected off toward the horizon, indicating British protection from above.

* * * * * * *

Before the noon hour, CTG dispatched the EDGAR G. CHASE, his last remaining escort, to try and locate the service tug LT 537 which had earlier picked up an adrift car float and had it under tow.[5] Now the tug was nowhere to be seen, visibly or on radar.

By 1530, the CHASE's skipper, Lt. Commander Russell V. Bradley, USNR, came upon LT 537, her tow still securely behind her. It was obvious, because of sea conditions, that catching up to the main group again was out of the question. By radio, Bradley contacted Lind. He was told to stay with the tug and operate separately.

Earlier at 1400, CTG had reported to British authorities the location of the then four scattered units of NY 119. He gave, via wireless, the following estimated positions:[6] †

MASON GROUP: 49° 29' NORTH, 09° 16' WEST

CTG ON O'TOOLE: 49° 11' NORTH, 09° 20' WEST

BERMINGHAM GROUP: 48° 16' NORTH, 12° 12' WEST

POWERS GROUP: 47° 16' NORTH, 14° 23' WEST

The CHASE was, at this time, at some point halfway between the main Convoy and the BERMINGHAM group. Had CTG sent in his position situation after 1530 hours, when he ordered the CHASE to stay with the LT 537, then NY 119 would have been reported as five separate contingents instead of four. Thus it was that by midday of the seventeenth the Convoy was no longer a controllable single entity. They were five separate operational units, each on their own but reporting to CTG whenever possible.

†Arranged here in order, east to west.

* * * * * * *

At 1930, the MASON began taking on some water—21 inches of it was sounded in her chain lockers.[7] The battering was beginning to tell. An hour before midnight, the MASON's radar picked up Lizard Head Light bearing eight miles distant. The termination of the trip for the lead group was almost in sight, but it would be another fourteen hours before the MASON had her charges safely behind a breakwater.

October 18

October 18 was the day on which the advance group of NY 119 was to make port. It also marked the worst weather the Convoy had experienced and the worst storm for October in the English Channel during the War. Before the day was over, there would be winds gusting to ninety miles per hour and seas estimated at fifty feet and more in height. Some men would die; others were to be filled with a fear that would last in their memories far down into the years. Clarke, of the LT 784 remembered such a man, a young AB whom he discovered kneeling with hands clasped in prayer on the spray drenched boat deck.[8] Ken Truelsen, a Motor Machinist on the BERMING-HAM remembered it as the day the "Mighty B" rolled so far no one thought she would ever right herself. Lt. Robinson McIlvaine (who years later became the Ambassador successively to three African nations) remembers registering the BERMINGHAM's roll at 62° off level keel.

* * * * * * *

At 0130 a TBS message crackled over the radio on the O'TOOLE's bridge. It came from the ST 511 reporting that one of her towing bridles had carried away. The O'TOOLE's Officer of the Deck queried the tug's skipper as to whether he would make out all right if he remained under tow. The answer was that the Master thought he would, all things being equal.

At 0325, Commander Lind entered CIC where, after viewing the interference specked radar scope, it was very clear that the Convoy was becoming widely dispersed. Then things began happening: First, the LT 538 parted her tow hawser. Next, there followed reports from other LTs with the same problem. Additionally, there were innumerable minor casualty reports concerning personnel and gear. A nightmare was developing.

Among the ships of NY 119: The officers and crews, from CTG down to the lowliest Messmen aboard the tugs, had by now one universal thought:

SURVIVAL. Gone were the previously dominating factors of fatigue, seasickness, irritation with others, worry over command difficulties—marks of a long voyage. The one single preoccupation was either the safety of their commands or, in the case of those without command responsibility, survival for themselves. For men off watch, sleep was almost impossible; some of those who tried it were thrown from their bunks to the steel decks. Aboard the STs, few dared to count the days of their lives past the present one.

At 0515, Lind, clinging to a hand hold near the TBS set, overhead the following messages coming over in quick succession:[9]

"LT 651, this is ST 511. Will you stop please?"

"ST 511, this is LT 651. What is the trouble?"

"LT 651, this is ST 511. We are turning over."

— SILENCE —

* * * * * * *

Aboard the ST 511 and backtracking to 0130:[10] When the port towing bridle parted, delivery Master Ivar Evensen started the tug's engine in an attempt to counteract the side angle at which the ST was being dragged along by the remaining cable attached to her starboard side. Under Evensen's orders, members of the crew stood by with an acetylene cutting torch ready to burn loose. A few minutes later, Evensen, apparently deciding that disaster was not imminent, ordered the engines stopped and the acetylene team secured from their precarious positions on the weather deck.

The night wore on as the little tug was dragged at a sideways slant astern of the last car float in LT 651's string. The rolling that the ST was experiencing was extremely heavy. She would stay over for terrifying periods of time to the starboard. When the hawser connecting her to the float ahead would slacken, she would hesitatingly roll back. One crew member entering the Head situated on the starboard weather deck witnessed, during his visit here, one of these delayed rolls. The tug went over so far that the porthole itself was completely submerged; solid water under pressure, not spray, squirted past the porthole gaskets. The Chief Engineer, Driscoll, also reported to Evensen that water was entering through the starboard engine room door. There was no inclinometer aboard, but it was obvious that many rolls were exceeding 50°. Yet Evensen continued on without any power to his engines or without any further thought of cutting loose from the potential death grip in which the broken towing bridle was holding them.

* * * * * * *

Following the brief TBS interchange between the ST 511 and the LT 651, Lind paused a few brief moments during which he anxiously awaited further word. Realizing that none would be forthcoming, he called the MAUMEE to tell that ship that he was pulling back from forward picket position to investigate. Ballard, "Rogering," then ordered the unencumbered LT 536 and LT 580 to assist.

After Lind had instructed Mauldin to swing the O'TOOLE to the Convoy's rear, it was discovered that to bring the DE directly to the scene via a run from the Convoy front, would be highly hazardous—this in light of what appeared on the radar scope to be a jumble of ships and barges all out of their respective columns. Deciding a less direct route was advisable, Mauldin brought her across the Convoy front, down its disoriented right flank, and up from astern to the estimated position where the ST 511 should have been. By the time the O'TOOLE neared the scene of the disaster, her radar indicated an absence of target—the ST had apparently gone under. Minutes passed. Finally, two small lights were intermittently sighted, their visibility hampered by the mountainous seas. Closing with her searchlights on, the O'TOOLE's lookouts reported what appeared to be two groups of four men each clinging to wreckage. Lind ordered the two LTs which had arrived simultaneously upon the scene to pick up the nearest group; the O'TOOLE proceeded to the second pod of survivors.

To get the DE maneuvered into a rescue position was difficult, but after a couple of abortive tries, the O'TOOLE was worked ahead to a position alongside what turned out to be a life ring with four survivors clinging to it. Lines were thrown out. The men, still clinging to their life ring, were hauled alongside.[11]

What happened next is not within the official record. It was described to the author by Edward P. Edmunds who was the O'TOOLE's Engineering Officer. It is related here not in the spirit of criticism but rather, as Edmunds himself described it to the author, as an illustration of "how necessary is perfect performance by everyone in a ship's crew when engaged in a critical operation."[12]

While Mauldin was bringing his ship up to the survivors, full power was kept on all of her shafts. It was necessary to give bell signals to the engine room which ranged directly from "All engines ahead" to "All engines back full," without pausing at "All engines stop;" for if he had done so, the power of the breaking seas would have broached the DE sideways and brought her down on top of the swimmers. At any rate, the Electrician's Mate, stationed at the control panel in the engine space, whose job it was to move the engine controller in response to the bell signals, reacted too fast. Instead of stopping momentarily with the controller handle, he swung it full reach from ahead to astern. As a result, No. 3 main engine took over from No. 4 main engine, causing it to reverse. According to Edmunds this brought about an air box explosion followed by a fire which immediately caused loss of power on the port propeller shaft. It was at this instant, that Mauldin was making his last critical maneuver to stay parallel to the swimmers so as to get them alongside the boarding net. With maneuvering ability thus limited, the O'TOOLE's stern rose sharply sucking under three of the four survivors. The fourth man, Able Bodied Seaman Joseph D. Holliday grabbed the boarding net in time and was spared the fate of his companions. The three who were sucked down under the DE must have been struck by its hull as it crashed down over them. The only evidence of them was their life jackets popping to the surface off the O'TOOLE's stern. The ship itself was never in real danger as the fire was extinguished and power restored within a matter of minutes.

The second group of four survivors, the rescue of which was delegated to the LTs, did not fare much better than the first. Only one man was saved; he was the ST 511's Chief Engineer, Maurice Driscoll, who was picked up by the LT 580 at about 0630.

After Holliday had been given time to partially recover, he was given breakfast and escorted to Commander Lind's cabin where the following interview took place:

CONVERSATION BETWEEN COMMANDER A.L. LIND, CTG 27.5 AND JOSEPH D. HOLLIDAY, AB, SURVIVOR OF ST-511 TAKEN ON THE USS O'TOOLE ON 18 OCTOBER 1944.†

LIND: We heard the 511 say to the 651, "Will you stop please?" Then the 651 said, "What's the trouble?" and the 511 said, "We are turning over." That is all I heard after that. The Delivery Captain was talking then, Evensen.* Who was the First Mate?

HOLLIDAY: "Cannon or Kannen, he died, he was with me. After he died I let him go." (Correct name, Horace M. Canning who was in fact the Permanent Master.)

LIND: "He didn't drown but died, is that it?"

HOLLIDAY: "He seemed to have, he was holding the light some of the time and I was but then when I looked at him he was all

*Spelling corrected by author.
†All materials shown in parenthesis are statements by the author of this book, taken from information supplied him through the files of the Office of General Services Administration.

doubled up and he went under in the water. That was all I saw of him. He was inside of the ring with me."

LIND: "What was the Mate's name?" (Josiah O. Wolcott, Jr.)

HOLLIDAY: "That I don't recall."

LIND: "What was the Assistant Engineer's Name?" (Richard J. Dunker.)

HOLLIDAY: "That I don't recall either."

LIND: "What was the cook's name?"

HOLLIDAY: "They called him Pete."

LIND: "It was just a ring life buoy that you had in the water."

HOLLIDAY: "We rigged up some floating material that we got ahold of and this 6 x 6 was full of spikes. We got it turned over and got it through the life ring so it couldn't slip back out and there was five of us to start with and then there was only four."

LIND: "How long was it before we came near, that Canning died?"

HOLLIDAY: "I would say about 3/4 of an hour."

LIND: "Were there four of you on it then?"

HOLLIDAY: "Yes, sir."

LIND: "Were they all hanging on?"

HOLLIDAY: "Yes sir. I let go and grabbed a life line and then I couldn't hold it. The sea took me under and when I came up I got another line and I went under again. The second time I came up I grabbed the ladder and hung on to it then."

LIND: "Were there many lines in the water?"

HOLLIDAY: "Yes, but they were small and we couldn't hold on to them because our hands were pretty numb."

LIND: "Did the ship come up and hit the men?"

HOLLIDAY: "No the ship didn't hit them, they may have hit the ship underneath the water by the suction of the big swell as it came alongside the ship which took us under but it wasn't the ship."

LIND: "You didn't see the other three after that?"

HOLLIDAY: "No, after I got ahold of that ladder I don't remember anything until I was in your Sickbay."

LIND: "Had you been having any trouble with the ship before this?"

HOLLIDAY: "Yes, we broke one bridle one night around 4:10 in the morning, they put the motors on and kept the speed up with the convoy and we changed bridles around 7 or 8 in the morning." (Not on the 18th.)

LIND: "Was there any strain on your bridle?" (Morning of the 18th.)

HOLLIDAY: "No, sir, the bridle broke about 1:15. I got up on the forecastle and had a look at it. She was steering very well then and I went back in the forecastle and put on my life jacket and then took a nap and the next thing I knew she was on her side. I opened the door and crawled up out on the hull on the port side. Yesterday the bridles were pretty well cracked. She snapped and then they turned the engines off. There was a heavy sea and it turned her over."

LIND: "You say it was around 1:15 when the bridles broke; did they start the engines then?"

HOLLIDAY: "Yes, I would say they started the engines around 2:00."

LIND: "Who gave the orders to turn off the engines?"

HOLLIDAY: "I don't know."

LIND: "How long after she went over did she stay on her side?"

HOLLIDAY: "Well it seemed like a long time but I would say about 10 or 15 minutes. I sat on the side until the sea washed us off."

LIND: "How many were there of you?"

HOLLIDAY: "About 10 of us, I am positively sure there were three that didn't get off. Hughes and Walker, two Britishers, I don't know the oilers name. I know he didn't get off because the oilers opening was right in the water. I never heard the Chief Engineer's voice so I think he was down in the engine room. (Oilers name was Emmet T. Carey.)"

LIND: "How many of the men on there didn't have life jackets on?"

HOLLIDAY: "Only one, I think he got one or he got a life ring. If I'm not mistaken he was picked up."

LIND: "One was picked by the LT 580 but I didn't get his name."

HOLLIDAY: "If he was a young fellow that would be the Navy Flags because the AB that was with me was as old as I am. The Chief Engineer wasn't very young neither but all the others that I could account for were only four young men on the ship. The two British boys, the oiler and the real young one was the Navy Signalman. I know that if he is a real young boy it is him. I heard him several times in the water, he was praying. I don't remember his name but he was an Irishman." ("Flags," the Navy Signalman was Charles L. Gallagher SM 3/C USNR. The Chief Engineer's name was Maurice A. Driscoll.)

LIND: "After you went in the water were you in two groups?"

HOLLIDAY: "No, sir, we were scattered, every man was for himself. I found this one life ring and this piece of timber and I worked them together. Captain Canning* came along and I got him in this life ring. That was the way we were when we picked up the cook, he had a life jacket on and there were five of us. We told them all to stay in a group so it would be much easier for them to spot us and pick us up."

LIND: "When you were floating did you see any other groups?"

*Spelling corrected by author.

127

HOLLIDAY: "I saw scattered lights, 3 or 4 of them."

LIND: "I thought there were 2 or 3 separate groups. It was still pretty dark and every once in a while we could see faces. What do you think the Captain died from, was he a sick man?"

HOLLIDAY: "No, sir, he was a little timid, he wasn't used to the sea. As far as a seaman is concerned he just wasn't. He wasn't rugged enough."

LIND: "Have you been to sea long?"

HOLLIDAY: "About 16 years." (Record indicates 9 years.)

LIND: "How old are you?"

HOLLIDAY: "Forty-one sir."

LIND: "What had the Captain done before he took this job?" (Assumed to mean Canning.)

HOLLIDAY: "He was a professor of some kind and the only boat he sailed was a small vessel on the Sound." (Canning had been a civilian instructor employed by the Coast Guard.)

LIND: "Was he a wealthy man?"

HOLLIDAY: "Yes, he was." (His past employment record indicates the unlikelihood of this.)

LIND: "What about the Mate?"

HOLLIDAY: "The Mate was an attorney from Wilmington, Delaware."

LIND: "What did the First Mate do?" (Meaning the "Mate.")

HOLLIDAY: "He sailed one time on a liberty ship; he was a graduate from some diesel school." (According to personnel records this is incorrect. Wolcott never sailed on a liberty ship, nor had he ever attended diesel school.)

LIND: "What about the cook?"

HOLLIDAY: "He had just signed on and he was a good sea cook."

LIND: "Where did he come from?"

HOLLIDAY: "Somewhere near Brooklyn." (Born in Norway; name was Peder A. Ambjornsen.)

LIND: "Now these people that went with you, who was in charge of them?"

HOLLIDAY: "Evensen* was." (Evensen was the Delivery Master.)

LIND: "Where did he come from?"

HOLLIDAY: "He was an old seaman from Scandanavia." (Same age as Holliday.)

LIND: "Who was the next highest?"

HOLLIDAY: "There was only one, then there was Larsen* and Flags." (Anders Larsen was an Able Bodied Seaman.)

LIND: "What did Larsen* do before this time?"

HOLLIDAY: "He had been to sea for sometime too. If it would have been 4 or 5 o'clock we would have cut the cable and we could have kept her in line. If they would have cut the cable at 1:15 and let her go on her own power she would have been all right." (This irrelevant answer indicates the state of shock Holliday was still in at the time of the interview.)

LIND: "That makes eight, do you remember who the others were?"

HOLLIDAY: "No, the others would consist of this group that didn't get out of the water."

LIND: "Yes, that would make the 12."

LIND: "When you spoke of sleeping in the forecastle it actually isn't on the forcastle, it is in the bridge structure isn't it?"

*Spelling corrected by author.

HOLLIDAY: "Yes, sir. All of our quarters are called forecastle."

LIND: "What had the situation been on food and water?"

HOLLIDAY: "The water wasn't so good, it was down low and was very rusty. Our food had been down since the fourth day out and about one thousand pounds of meat went bad around the fourth day out. When we left they only put fifty pounds of dry ice for us to make this trip to keep all our meat fresh with. We threw cases of chicken, beef, loins and everything else over the side because they went bad. I saved the hams and bacons and swung them to the mast out in the air. The last of the ham went last Sunday."

LIND: "You had plenty of canned foods so you weren't starving?"

HOLLIDAY: "No, sir we had plenty to eat even under those conditions." (This statement can be viewed questionably as if it is correct, then the conditions on the ST 511 were considerably better than was the case on the other STs.)

* * * * * * * * * *

The search for the ST 511 survivors continued until 0740. The O'TOOLE was assisted by the LT 580 and the LT 536. During the search, several life jackets were seen as was the top of the deck house of the ST 511. The deck house was thought by the observing vessels to have become separated from the sunken ST's hull, but they were obviously unaware of the construction specifications of an Army ST. The separation of a deck house from the rest of the hull would have been next to impossible—both units were steel and welded together at the deck line. Even if the deck house had come unattached, it could not possibly have floated. What the searchers probably saw was the top most super structure of the little tug, her hull lying just submerged beneath the surface.[14] Such being the case, were there still men left alive aboard her? Possibly, but if there were, they would have been beyond rescue due to the heavy seas running. Most likely, the air pockets which were keeping the vessel afloat were soon displaced by sea water. The ST 511, following this last sighting, must have soon joined the scores of Allied and German vessels sunk in two World Wars which pave the bottom of that maritime commerce funnel known as the Western Approaches.

* * * * * * *

Following the overturning of the ST 511: CTG ordered Blackford, commanding officer of the MASON group, to disregard his earlier instructions to stay within five miles of the O'TOOLE. Instead, he was to go ahead, getting his unit into Falmouth as best he could.

At 0920, Commander Lind handed his bridge runner the following message for immediate radio transmission:

"ACTION CINCWA INFO ADMIRALTY FROM COMTASKGROUP 27.5 X REF 180044 AND 180052 X 2 ST TUGS SUNK DURING NIGHT X DUE TO SEVERE SEAS X TOWING GEAR ON TOWS PARTING X INTEND TO SEND SEVEN STS AND POSSIBLY OTHER SMALL CRAFT INTO CROWS SOUND SCILLY ISLES WITH LT 580 X WHICH WILL REJOIN TASK GROUP X UNLESS YOU SUGGEST BETTER TEMPORARY ANCHORAGE TO RIDE OUT STORM X USS MASON WITH ALL Y OILERS PROCEEDING TO FALMOUTH X WILL MAKE LATER REPORT ON LOST TUGS X INFORM ALL PORT AUTHORITIES X"

By the time the message had been sent off, all of the tows had parted from the LTs. This caused most of the tugs to lose their usefulness since their towcables were, in the main, completely stripped out. One or two did have enough cable left to pick up barges, provided the weather broke, an occurrence that did not appear likely immediately. The STs had meanwhile cast off from the derelict car floats. Their skippers took this action without orders. Yet to them, it was in the best interests of their vessels and an obvious step upon finding oneself tethered astern a massive object which might sink without a moment's notice.

Lind, looking over the turbulent scene, decided to send the SS SUERTE on alone to England. Her Greek skipper, free at last, headed his vessel toward Barry Roads where she arrived safely the following morning.

Next, Lind TBS'd the MAUMEE, the remaining seven STs and the LT 580 to fall in behind the oiler under O'TOOLE escort on a course set for the Scilly Isles. The remaining LTs, believed to be safe from submarine attack because of the heavy sea conditions, were ordered to stand by their tows awaiting favorable weather for salvage.

Soon after the O'TOOLE group had set its course for the sheltering islands, it found itself wallowing dangerously in the trough of a broadside sea. After a few minutes of this punishment, CTG ordered a change of heading back toward Falmouth which again put the seas more comfortably astern.

* * * * * * *

The O'TOOLE left behind a desolate and inhospitable scene. The LTs' skippers, feeling very much alone, tried to stay within sight of their former tows by cruising back and forth, now with the seas and then back against their punishing force. The windward course legs were brutal rides for the crews, the bows of the stubby tugs crashing into solid walls of water. Consequently, the order to swing ship for the leeward course leg must have often been given before the lost ground back to the car floats had been regained. A combination of the latter and other factors resulted in a widening gap between the tugs and their former tows.[15]

* * * * * * *

Apparently oblivious to the off-shore situation was Major Charles Hurst, Commanding Officer of the 343rd Harbor Craft Company. The 343rd consisted of twenty men and three officers which had overall American Army port command of Falmouth and an up-river facility at Truro.[16]

Before the invasion of Europe, Falmouth had been an important coastal port. One of its more interesting functions was that it served as the home basing of a fleet of Free French trawlers which operated from there subversively to the French coast. They carried arms and explosives along with British and Free French intelligence agents.[17] Shortly before the invasion, the port had become a major staging area for landing craft and continued to be so until after the major northern French ports of Cherbourg and LeHavre were opened to conventional shipping thus negating the necessity for over-the-beach supply.

By October, Falmouth's function had depreciated down to a patrol base for small British Naval craft and as a coastal port for British shipping. Under Hurst's responsibility, it was also used as a trans-shipment point for wooden barges which were being constructed by the British under U.S. Army supervision up the River Fal at Truro. Hurst's 343rd had as its major responsibility the barge construction program. Consequently, Hurst spent most of his time at Truro in the company of three enlisted men, all of whom acted as inspectors over the British contractors. The rest of the 343rd, which consisted of two Lieutenants and seventeen men, were based at Falmouth where their major activity was the down river hauling of the barges. They then turned them over to U.S. Army towing craft for transport either further east to Plymouth or directly to the French coast.[18] The 343rd Harbor Craft Company was not equipped to handle the succoring of a bruised and beaten convoy. NY 119 was in such a condition, and it would desperately need repair and provisioning once it arrived at Falmouth.

It appears, in retrospect, to be quite doubtful that Hurst was ever informed of the pending arrival, despite a continuous string of messages which were sent by Commander Lind announcing the Convoy. Unfortunately for the mariners of NY 119, the Army had just recently made a command switch. This was a transfer of the 13th Port, which had controlled the southern English sea ports from Falmouth eastward to Southampton. The 13th Port had been sent to France while the 14th Major Port had taken over the 13th Port's prior responsibilities. The 343rd Harbor Craft Company, although remaining part of the 13th Port, was put on detached service within the bailiwick of the 14th Port.[19] Hurst and his Company had been left behind because of their personalized knowledge of the barge construction program and because of the rapport which had been established between them and the British contractors. It was felt that to transfer the Company might upset the program substantially. The command switch had occurred on October 13, and it is probable that an efficient line of communication had not yet been established. Because of the latter, it appears that Hurst, busy as he was supervising the British contractors working on the barge stocks, either was not informed of the role of host he was expected to play, or, if he was so informed, disregarded any needs in planning for the Convoy's arrival.[20]

Meanwhile, NY 119 fought its battle against the elements, anticipating that if it survived, it would be welcomed and cared for by an appreciative Port Command.

* * * * * * *

At early post noon, the MASON group was becoming badly dispersed. Despite the PRETEXT's assistance, Blackford knew he needed help, and he needed it fast. At 1303, he sent the following radio message addressed to Admiralty, Falmouth:

"REQUIRE IMMEDIATE ADDITIONAL ESCORT ASSISTANCE FOR ADVANCE SECTION NY 119 OFF LIZARD HEAD X SECTION SCATTERED BADLY DUE TO HIGH SEAS X"[21]

At 1314, the MASON intercepted an Admiralty verification for the dispatch of the HMS ROCHESTER and the HMS SALADIN. They were to proceed at their best speed to assist the MASON.

* * * * * * *

Rejoining the CHASE in the early hours on the eighteenth: At 0425, it was reported to Russ Bradley that his charge's (LT 537's) tow was adrift. Unable, because of the weather, to effect a pick up, the escort and the tug stood by the adrift car float until noon. At that time, Blackford, feeling the smaller vessel was in danger, ordered her to proceed toward port while the CHASE rejoined the O'TOOLE. To the amazement of those aboard the CHASE, Waaler, the LT's skipper, told Bradley that this was impossible since his ship had no charts of the United Kingdom coast and that he had not the faintest hint of where he was.[22] A conference of the CHASE's officers resulted in the decision to lead the LT into the Scillys since that group of islands was the closest point of land affording shelter. Bradley and his navigator huddled in the chart room studying the detailed chart of the Scillys and the related Coast Pilot. The latter warned against approaching beyond the one hundred fathom curve during a westerly gale—according to the Fathometer, they were now in less than fifty fathoms. The astern quartering seas developed their size in the open Atlantic. They were now frictionalized by the coastal shelf, thus being shortened between crests but heightened in size. The resultant effect against the CHASE was a tendency to make her broach to. Fortunately, Bradley was to find out that he had a good ship under him, yet, "they were anxious hours, with those great foaming crests towering over our bridge."

The visibility had by now become so poor that, despite extra lookouts, it was difficult to keep the LT 537 within sight. Consequently, TBS conversation was kept up on a continuous basis. At one time, audio contact was lost for fifteen to twenty minutes. After an anxious interlude and to the relief of the worried Bradley, Waaler came back on the air apologizing for his silence. He explained that his ship had taken a cresting wave down the funnel. The same sea had also wet down the main electrical panel which robbed the LT of all electric power until the damage could be repaired.

By 2110 that night, the CHASE and the LT were in the lee of one of the Scillys. Bradly ordered Waaler to stay put—an order no doubt welcomed by the recipient. The CHASE paused just long enough for her cooks to serve the crew a hot meal (impossible during the bad weather of days past) before heading back to search for more stragglers.

* * * * * * *

Shortly after midnight on the eighteenth: Lieutenant E.O. Ross, USNR, Executive Officer and Navigator on the MASON, identified Bishop Rock Light bearing 052° true. (That light is located on the outside shoals of the Scillys.) By this time more cracks had appeared in the ship's deck welds. As if this wasn't bad enough in itself, two longitudinal strength members in compartment B4 were adrift. Additionally, the radio antenna had blown away. A jury rig antenna was set up, but this makeshift arrangement gave only a limited transmission capability.[23]

Despite the earlier offer of British help, the MASON had not received any yet. By noon, the Falmouth entrance buoy was sighted. Blackford devoted the next four hours to directing the Ys and the four STs from a point near the buoy in toward the Falmouth harbor entrance. By 1550 the last of the MASON's section had headed for the safety of the sheltering breakwater.

Without the luxury of sampling what smooth water could be like, the MASON, in company with HMS ROCHESTER and HMS SALADIN, headed back to rejoin the O'TOOLE. Shortly after the establishment of the return heading, both Britishers (now under the formal control of Task Group Commander 27.5) requested permission to turn back rather than subject their vessels to the force of the forty-foot seas. Lind, by radio gave a "permission granted" but added some sentences unfavorably comparing the Englishmen's ability to withstand punishment when compared to the crews of TG 27.5.[24]

At 2016, the MASON, alone again, sighted a single blue light to port. This was subsequently identified as the LT 653, one of the tugs which earlier had been with the O'TOOLE group. The LT 653 was given directions to Falmouth.

By 2200, the best speed that could be made was between seven and nine knots; Blackford forced his vessel onward. The sonar soon became unusable because of the sea's turbulence, and it was ordered secured.[25]

* * * * * * *

The O'TOOLE bunch, consisting of the seven STs, the two hawserless LTs, and the mothering MAUMEE, had arrived off the entrance to Falmouth Harbor. The time was 2230. Despite CTG's earlier requests for a pilot, none was waiting.

Lind, anxious to return to what was happening off shore, requested Blackford on the MAUMEE to take over. That officer, conning by radar with all the tanker's running and cross tree lights burning brightly, and the storm shrieking around him, led the smaller vessels into the outer harbor. Once safely inside, the MAUMEE's anchors rattled out, and she swung peacefully, her engines on "Stop" for the first time in over thirty days. The dependent STs, a few of their crewmen near emotional breakdown from fear and fatigue, anchored close around.

Lind messaged "THANK GOD ALL SMALL CRAFT ARE NOW SAFE." And then the O'TOOLE, her crewmen gazing with envy at the MAUMEE, fast disappearing astern, headed back into the wind-whipped English Channel.

October 19

At 0100 hours on October 19, the POWERS' log book recorded the wind out of the west at 40 knots steady, with stronger gusts. Seas were extremely steep and steepening as the DE, the ABNAKI, and the LT 538 approached into shallower water. Lt. Commander Loew, leery of the reliability of his radar because of the high seas and the spin-drift, ordered all running lights turned on.[26]

* * * * * * *

At 0205, Commander in Chief, Plymouth sent a message addressed to CTG informing him that the U.S. Navy tugs, OWL and CORMORANT, which were then at Falmouth, were available if CTG required them. Lind immediately requested the assignment of the OWL and any of the former Army tugs of the Convoy that could be sent back to him. Within the hour, the OWL was at sea.

* * * * * * *

At 0545, by TBS, the MASON contacted the CHASE which by radar bearing was then fourteen miles to the west southwest. At the same time that the contact was made between the two DEs, the CHASE had just come upon the LT 581 and was proceeding to escort her into the shelter of the Scillys, there to join the anchored LT 537. After the CHASE brought in the LT 581 and Bradley had assured himself of the tug's condition to proceed, he ordered her Master to set a course for Falmouth. The CHASE and the LT 537 began a search for lost barges which were believed to be missing in the area of the Scillys.

* * * * * * *

The MASON's present mission was to find the BERMINGHAM. Blackford felt it was reasonable to assume that since the LT 581 had previously been with the BERMINGHAM, he at least was in the correct area. This assumption was arrived at without the knowledge that the LT 581 had some time earlier departed from the BERMINGHAM's control.

* * * * * * *

Aboard the POWERS at 1600: The barometer was dropping with the wind shifting to south southeast and increasing in velocity.

Radioing CTG for approval, Loew sent the LT 538 on ahead toward

Falmouth—her skipper under orders to report to the MAUMEE upon arrival.

An hour and twenty minutes later, the POWERS was pacing the ABNAKI and her tow and would soon pass the MASON on a reciprocal course.[27]

* * * * * * *

By voice radio from the MAUMEE which was lying at Falmouth, Ballard disclosed to Lind that Army authorities there were refusing to resail any of the LT tugs that were available in that port. In the words of Lind, then subjected to the punishment of the stormy Channel, "The situation looked hopeless as we were standing by drifting barges but could do nothing without tugs." To get an answer as to where he stood and inform those "who needed to know," he sent the following secret dispatch to Commander in Chief, Plymouth:

"REQUEST ALL VESSELS THIS TASK GROUP REMAIN SUBJECT MY ORDERS UNTIL TASK ASSIGNED COMPLETED X ALL LT TUGS BE FITTED AND READY TO PROCEED TO SALVAGE BARGES X TRANSFER SPARE TOWING EQUIPMENT WITH LT. PHIPPS NOW ON MAUMEE TO CORMORANT KK WHOSE USE WE REQUEST KK AND REPORT TO ME 200700 AT LAT 49° 31' LONG 06° 06' FOR FURTHER ORDERS X ESCORTS ARE SPOTTING FLOATING TOWS AND WILL DIRECT SALVAGE X REQUEST PLANES BE ASSIGNED TO AID IN SEARCH X PLEASE ADVISE X ACTION ADEE PLEASE PASS THIS TO CINCWA AND COMNAVU"[28]

Thus Commander Lind had established for the record that: 1. The Army vessels must remain under his command until notified accordingly. 2. He fully intended, come what may, to bring in all of NY 119 that he possibly could.

* * * * * * *

The OWL reported to CTG at 1919 that she had picked up the car floats 3212 and 3208—their top wooden lighters still secured in position. Further, she was proceeding with her tandem tow at best possible speed toward Falmouth. Her hull had been damaged during the salvage, and she had lost one of her anchors.

* * * * * * *

The BERMINGHAM contingent was making a steady 5 knots toward Falmouth. With her were the LT 579 with wooden barge in tow and the LT 63 standing by her. It was the LT 579 that was to have the distinction of being the only tug of NY 119 to successfully deliver her tow into port.

* * * * * * *

The CHASE, in company with the LT 537, sighted and began a salvage attempt of a double float, car float unit 3302, just before darkness settled in. Hooked on and with full power on her engines, the LT 537 was unable to budge it. It was thought at the time that the astern bridle must have either been fast to a wreck or to the other barge (the sunken 3202) which had originally been in tandem. It was far too dangerous to think of putting men back on the barge to cut the bridle, so the CHASE dropped astern and let go two depth charges in an attempt to free the float. The depth charging proved futile. The LT 537 hung on throughout the night, her skipper and Bradley reluctant to lose the LT's towing cable. They hoped that in the morning men could be put back aboard to cut it free.

* * * * * * *

Just before darkness settled in, the O'TOOLE's lookouts, who were scanning for other lost barges, saw flashes of gun fire reflected against the leaden sky. Proceeding to investigate, Mauldin brought the O'TOOLE into blinker range of the HMS ROCHESTER. That ship obviously had taken second thoughts regarding the honor of the Royal Navy and had put back to sea following the American Task Group Commander's earlier, sarcastically phrased remarks. Asked as to what he was firing at, the Britisher stated that he was attempting to sink a "derelict," but was having difficulty in so doing and requested the O'TOOLE to give assistance. Lind, taking a closer look, saw that the ROCHESTER's target was one of NY 119's missing barges. The "derelict" turned out to be BCF 3207, still afloat though punctured like a sieve from the ROCHESTER's guns. Lind messaged the ROCHESTER, "After fighting heavy seas for thirty days to bring this barge to England, I don't want it sunk now." The ROCHESTER pulled away leaving the O'TOOLE standing by the well-ventilated lighter.[29]

At 2328, while in the vicinity of the car float, a sound contact with very clear echoes was picked up by the O'TOOLE. Since there were possible doppler indications, a deliberate attack was carried out. Twice, attack runs were made, whereafter it was assumed that the submarine was still lying on the bottom.

October 20

Thinking he had the real thing, Mauldin ushered in the new day with three more attack runs on the suspected sub. At 0113, he lost sound contact. Fifteen minutes later, it was regained whereupon the fantail crew rolled off a 5-charge pattern. This was soon followed by another pattern of depth charges, a total of thirteen. Target movement was then noted. Despite the fact that the depth charge and hedgehog crews were working on a deck knee-deep in green water, both Mauldin and Lind agreed that they should hang over the target, awaiting daybreak and better working conditions.

By 0500, the sea was getting so bad that both officers, fearing for the ship's safety, decided that close contact would have to be temporarily abandoned in favor of long sweep legs on safer headings.

At 0930, the O'TOOLE was back over the original contact point reconducting a close pattern search. At approximately 1115, she picked up a promising return signal but soon lost it. Another hour went by with no further contact; the search was given up. Despite CTG's request, a tug never turned up to haul in the BCF. When later in the day the O'TOOLE departed the area, she left behind the still-floating BCF 3207 with its wooden lighter securely lashed down. It was taking on an increasingly water-logged appearance, due, no doubt, to the entrance of sea water through the shell holes. It is believed that it went to the bottom somewhere near 49° 33'N; 06° 58'W.

* * * * * * *

A Navy tug, the USS CORMORANT, was on a search for two barges, believed to be in tandem and reported by a British patrol vessel at latitude 49° 17' N, longitude 05° 48' W.

* * * * * * *

The POWERS, in escort to the ABNAKI, which was towing a barge, greeted a menacing dawn. The escort was already showing heavy weather damage. By the time she gained harbor, fourteen of her major and minor frames were broken.[30]

Lt. (JG) Henry G. Wenzel III had just come off watch and was asleep in his bunk. Suddenly, he found himself lying on the bulkhead instead of on his mattress. Groggy from approaching sleep and just beginning to realize that the ship must have taken an extraordinary roll, he was suddenly "deluged with icy water." In the unlighted compartment, he thought that the ship had capsized. Conditioned as he was to the stories told by the ST survivors who had fought their way out of their capsized vessels, the young officer felt a moment of outright and justifiable panic. Rushing into the companionway, he ran head long into a mass of men pouring from an adjoining crew's quarters. In what to all of them was a struggle for life, they were wildly trying to push onto a ladder leading to a deck manhole. No sooner had the rush started than the POWERS righted herself. Wenzel, gathering his equilibrium, switched on the lights to discover that the source of his icy bath was a ventilator directly over the bunk on which he had been lying. What had happened was that in her extreme roll, the ship had taken green water into some of the ventilator cowls. Wenzel, a judge of human nature and in a mastery of understatement noted that, "Apparently, the scramble for the ladder which followed the extreme roll and the subsequent fight to get through the manhole was rather demoralizing to the men who participated."

Unwilling to subject himself to the coffin-like confines of his quarters, Wenzel struggled forward and then topside to the bridge. He stood there in the half light of dawn watching the great seas—mast high while in the trough. The ship, hesitating for what seemed like an unrecoverable period of time, would shudder and then start up at an express elevator velocity. "Suddenly, we would see the horizon and the great waves rolling toward us."[31]

The ABNAKI, which was then close off the POWERS' stern, still had her barge, but the going was getting tougher by the minute. Lind, in radio contact with Loew on the POWERS, ordered him to instruct the ABNAKI to cast loose the barge and head for shelter. The freed barge, BCL 3162, dropped astern, dragging with it two thousand feet of 1½-inch cable.

At 1400, the POWERS and the O'TOOLE came in visual contact with each other. Lind, standing on the bridge wing of the O'TOOLE, snapped a picture of the POWERS when she was in the trough of a sea. Nothing except her radar antenna was visable above the water when the picture was developed. Later, Lind said that he believed the seas to be sixty feet in height at that time.

* * * * * * *

At 1420, CTG sent out the following message addressed to CINCWA:

"ALL TUGS ORDERED FALMOUTH X ESCORTS TO SHELTER OFF PLYMOUTH X WILL RESUME SALVAGE OPERATIONS WHEN WEATHER MODERATES X ETA PLYMOUTH HARBOR 2030 X REQUEST PERMISSION TO REFUEL AND PROVISION FIVE ESCORTS PLYMOUTH"

Subsequently, Lind directed Mauldin to proceed to Plymouth. Following this, he sent out messages to all LTs still at sea in which he ordered them into Falmouth where they were to take on water and provisions together with any towing gear replacements they were able to obtain from the MAUMEE and shore facilities.

* * * * * * *

Prior to when CTG had sent out his instructions to head for the barn, Bradley of the CHASE had ordered the LT 537 to cast loose from her anchored barge. Escorting the LT, the CHASE made sonar contact on what, at the time, was thought to be a moving submarine. She made several runs, firing one full pattern of depth charges before evaluating the contact as false.[32] Rejoining the LT 537 and Falmouth bound, together they overtook the BERMINGHAM group. The former free traveling LT 63, which was with the BERMINGHAM, had the disabled LT 643 under tow. By sunset, both escorts and the three tugs were safely dockside at Falmouth.

* * * * * * *

During the mid afternoon, Commander in Chief Plymouth sent out HMS SKATE to patrol and the USS CORMORANT to pick up two barges, the location of which had been reported to the shore authorities by aircraft. The OWL was unable to accompany her sister tug due to the damage she had sustained the day before.

* * * * * * *

By 2300, the O'TOOLE, the POWERS, and the ABNAKI were anchored in Cawsand Bay Anchorage, Plymouth Sound. The MASON had arrived earlier by some few minutes.

* * * * * * *

The last hour of October 20, 1944, marked that point at which all the remaining crewed vessels of Convoy NY 119 reached English ports; yet the flotsam and jetsam of their passage drifted behind them. The responsibility to recover it still lay before many of the ships and their crews before the curtain could be brought down on Convoy NY 119.

Chapter X

THE SALVAGE

Unbeknownst to Commander Lind, aboard the USS O'TOOLE which was still at anchor in Plymouth Bay in the early morning hours of October 21, the next six days were going to be loaded with more worry, frustration, and downright hard work than any of the storm-wracked ones which just transpired.

While the O'TOOLE was quietly lying at anchor, the duty officer, Commander, Plymouth, was beginning to put into action the steps necessary for the fueling of TG 27.5's escorts. Through Commander, Plymouth, the U.S. Naval Base at Queen Anne's Battery was alerted for the delivery of provisions. While in conversation with U.S. Shore Command, the British, together with CTG, agreed that for the escorts to take to the sea without service tugs would be a useless endeavor. Every effort would be made so that on the following day the necessary tugs would be provided—or so the shore people had promised.

It wasn't until 0330 that morning that Lind was able to arrange for a car to meet him quay side. He was offered a bed at the Royal Naval Barracks which he accepted. Exhausted from lack of sleep, he remained in it in a state of blissful unconsciousness until 0900 the following morning.

Upon arising, CTG traveled to the other side of the port and called on Commander, Amphibious Forces, United Kingdom. This was the most likely agency to provide the necessary logistical support for refurbishing the Naval ships of the Task Group. While there, Lind received helpful advice as to whom it would be proper to contact for assistance on various problems.

Returning to the Naval Barracks, Lind next called on Commodore Beaverly, Chief of Staff to Admiral Ralph Leatham, RN, the British Commander for the Western Approaches. Beaverly informed Lind that Admiral Leatham had requested a visit from CTG later that afternoon. This request Lind gratefully accepted. Much to the American officer's surprise, Beaverly seemed to be fully informed on all the problems then facing TG 27.5. Lind questioned him as to the overall efficiency of the U.S. Army people at Falmouth and what could be expected of them. The Commodore, either not knowing of the situation there or too polite to remark about an Allied group, declined comment. Lind sensed that things in Falmouth might not be as they should. When asked as to whether the dispatches from CTG had reached Major Hurst at Falmouth, Beaverly called in four senior Royal

Naval Officers who confirmed the fact that dispatches received by them had been forwarded through regular channels to Hurst, but receipt could not be guaranteed without further checking. Insofar as Admiralty was concerned, Lind was told that all possible action had been taken to provide escorts and tugs for the Task Group's assistance. Asked as to what the sources of supply concerning Naval tugs were, the Britishers replied that the only ones available and not at sea were already under the control of CTG and were berthed to the westward at Falmouth. A phone call was then put through to Hurst, but that officer could not be located. A message was left for a return call which never came through (although CTG stood by for several hours awaiting it). Exasperated, Lind eventually put through a second call; this time he managed to make contact with a Lt. Verrinder and a Lt. Herman, both of the U.S. Army's Transportation Corps. Lind's interpretation at the time was that these officers were extremely confused over the whole situation and were apparently reluctant to act without Hurst's authorization. Inquiring as to where Hurst was, Lind was told that that officer had been out of contact with the Lieutenants for several days. Perhaps because Lind began showing irritation with them over their lack of initiative, the conversation ended with an assurance that steps would be taken to have the tugs made ready to sail by the next morning.

On schedule, Commander Lind arrived at the office of Admiral Leatham for his afternoon appointment. He found the Admiral to be a most pleasant gentleman; their conversation brought out the fact that the Admiral had been keeping a close personal watch on the progress of NY 119 while it had been at sea.[1] Nothing really new came out of the meeting, but it did serve the purpose of lifting Lind's morale above the plane on which it had earlier been.

* * * * * * *

During the day, a message report came in stating that HMS RUBY, escorting HMS GOLIATH (tug), was standing by BCL 3162 at latitude 49° 11' north, longitude 07° 32' west.

October 22

By the morning of the twenty-second, there were indications of things finally beginning to happen; Lind was greeted with the news that the LT 651 had been made ready and was then preparing to sail from Falmouth. The LT 374, a vessel assigned to the Army Transportation Corps docks, Plymouth, was going to be dispatched to the area where some of the drifting barges had most recently been reported. During the early morning hours, the BERM-INGHAM, the CHASE, the ABNAKI, and the MAUMEE left Falmouth; by dawn they had arrived at the fleet anchorage in Plymouth. Both escorts and the Navy tug were in the process of taking aboard fuel and stores in order to join the salvage effort. By 1300 hours, the three ships were bunkered and provisioned and on their way to sea. In their company was the LT 374.

No sooner had Lind been informed of their sailing than a message arrived stating that at the last minute the LT 651 had been unable to depart due to some unexplained deficiency. Shortly after this, as if to counteract the bad news, Falmouth reported that the LT 581 was on her way out in company with HMS SKATE.

Lind, believing it useless to send out his three remaining escorts, O'TOOLE, MASON, and POWERS, ordered them to remain at anchor but to hold themselves on a 2-hour standby basis, ready to meet with any tugs that could be sailed.

CTG and staff spent their day at the offices of Commander in Chief, Plymouth. There they continued to harass British and American Naval and Army commands for any tugs that might be scraped up. Allied tug command at Portsmouth was contacted, but the excuse was given that every one of their vessels had already been assigned missions and could not be spared. Inquiring of Army command Plymouth, Lind was again told that with the exception of the LT 374 all the tugs within that command had already been assigned elsewhere and were standing by for definite duty.

A suspicion was beginning to develop in Lind's mind—how really desperate was the military need for the car floats for which he had risked so many lives and for which he was preparing to risk still more? If the need was as great as he had been told, back in New York, then why weren't shore authorities showing more concern?

Since Falmouth had sent out only one tug of the twelve that were moored there, Lind put a third call through hoping to locate Hurst. This only resulted in the continuing news that the man "was still among the missing." Both Verrinder and Herman were apparently having no luck in expediting matters. Lind believed that they "were putting forth much effort but accomplishing nothing." He decided that the only thing for him to do was to go to Falmouth personally and try to straighten things out. Arrangements were made for a car with driver to leave the next morning at daybreak. (British regulations did not permit driving up the coast in the blackout after nightfall.)

* * * * * * *

At 2150, the BERMINGHAM reported by radio that the ABNAKI had hooked onto a wooden barge (BCL 3210) in latitude 49° 8' N; longitude 04° 28' W. The two vessels then headed toward Falmouth where the barge was delivered early the next day.

The CHASE and the LT 374, finding nothing, spent the night at sea.

October 23

Lind arrived at Falmouth the following day, October 23. His first stop was to check with some U.S. Navy people who were remnants of an Amphibious group. He found their facilities extremely limited with no tugs available except for the OWL and CORMORANT. The former was at sea; the latter was being repaired. The Navy men's localized opinion of Hurst and company being able to deliver what CTG wanted was not the best. Lind was advised to concentrate his efforts on the two young Army Lieutenants, who, unlike Hurst, were at least physically locatable and appeared willing to try.

A short walk through the dock yards brought Lind to the offices of Army Transportation Corps, Falmouth. His first contact there was with some of the survivors of the STs that had been lost in Convoy NY 119. They told of being ashore for as long as four days; during that time they had not received any new clothing, food or shelter—or money with which to purchase any. The men said their only means of getting by had been through the charity shown them by the crew members of the other Army tugs. To CTG, already frustrated and angry at what appeared to be a complete lack of efficiency or "give a damn" on the part of the Army port authorities, this dereliction in the caring of shipwrecked survivors was the last straw. To the ATS civilian Port Captain, he gave outright "Hell" and told him to "get busy and do something about it or I will." Continuing the "butt chewing" session, Lind asked why, after four days, only one tug had been made ready to salvage the barges. The excuse was given that the Masters of the tugs had claimed that their ships were not fit for sea.

Lind pulled out a copy of the dispatch from Commander·in Chief, Plymouth, which gave him authorization to take command of all the former ships of TG 27.5 until salvage operations were complete. Upon reading it, the Port Captain claimed that this was his first knowledge of any dispatch, including the ones which Lind had sent ordering out the LTs. The Port Captain protested that they must have been passed directly to Major Hurst who had not bothered to inform him. He also volunteered the information that he had absolutely no knowledge of the arrival of NY 119 until the first contingent of small craft arrived on the eighteenth.

CTG, now in full psychological command over what appeared to be a cowed and cooperative Port Captain, asked him to have all the LT Masters report to the office at once. All assembled, CTG informed them that their duties involving the Convoy were not to be considered complete until all hope of salvaging the barges was gone. The Masters were then asked to state why their vessels were unable to sail. They were warned before answering that he, Lind, intended to send a crew of Navy experts to inspect each tug. If their report indicated that anyone had lied as to the condition of his ship, that person would be placed under military arrest, along with every member of the crew who shared responsibility. The charge would be "willful sabotage in a war zone." Lind wasn't too sure whether he had enough legal backing to make good these threats, but the point he was trying to get across appeared to be heard. When he asked each of the Masters what his tug required, most of them came up with a rather uncomplicated bill of particulars. A few did claim serious breakdowns that only a shipyard could correct; yet out of a total of eleven, six Masters said that their tugs could be ready as soon as parts were interchanged from the five downed vessels. Ships' crews, co-operating with Port Captain personnel, were put to work on this immediately. The outcome was that it was soon generally agreed that by daybreak the next morning the six tugs could be back at sea. Appearing on the scene, Lt. Verrinder assured Lind that he would have provisions brought dock side in ample time for loading aboard before the daybreak deadline had arrived.

In the presence of the Port Captain and Lt. Verrinder, Lind called Commander in Chief, Plymouth, requesting that orders be issued to sail the O'TOOLE, the POWERS, and the MASON from Plymouth at 0700 the following morning. Lind told Plymouth that the six LTs from Falmouth were to rendezvous at a designated point two hours later. Wishfully thinking that he had solved the command problems then existing at Falmouth, Lind climbed back into his car for the return trip to Plymouth where he was to rejoin the O'TOOLE.[2]

After CTG's departure, the Port Captain dispatched the partially provisioned LT 536, in company with a British escort, HMS ELLESMERE, to pick up a barge spotted by the BERMINGHAM.

The ABNAKI, after bringing in the BCL 3210, again went out into the Channel. Winds were now blowing at 20 to 30 knots, further riling a mixed-up although somewhat moderated sea as compared to conditions of the past day.

* * * * * * *

At 1640, the BERMINGHAM sighted one section of a broken up car float tandem. The number of it was not visible due to the low position in which the float rode in the water. Determining that the unit did not appear salvageable, Beerman ordered it sunk by gun fire to remove it as a menace to navigation.[3]

While the shooting was taking place, Lt. Robinson McIlvaine, the BERMINGHAM's Navigator and Executive Officer, overheard the conversation of a British task force thought to be probably working near the northerly entrance of the Irish Sea. It was carrying on a more conventional mission than that in which the Americans were engaged. To those listening on the radio, the British group appeared to be working over a U boat sound contact. Via the radio circuit came the following message which is quoted from a letter addressed to the author from McIlvaine. In clipped British accent, it began:

" 'RASPBERRY, THIS IS BLUEBERRY. OVER.'
After what seemed an eternal delay, a deep phlegmatic voice replied,
'BLUEBERRY, THIS IS RASPBERRY. PASS YOUR MESSAGE.'
BLUEBERRY, by this time in a high state of excitement, came crashing in.
'RASPBERRY, THIS IS BLUEBERRY. HAVE CONTACT AND HAVE DROPPED CHARGES. LOOKS GOOD. LOTS OF DEBRIS, INCLUDING ONE WATER CLOSET SEAT – UNFORTUNATELY NO ONE ON IT. OVER!'
To our great disappointment, all RASPBERRY could muster in reply to this gem was,
'ROGER, OUT.' "[4]

While the above added little to the concerns of TG 27.5, it did provide a note of levity to the day. For the "flotsom and jetsom" "Picker-up-ers" it must have been nice to know what the War was like for someone else.

* * * * * * *

At 1700, the LT 374, accompanied by the CHASE, came upon car float BCF 3201, its wooden lighter still in place. It was approximately forty miles south of the Scillys at a position near the one from which an RAF plane had reported "a barge-like object." This float was in the same predicament as the one which the O'TOOLE had stood over earlier. It, too, was anchored fast, with its stern bridle either hooked onto a sunken wreck or the tandem barge to which it had originally been attached.

Bradley, like Mauldin before him, tried a series of depth charges in an attempt to shake it loose. He, too, found this proved useless. Bradley then tried sending over a boarding party from the CHASE via rubber boat, with the intent of cutting it loose. No sooner had the men left the CHASE enroute to the float than the sea began to act up again making boarding impossible. Close-tethered as it was to the bottom, it was acting like a break water—immobile to the force of the elements. It was only with difficulty that the boarding party managed to get back aboard the DE. The problem was compounded when the LT got too close to the rubber boat. This provoked a loud protest from Bradley. In attempting to clear the area, the LT swung her stern to the seas; this accidental maneuver caused a back splash which knocked one end of the tug's manila hawser overboard. As the skipper attempted to back away, the hawser wrapped itself securely around the LT's screw, immobilizing the tug completely.

Now there was a new problem. The LT began drifting helplessly with the current, the set of which was toward a section of still German-held French coast—obviously, new arrangements were called for.

Knowing the ABNAKI was somewhere in the area, Bradley placed a general call. Lt. Walley answered, promising to arrive at the scene as soon as possible. By 2032 hours, the ABNAKI showed up. This allowed the BERMINGHAM to also go off in search of the disabled LT 374.

October 24

Before dawn on the twenty-fourth, the drifting LT 374 was located by the CHASE. She was much further to the south than had been anticipated. As soon as first light made visibility possible, Bradley brought his ship in close. Using his Lyle gun, he proceeded to try getting a light line across the LT's fantail. Down to the last shot, the salvagers finally managed to get one over. Bradley remembers what followed:

> The tug crew completed their part of the comedy by attaching a heavy manila messenger line to our light piece of cotton which had been fired from the gun. Of course, it parted, and we were forced to maneuver close enough in the bouncing seas to get a heaving line over.[5]

The unfouled end of the LT 374's towing hawser was taken aboard and secured to the stern bits of the CHASE, whereupon the LT began a "whipping ride" at 15 knots behind the plunging DE on a course set for Plymouth.

On the way in, Bradley called Walley of the ABNAKI to inquire as to how he was getting on with the bottom hooked BCF 3201. The reply came back that it was still too rough to attempt putting men aboard via rubber boat. Walley intended to stand off for the remainder of the day waiting for better weather—a prediction for the following morning.

The CHASE, with the LT in tow, made it into Plymouth without mishap, arriving there the following morning.

*   *   *   *   *   *   *

At daybreak on the twenty-fourth, CTG on the O'TOOLE and in company with the MASON and POWERS, left Plymouth Harbor for their appointed 0900 rendezvous with the LT tugs from Falmouth. Arriving at the spot (designated as Point Able) there was no sign of an LT. Contracting the LT 537, CTG inquired of Lt. Phipps as to what had gone wrong this time. The answer came back that the LT 537 and the others had been ready to sail at 0700; however, no pilot had appeared to guide them out of the harbor. Phipps had been told it was compulsory with local Port Command to have such a person aboard. Saying to hell with regulations, he proceeded without one but was told to turn back or be fired upon. As to the other LTs, "they still had not received the provisions promised by Verrinder and could not be made ready to sail before 1100."

At this point, Lind had really had it. What was going on ashore remained somewhat of a mystery. He knew that the only way to straighten it out was by strong and drastic action. After a careful drafting, a message was sent out addressed to: Commander, Navy Europe; with informational copies to Commander in Chief, Plymouth; European Chief Naval Operations; Commander in Chief, Atlantic; and Chief Naval Operations.

"27.5 BARGE SALVAGE OPERATIONS DELAYED AND THREATENED BY INEFFICIENCY OF U.S. ARMY AUTHORITIES FALMOUTH AND PLYMOUTH X NO PREPARATIONS MADE TO RECEIVE CONVOY X SINCE ARRIVAL NO EFFECTIVE ACTION TAKEN TO EXPEDITE SAILING TUGS TO AID IN SALVAGE X TWO OUT OF THREE TUGS READY AND ORDERED TODAY FAILED TO SAIL FOR LACK OF FOOD X TUGS MUST BE FURNISHED OR BARGES WILL BE LOST X SURVIVORS LANDED AT FALMOUTH STILL UNCARED FOR X C AND C PLYMOUTH IS GIVING EVERY POSSIBLE ASSISTANCE X REQUEST ASSISTANCE PROVIDING TUGS X"[6]

To further degrade Lind's morale, a radio message was soon received that the aircraft which was requested to aid in the search for the barges was going to be withdrawn due to submarine activity elsewhere.

At 1217, CTG received word that the LT 653 and LT 537 were at last being sailed to rendezvous. Word came in at about the same time that the ELLESMERE with the LT 536 had located the BCF 3214. Recovery was being prevented by the presence of a mine field. Both vessels were standing off waiting further developments.

CTG decided that it made little sense for three destroyer escorts to circle around a blank spot in the ocean known as "Point Able" to await a group of Army tugs that might or might not arrive. He ordered the MASON and the POWERS to peel off in a screening search for barge units. The O'TOOLE lay to, awaiting the arrival of the LT 653 and the LT 537. Feeling his earlier message regarding Army authorities may have had time to percolate, Lind fired off a direct communique to Falmouth informing them that their inefficiency and lack of cooperation had been reported to higher authority.

At 1336, a sound contact was picked up bearing 170° true, range 2,000 yards. The O'TOOLE crew went to Battle Stations. "Foxer Gear" was streamed. By 1355, the sound contact had been evaluated as a probable submarine. Depth charges were dropped with resultant contact explosions coming after the first run. In CIC, it was still being evaluated as a submarine. The timing of the explosions agreed with the depth of water—about 60 fathoms. No wrecks were reported in this area, so there was no slackening off of attack runs, especially after a large number of oil patches began to surround the contact point.

While this was going on, whom should unwelcomely show up but the LT 653 and LT 537. Told to stay clear, the runs were continued. Near sunset all hedgehogs had been expended. The O'TOOLE stayed on—maintaining contact, carefully evaluating it, and observing for possible movements.

At 1800, the O'TOOLE, still laying close over the possible submarine, received a message from Falmouth stating that the HMS ST. HELENA had just departed escorting the LT 538, LT 581, LT 492, and LT 579. She had orders to rendezvous at "Point Able."

* * * * * * *

Not long after leaving the company of the O'TOOLE, the POWERS and the MASON sighted the BERMINGHAM. She bore southeast of them at a distance of 10 miles. The two skippers, consulting with Beerman, decided that the best method to use in locating the barges was to form a scouting line with intervals of eight miles between each ship.

Shortly after dark, the POWERS left the others upon the request of CTG. He had asked Loew to come to his assistance and help evaluate the contact over which he was maintaining surveillance.

At 2200, the POWERS joined the O'TOOLE. Both vessels' ASW people were uncertain as to what they had below them. While engaged in evaluating the contact, a large convoy appeared; it was heading directly toward the scene. CTG warned them as to what they were running into, and the convoy neatly split. Half passed to starboard; half passed to port of the target area.[7]

By 2300 the wind had swung from a little east of north to 350° with a velocity of 20 knots. The barometer was rising, and air temperature stood at 56° Cloud cover was six tenths complete with visibility at six miles.

October 25

By the morning of the twenty-fifth, the communications specialists aboard the O'TOOLE had just about given up trying to repair the radar and ship's radios. This gear had been badly jarred out of kilter during the depth charging of the afternoon and evening before. Appearing on the scene to join the two attacking Americans, was the HMS ROCHESTER. The latter ship made a number of runs on the target, dropping depth charges. The ROCHESTER had no information of a wreck at that position. Her skipper's evaluation, like 27.5's, was a possible submarine. The Britisher, having urgent business elsewhere, left the American DEs to decipher the puzzle below. Loew was the first to decide that the contact could be classified as doubtful and was most likely an uncharted wreck.[8] Lind and Mauldin soon concluded that since the communication and radar equipment on the O'TOOLE was inoperative, the best bet would be for the O'TOOLE to return to Plymouth. Once there in person, Lind could go "all out" in a search for aircraft to assist in a reconnaissance to locate the barges.

At 1115 hours, CTG placed Lt. Commander Loew in charge of the barge search. He then proceeded to Plymouth in the O'TOOLE.

* * * * * * *

At 1330, the O'TOOLE was moored to the starboard side of the CHASE at Buoy 7, Plymouth Harbor. Repair parties came aboard as soon as the ship was secured.

Lind immediately left for dockside in the ship's whale boat. Once at the offices of Commander in Chief, Plymouth, he began arrangements for an air search the following day. Two planes were assigned. Via telephone, Lind went over the details concerning wind, tide, and probable locations with the local RAF Wing Commander.

* * * * * * *

Word came in to Loew that the ABNAKI had at last been able to place her men aboard the BCF 3201. After cutting loose the cable, they had hooked on and were proceeding to Plymouth. During the morning, sightings were made of LT 653 and LT 537 and also the OWL, her hull having been repaired. All that was needed now were barge sightings.

* * * * * * *

By mid afternoon, Loew, alarmed by the constant radio reports of suspected "Snorkelers" in the area, ordered all escorts and those tugs not engaged in towing, to zig-zag.[9]

The LT 536, accompanied by her British escort, was keeping close tabs on the BCF 3214. It was clearly in sight but out of reach. Its drift path had put it well within the confines of the barrier mine field.

* * * * * * *

Shortly after 1700 hours, the MASON's radar picked up a floating object. Upon close visual investigation, it appeared to be a type of mine. Firing was commenced with main battery and 20 millimeters; no explosion resulted.

* * * * * * *

At 1945, sonar on the POWERS had a sound contact at about 1150 yards out. After an hour of sound runs, Loew and his ASW officer analyzed it as non-submarine.

Continuing their search, the ships zig-zagged throughout the night.

October 26

At one bell, during the first watch of October 26, the MASON's log recorded the wind down to 15 knots out of the north.

Fifteen minutes later, MASON's radarman picked up an unidentified surface contact at 17 miles, bearing where no known ship was supposed to be. Trying various radio channels, contact was attempted without luck. All hands were called to battle stations. At 0206, by blinker light, a challenge was made; no answer. The MASON's 3-inch gun then fired off star shells. This did the trick; the challenge was immediately recognized. The "target" identified herself as the British tanker VINERIVER outbound from Gibraltar to Barrow, England.

At 0530, another radar contact bearing 125°, distance 15 miles, was made. Contacted on TBS, it proved to be the POWERS. Once reunited with the MASON and the BERMINGHAM, together they recommenced their scouting search at intervals of eight miles between ships.

At 1218, the MASON sighted an 8-man life raft, empty of occupants—an eerie sight in a war zone. At 1333, she changed course to investigate an alleged barge sighted by aircraft at 49° 39'N and 06° 48'W. No sooner on her way, she was called to the assistance of the BERMINGHAM who had picked up another sound contact and was attacking. Before the MASON could arrive on the scene, the BERMINGHAM had evaluated the contact as a false one.

Back on course toward the reported barge, the MASON arrived at the position; there was nothing in sight.

* * * * * *

A report was received by the POWERS that the LT 536, with the HMS ELLESMERE in escort, had at last seen the barge for which they had waited drift out of the mine field. Hooking onto it, the LT 536, with the rescued BCF 3214 in tow, departed at a good rate of speed toward Falmouth. She was eased on her way by a flattening sea. For Lind and the anxious eavesdroppers in Plymouth who were monitoring the search, this was the only definite barge sighting for the day.

At 1300, Lind, in conference with the staff of Commander in Chief, Plymouth, decided that if nothing was sighted by 1500 hours, the search would be called off as far as Task Group 27.5 was concerned. Any future salvage operations that might develop would have to be handled by the local authorities at Falmouth. By mid afternoon, no new reports had come in; orders were immediately issued to all craft of Army and Allied Navies to return to base.[10]

At 1500 hours on October 26, 1944, NY 119 ceased to exist as an official entity. To many of those who participated in it, it was the truly great adventure. To others, it was but another episode in a long, hard war. To the historian, it is a unique chapter among the hundreds of operations which, taken together, have been called "The Battle of the Atlantic."

THE END

EPILOGUE AND CONCLUSIONS

Post-voyage computations analyze the losses of NY 119 as follows:

MEN — 19 LOST AT SEA — all ST crewmen—represents 11% of Total ST crew lists.

MANNED SHIPS — 3 ST TUGS—ST 719, ST 720, ST 511†

STEEL CAR FLOATS (BCF) — 8*

WOODEN CARGO LIGHTERS (BCL) — 5*

†ST tug losses totaled 22% of number of STs sailed.
*The BCF and BCL losses totaled 46%.

Safely delivered to England in a somewhat battered but still usable condition were six BCFs and nine BCLs out of a starting total of fourteen and fourteen, respectively. The Report of Convoy NY 119—TG 27.5, in which Lind discussed the lost car floats and lighters stated: "That all steel barges are accounted for (either delivered or sunk) as are the wooden BCLs, except one which was sighted near the coast of France south of Brest and which may have floated on the beach still occupied by enemy forces, where no doubt it was broken up by the sea." This is probably the barge which provoked a series of telegrams between the American Legation people in Spain and the State Department. The text of the first of such messages follows:

"FROM: ALUSNA MADRID 021233 NCR 37111 3 MARCH 45 WOODEN BARGE LENGTH 53 METERS X NO ENGINE X GOOD CONDITION X FOUND ADRIFT NEAR SILEAO ON 12 FEBRUARY AND TOWED TO PORT OGALETE X ONLY MARKINGS REPORTED BCL 1356 WITH NO INDICATION NATIONALITY X SPANISH STATE CLAIM SHOULD BE SUBMITTED PRIOR MARCH 12 X REQUEST INFORMATION IF U S CRAFT SO NECESSARY ACTION CAN BE TAKEN X"

Following much bureaucratic unsnarling and tracking down of the facts, this return message was sent back to the Legation in Spain; dated 9 March 45, from the U.S. Chief of Naval Operations:

"BELIEVE BARGE IS U.S. ARMY BCL 3156 INSTEAD OF 1356 X CONVOY NY 119 X REFER HM COUNSEL BILBAO 121445 NOVEMBER TO ADMIRALTY BEING PASSED TO YOU FOR INFO AND CTG 27.5 SERIAL 002 OF 8 OCTOBER 44 X ETOUSA REQUEST NECESSARY ACTION BE TAKEN FOR RECOVERY OF BARGE AND ONWARD MOVEMENT TO UK OR FRANCE IF PRACTICABLE XX"

Whether the barge was ever towed to the United Kingdom or France is not a matter of locatable record.

* *

Another wooden lighter (BCL) which Lind thought to have been sunk was the one which had been the recipient of the combined fire power of the MASON and the O'TOOLE when they had tried to sink it on October 13. As the reader will recall, the barge was left perforated and smoldering but very much afloat after being treated to all the O'TOOLE and the MASON could dish out. This barge is thought to have been responsible for an incident involving the MASON some weeks following Convoy NY 119.

It was the first week of January, 1945; the MASON was in the company of her old companions, the O'TOOLE, the POWERS, the BERMINGHAM, and the CHASE, plus an additional DE, the ANDRES; in composite, they made up Escort Division 80, skippered by Commander Alfred L. Lind. The DEs, in conjunction with a Destroyer Division, were escorting Convoy GUS 64 bound from Oran, Algeria, to Norfolk, Virginia. Following an attack in December on the returning escorts of CK 4, there had been consistent reports of enemy submarines in the approaches to the Straits of Gibraltar. Because of this, the escorts of GUS 64 were keyed up and ready for anything. At 2100, January 3, the Task Force received word that the convoy just ahead of them, GUS 63, had had a ship torpedoed that evening. For the next eight days, a number of sonar contacts were made and evaluated, but proven false. No definite indications of enemy presence were logged between the 3rd and 10th of January.

The peaceful scene remained until ten minutes past midnight, January 11. The MASON, which was on screen off the starboard front of GUS 64, made contact at that time on an object bearing ahead of them at a range of 2400 yards. Battle Stations were ordered, and the ship made preparations for a depth charge attack. However, by the time the target was fifteen hundred yards off, it was evaluated as non-sub due to mushy echoes, narrow target, and a lack of bearing movement, along with erratic recorder traces. As the MASON's crew was about to be secured from Battle Stations, Radar reported a contact at a distance and bearing toward the point of earlier sonar pickup. The contact appeared to have "such remarkable resemblance to periscopes seen during training exercises, that the decision was made to attack, regardless of the previous evaluation." Full speed was rung up as the MASON headed toward it. At seven hundred yards, headway was reduced to about 15 knots; the target was still very much in evidence, both on radar and sonar.

What was to follow can best be described in the words of Lt. Leonard Barton, then the Gunnery Officer of the MASON. He recounted the episode to the author in a letter dated November 21, 1969. It coincides remarkably well with the official record; despite the passage of the years, it also agrees with the recollections of other former crewmen:

> I was then busy trying to establish communications. If you think it's hard to communicate between generations or between races, you should be on a ship sometime at Battle Stations in the dark. There seems to be dozens and dozens of wires twisted around you, control talkers, lookouts, your own head phones and Lord knows what other wires seem to be about. All the time the 'ping-ponnnggg' of the sonar seemed louder and more insistent than ever—meanwhile Radar is trying to estimate the distance while the Captain is trying to intercept the sub. The Captain and the Executive Officer were giving steering orders and whatever else they do at such a time. Most of the Gunnery Talkers and myself were shaking and stuttering, partly from the cold.
>
> The 'submarine' got closer and closer, on a intercept course— and I kept yelling (no, asking) the Captain what depth to set the charges on. Whether he answered or not, or I did not hear, or whether it finally came down to the point that someone had to make a decision—when almost upon it, I sent word down to set charges at something like fifteen feet, as it seemed that CIC yelled out that they were very close to the surface. I also sent word for the gun crews to fire, using local control when I gave the word. Fifty yards from it and still no orders from the Captain. Then 'CRASH,' a shudder went through the whole ship which seemed to rise up in the air, then shudder some more—and a hundred thoughts raced through my mind, we've rammed the sub, we've sunk it, or have we? Then the ship settled back, and I thought what if we hadn't sunk it. I was going to make sure. 'Fire number one depth charge.' BOOM. 'Fire number two.' BOOM. 'Fire number three; fire number four.' As I was yelling fire four,

the first charges went off 'whoom', and the ship shuddered again and again as numbers two, three, and four went off. I thought, 'boy, we're stopped dead in the water and now we're going; well, that's all right, we've got the sub!' I don't know what the others were thinking.

Immediately, lookout reports began coming in stating that there was wreckage floating down both sides of the ship. With his ship back under way but vibrating, Blackford sent out a status report to the O'TOOLE, whereupon CTG ordered him to stay over the target for the next sixty minutes before rejoining.

Unable to regain sound contact, Blackford called back the O'TOOLE to ask for assistance in conducting an "Observant." Minutes later, an unidentified radar contact at a distance of seven hundred yards and in the direction of the original collision point, was made. Closing, and under illumination by searchlight, it was revealed to be a wooden derelict which, in the words of the MASON's War Diary, "was probably a barge about a hundred by fifty."

Evaluating possible hull damage, the MASON's sonar technicians found that their sound gear was totally inoperative. The next morning, Lind ordered Blackford to proceed independently to Bermuda for repairs.

A plot made following the ramming determined that the barge was most probably one of the BCLs lost from Convoy NY 119—specifically, the one which the MASON and the O'TOOLE had attempted to sink on October 13. By computing the time and normal drift, it would have been at the approximate location where the ramming occurred on the 11th of January.

* *

It may be of interest to know what happened to the Army ships and barges of NY 119 after they arrived in Europe:

Despite energetic attempts to locate records of the disposition of the wooden lighters and the steel car floats, the author could find nothing in the official record concerning them. A former ATS man did remark to the author that following the War he was in a barge convoy containing car floats which were being returned from northern Europe to New York. The rumors were that the floats were to be returned to their former owners. Since there were towings of car floats to Europe prior to NY 119, there is no way of knowing what floats were returned to the United States.

The Y boats remained in Europe at least until the end of the War. The Y 17, (formerly of NY 119), was lost along with most of her crew in a mine explosion off Ostend on April 8, 1945. She was one of three Y boats lost by enemy action. One other, like the Y 17, fell victim to a mine off Ostend. Another capsized and sank in the Bristol Channel after being allegedly torpedoed. (The latter two did not come over with NY 119.)

The surviving STs of NY 119 seemed to fare quite well. None of them were among the four STs that the Army lost before the end of the War while either en route to or operating within the English Channel. Of interest concerning the four lost STs was one in particular, the ST 75, which carried a military crew. Traveling through fog, it stumbled into artillery range of the occupied Guernsey Islands; a shell from a German "88" sent her to the bottom. Most of the crew swam ashore; there to be rescued and hidden from the Germans by the local Underground.

Research dealing with the post-war disposition of some of the STs which were in NY 119 discloses: ST 752 was transferred to the Maritime Commission in 1947; ST 676 was transferred to Belgium; ST 677 was sold to Greece. The STs 742, 747, and 748 were sold to Finland in 1946. As for the others, there are no records.

Most of the LTs which sailed from New York in NY 119 returned to the United States with the escorts of TG 27.5; two or three remained in Europe. None of these were victims of enemy action or marine casualty up and through the conclusion of hostilities.

Within the northern European Theatre, the Army lost three LTs (none of which had been in NY 119) two by enemy action and one by marine casualty. Of the two sunk by enemy action, the LT 389 was reportedly torpedoed en route to the United Kingdom on November 28, 1944. It was probably in company with conventional cargo vessels at a point somewhere in the Western Approaches.

* *

The personnel of Convoy NY 119 were decorated for their services therein; both Navy and ATS are listed as follows:

COMMANDER ALFRED L. LIND, USNR—THE BRONZE STAR

ENSIGN ARTHUR MC CARTHY, USN—NAVY AND MARINE CORPS LIFESAVING MEDAL

BOATSWAIN MATE 2/CLASS DUSSEALT, USNR—NAVY AND MARINE CORPS LIFESAVING MEDAL

VALENTINE B. SWARTWOUT, MASTER ST 719 — THE MERCHANT MARINE MERITORIOUS SERVICE MEDAL

* *

Only one east-bound tug and barge Army convoy followed NY 119. This was CK 4 (in which the author sailed) which arrived in Plymouth, England, on December 2, 1944. That convoy lost one crane barge while en route; no lives were lost. While in the act of returning to the United States with a group of disabled landing craft under the tow of Army and Navy tugs, the escort group was attacked by a U boat off the Azores. Two landing craft were sunk and one of the escorts, the USS FOGG was badly damaged.

* *

The question was never officially settled as to whether Major Charles Hurst carried any blame for the apparent inefficiencies at Falmouth. If it was, then the answer remains unavailable to the inquiring historian. There is no record to be found of a Court of Inquiry specifically convened by the Army to inquire, with relation to Hurst, into the events at Falmouth between the 18th and 26th of October. The Army did hold an investigation of sorts into the loss of the three STs. A report made by Lt. Verrinder was included in the findings. A copy of this can be found within the Modern Military Records Section, National Archives; for the interest of the reader, it is reproduced as follows:

File 91011

SECRET

Section—subports—14th Port

Harbor craft "NY 119 in late Oct.: 39 ships entered harbor from this convoy, while another group of heavily laden barges broke away and drifted round the sea in the general region of the Scilly Isles. The 343rd was successful in recovering eight of the sixteen barges which were lost in the storm.

CONVOY NY 119

1. 1800 18 Oct., First ship of Convoy NY 119 arrived at boom in Falmouth Harbor. Three days later the last of 39 ships entered harbor.

2. Morning 19 Oct., Operations Office on the Prince of Wales Pier was besieged by requests for food, deck and engine room stores, fuel, water and clothing. Also on 19th, Convoy Commodore

requested LTs to sail from Falmouth to help in salvage operation of BCF barges from Convoy that were adrift. Since ships had been at sea for 30 days, plus rough crossing, almost impossible to find tugs with towing gear, food, water or fuel to go out again for five or six day salvage operation. Many of crew needed medical attention. By getting food from Plymouth by truck, and medical attention from 61st Field Hospital in Truro, we were able to get two prime considerations taken care of.

3. Borrowed engine parts from other LTs, emergency food and water, and in many cases towing gear and hawsers to get tugs operational.

Only 16 EM and 2 OFF, working 16 hrs. a day, managed to see the first of 7 operational LTs sail from Falmouth within a few days after they arrived.

4. Total of 8 barges of original 16 were recovered and the balance were either sunk or lost on the rocks of Scilly Isles.

A.J. Verrinder
2nd Lt. TC"

Apparently, Lt. Verrinder did not research his material too carefully when composing his report. The number of barges (tandem units) is incorrect. (There were 14 not 16 as he states.) The number recovered does not jibe with the facts, nor does Verrinder's statement that some of the barges were lost on the rocks of the Scillys—the wind directions and current drift make this seem improbable.

In fairness to Lt. Verrinder, there is a very real likelihood that the spirit of his report, in which he portrays the desperate attempts on the part of the 343rd to refit the tugs, is correct. The difficulties he encountered are familiar to the author, in that the working relationship between ATC crews and their civilian Port Captains with military Port Commands was often unclear, ill-defined, and without a clear demarcation of authority. Verrinder's statement that "the 343rd was successful in recovering eight of the sixteen barges which were lost in the storm" is absolutely incorrect. The numbers are wrong and without foundation; neither the 343rd nor any of its vessels which were mainly Motor Launches (MTLs) played a part in recovering the barges out at sea.

Whether Hurst ever appeared at Falmouth between October 18th and the 26th is unknown. Neither do we know if he played a role by telephone.

For that matter; was he ever located by Verrinder and even told of the Convoy? The author, during the research for this history, conducted an extensive hunt for Hurst. Despite contacting a number of former Army officers who had served with him, the best information as to his whereabouts was ten years old at the time of this writing. When last heard of, the former Major was in British Honduras. There, he was alleged to be engaged in some form of mining operation. Attempts to reach him via the American Legation in that country were of no avail. CONSEQUENTLY: Having no official verdict as to the responsibility of Hurst or what occurred at Falmouth and failing to gain Hurst's own firsthand account, it would be historically inappropriate for the writer to make a firm conclusion. Even as to whether Hurst was personally prone to gross inefficiency, or for lack of a better term, lack of concern, is a matter of opinion. The officers who had earlier served with him were of mixed opinions as to the man's ability and personality.

It is known, though, that shortly following the Convoy, Major Hurst was ordered to London. This excerpt from the History of the 14th Port relates to the travel orders in question:

"Orders dated 13 Nov. '44

SO: 264

The VOCO, 12 Nov. 44 directing that Major C.H. Hurst, 0923954 proceed to London from present station, Port TC 231 on 12 Nov. '44 for approximately 4 days, having been of such urgency to preclude issuance of orders in advance. Upon completion he will return to proper station."

The absence of return travel orders would indicate that Hurst never returned to Falmouth. This may be indicative of the Army's attitude over what had happened there. It is the author's personal opinion that the 'system' more than any individual was to blame for the 'snafu' situation which occurred within Army Command over the attempts to salvage the barges and the caring for survivors. The Transportation Corps was a new organization; its command structure was in need of revision through experience gained—NY 119 possibly being one of those experiences. The somewhat independent command structure of the civilian ATS Port Captain sections and the question of how they related to the military were probably the foremost contributory elements to confusion, along with the lack of established communications between a brand new Port Command, the 14th Major Port, and an attached element, the 343rd Harbor Craft Company.

The before mentioned "Army Investigation" as conducted in England, fully accepted criticism brought against responsible parties of the New York Port of Embarkation (Army) by Commander Lind. The following specific recommendations were made by the Army: "That more care should be taken in hiring qualified personnel; that kick-out hatches be installed aboard STs; that preferably STs not be sailed transAtlantic with crews aboard; that better refrigeration be provided aboard STs."

During the investigation, the Marine Casualty Investigative Officer, Lt. Col. C.L.T. Triplett stated, "In the case of the loss of the ST 511, it was probable that the failure to cut the bridle was the major cause for capsizing." He qualified this by saying that there was, "reasonable doubt as to whether she would have definitely ridden out the storm."

The only other documentation which could be located by the author relating to the Army's interest in what went wrong with NY 119 was a 'one way' piece of correspondence from a civilian NYPOE official who attempted to 'whitewash' his office of any responsibility over the manning and equipping of the Army vessels. Considering that NYPOE was where the 'buck' finally came back to rest, the author feels that this is where it belongs, despite the fact that NYPOE was laboring, in 1944, under the greatest of handicaps in recruiting personnel and assembling materials.

End of Epilogue and Conclusions

NOTES — Introduction

1. *This tug and barge was later canceled. The tug was the LT 785 which was routed in later Convoy CK 4 bound from Charleston to Plymouth, November-December 1944. The LT 785 was the Service Tug in that convoy and the crane barge was towed by another LT.*

2. *Commander Lind, by the summer of 1944 was a seasoned officer having begun his naval career in World War I. He was first commissioned an Ensign, USNR in 1919 after completing a Midshipman's training program which included a stint of sea duty aboard a merchant ship. Shortly after receiving his reserve commission he took the offered opportunity of being examined for appointment to the Regular Navy. Passing, he was re-commissioned USN and settled in to making the Navy his life's work. When "the war to end all wars was over", Lind was assigned to the USS ASHVILLE whereupon he spent the next two years on good will cruises along the coasts of South America. Following this came an assignment to a destroyer undergoing de-commissioning at the Philadelphia Navy Yard. Here, Lind witnessed events that must have been discouraging to any aspiring young officer. Ships, many of them with their first coat of grey, were being towed to sea and sunk in conformity with the naval disarmament treaty. Assessing this policy as not conducive to a bright naval future, Lind applied for permission to resign his commission. Permission being granted, he was transferred to a reserve status and in 1922 Ensign A.L. Lind became Mr. A.L. Lind of The Travelers Insurance Company, operating his own agency. Lind remained in the active reserve, commanding the 46th Division, Org. Naval Reserve in Minneapolis and in addition to weekly drills, participated in two week annual training cruises.*

   In October of 1940, Lind, then a Lt. Commander USNR, was recalled to active duty. There followed a series of assignments on naval transports as Assistant Navigator and Gunnery Officer. In February of 1943 Lind, was ordered to Baltimore to supervise the commissioning of the USS SANGAY, a mine supply ship. The SANGAY was ordered to the West Coast to begin a series of shuttle runs to Pearl Harbor from California carrying mines for the depot at Pearl, with Lind as her Executive Officer.

   After this duty, Lind attended Submarine Warfare School and in November of 1943 received command of the brand new Destroyer Escort, USS CURRIER, which engaged in trans-Atlantic escort duty. Lind had been promoted to Commander in July of 1943 with date of rank July 17, 1942.

   By now Lind had caught the eye of Admiral Jonas Ingram, Commander in Chief, Atlantic, who appointed the three stripper as C.O. of Escort Division 80 on June 30, 1944. Shortly followed the assignment to CTG 27.5 which Admiral Ingram bestowed on Lind with the following remarks, "I am giving you the most responsibile command at sea of any naval reserve officer under my command—and I think you can do it."

   Lind was released from active duty in April 1947 with the rank of Captain USNR. He owns and manages the A.L. Lind Company.

3. *An interesting sidelight as to the origins of some of the Norwegians who sailed on ATS small craft is contained within a letter to this author by Jack Thebus, a survivor of the ST 719: "You may recall that most of the skippers of the LTs were Norwegian sailors that were on whaling boats at the time of the invasion of their country by Germany, and they filled the bill, so to speak, for the ATC as qualified men on the LTs." (Norwegian Antarctica Whaling Fleet—Author)*

4. *Postwar German records confirm this claim, the sub being the U-986.*

5. *Selective Service policy was to defer all Merchant Seamen from draft call-up provided*

they remained active. A leave system was inaugurated which allowed a one day leave for each three days assigned aboard a vessel—leave time not to exceed thirty days. If a seaman exceeded his allowable leave he was immediately liable for call-up.

6. *To illustrate the reaction of men, some past their prime who are subjected to the usual rigors of the open ocean in small craft, one may consider an excerpt from the report of Convoy NY 118: An Army Master, referred to as Captain Wilson, was temporarily relieved of command during a period of moderate weather. Wilson had returned to sea early in 1941 after twenty-five years ashore, in the belief that to do so was his patriotic duty. He had given his age at 67 but "in the opinion of most, was nearer 76." The Captain, "a very fine old gentleman," in the words of Simmers, "had just reached a point, where, without rest, he was in danger of a physical and mental breakdown." After a few days, the old Captain, "was back on his bridge and served out the voyage in the best of spirits and good health."*

7. *The steering gear on the Y Boats was manufactured by an elevator manufacturing company. This firm had had no experience in the production of marine equipment prior to the War but like many others had been selected to produce components with which they had no background—this due to the overwhelming wartime demands on experienced marine manufacturers. Of interest is that the USS PUEBLO, the illfated U.S. Navy "spy" ship captured by the North Koreans in 1968, was an ex-Army WW II freight supply boat (FS). She, like the Y Boats, had the same steering gear, which had never been replaced, and it gave continual trouble until the time of her capture.*

   This same report of Simmers also lists in paragraph 3, a complaint that spare parts were deficient in Army craft. This can be partly attributed to the demand for such items for the Navy's Amphibious Command's small craft—a construction program then having manufacturing priority over the Army's small boat fleet. The Army was aware of this shortage and correspondence relating to it is contained in Box 16, Reference A 56-312, Modern Military Records, Archives. NYPOE statements refer to "Wet Storage" depots in which the vessels were moored awaiting crew—thus moored; security was insufficient to prevent pilferage of what parts the vessels did have aboard them at delivery. (Meeting of Supt. Water Divisions on 7 July '44—Ref. A 56-312—Box 16)

NOTES — Chapter I

1. *See Figure 1 of the text. As given therein is a reproduction of the Convoy Plan as finally set once the Convoy was at sea. The original plan that Lind reviewed on August 22nd, was to be later revised.*

2. *The shortage of French rolling stock was caused by wholesale damage arising from espionage and bombing raids prior to the Invasion. This had been essentially necessary in order to prevent the Germans from supplying and reinforcing their garrison defenses. This destruction on the other hand, caused Allied logistical headaches once Allied forces had stretched their own supply lines as they penetrated "Fortress Europe".*

   In the months just before the Invasion, the Marquis, FF1 and Allied saboteurs had destroyed or badly damaged 1,822 locomotives along with 10,500 freightcars (Cf. Les Resultats de L.Action de la Resistance dans la SNCF — History of the FF1, pp. 1364). Allied bombing had taken an additional, though not as heavy a toll—aerial bombing did the damage to the port facilities since these were not targeted as objectives of the saboteurs.

3. *(Prior to NY 118) ST Tugs were loaded aboard Liberty Ships since it was not felt that they were sea-worthy enough for trans-Atlantic passage. The USS KEARSAGE (a former Battlewagon equipped with a large deck crane) was used to load the tugs at*

NYPOE. Over 50 tugs were transported in this manner prior to July 1944. (STs sent to Europe after NY 119 were again handled this way.) Ref: Meeting of Supt. of Water Divisions, Stevens Hotel, Chicago - Box 16 - A 56-312 Modern Military Records Div. - Archives.

4. A Soldier's Story by General Omar N. Bradley—Henry Holt and Company; discusses the ammunition shortage on page 306. It also covers the queuing up of Liberty Ships awaiting unloading. Within Bradley's book, on page 304, is an amusing account which refers to the barges of NY 78. These barges were personally requested by Bradley due to the need for large barges on the beach heads in France; their usage to be that of providing a ready source of ammunition.

5. Taken from a letter addressed to the author by A.L. Lind. (12/26/69)

6. Lind's request for rubber rafts was based on a projected usage that would eliminate the two other common methods of transferring men and equipment. The others are: 1. The use of breeches buoy or messenger line transfers which are time consuming and can be dangerous in heavy seas due to the necessity of having to put vessels close aboard each other. 2. The transfer of men by the method of jumping from one vessel to another—dangerous to say the least. In later Convoy CK 4, the author witnessed a serious accident occurring to a Navy Machinist Mate when he attempted jumping from the well deck of the Convoy's oiler to the deck of the LT 785.

7. Task Group Commander's Report—TG 27.5.

8. "Quotations": From a letter; McIlvaine to author. 11/12/69

9. Task Group Commander's Report—TG 27.5.

10. The USS MATOLE shortly thereafter reported to Charleston, S.C. where she was assigned as Task Group Oiler in Convoy CK 4—another ATS barge and tug convoy bound for the United Kingdom. CK 4 in addition to ATS craft, had within it two WSA tugs; each towing a floating Power Plant. The Power Plants were contained within the hulls of converted Liberty Ships and were under the operational control of the Corps of Engineers, U.S. Army. The plants were to be used as emergency power sources at the Port of Antwerp, Belgium.

11. According to William Nelson in a telephone conversation with the author; this was a U.S. mine that had broken loose from the defensive mine barrier then maintained at the entrance to New York Harbor.

12. The wisdom of this plan can be bourne out by the author's own experience in Convoy CK 4. In that convoy he was aboard the LT 785 which acted as the sole convoy service tug. The LT 785 did not carry a repair team aboard, but rather picked up naval repair personnel from the MATOLE when needed. The time spent so doing was excessive and contributed to a work day on the tug which sometimes ran 18 hours at a stretch; the result of which severely strained the efficiency of the LT 785's crew and bringing members of her deck force to a point of exhaustion before the voyage was over.

13. During the war; because of the shortage of licensed officers, waivers to serve in licensed capacities were issued by the Coast Guard to rated personnel for filling officer's vacancies on U.S. merchant vessels.

14. Monthly Weather Review: Vol. 72 - No. 9 - WB No. 1419; The North Atlantic Hurricane of Sept. 8-16, 1944: U.S. Weather Bureau.

NOTES — Chapter II

1. The term "Sortie" in Navy lingo applies to a going out of ships from a harbor— usually in line of file.

2. As explained in Chapter I "Preparations", this was the call-sign for NY 119 when spoken to as a unit by voice radio. CTG Operational Order 27.5 - NY 119 gives this

in detail.

3. *Mention of the attempted suicide of the ST 719's cook can be found in a tape recording made by Captain Swartwout for the author and in the custody of The South Street Seaport Museum. The acuteness of Thomas Janos' seasickness is apparent within the official records which include survivors' testimony given aboard the rescue vessels after the sinking; Office Report CTG 27.5 - NY 119.*

NOTES — Chapter III

1. *This is a general assumption by the author derived from interviews with four former enlisted crew members of the MASON. The author also interrogated some of the Mason's former officers as listed under "Acknowledgements" who attested to a "reasonably happy ship". Examination of the Mason's long book for the period of Convoy NY 119 will confirm, that although there were disciplinary problems, they were not excessive nor any more frequent than (as an example) were such problems aboard the ABNAKI.*

2. *The activities of the MASON as given for September 23, are taken from her log book.*

3. *This exact conversation is ficticious, but it accurately reflects German submarine activity for that period and that area and its content was no doubt expressed in bridge talk. Further research on this subject can be carried out by referring to any of the volumes that are listed in the "Bibliography" under "Suggested Reading". That part of this conversation that refers to vulnerability of the various vessels was taken from the "Operational Orders; CTG 27.5 - NY 119.*

4. *Taken from Report CTG 27.5 - NY 119; when referring to the attempts to repair the fuel pumps of the ST 719.*

5. *Telephone conversation between author and C.V. Harding 11/69.*

6. *The fact that Swartwout had by this time assumed the leadership role was attested to by Harding, Leonard and Thebus in telephone conversations to the author in 11/69. The tape recording by Swartwout also brings this out.*

7. *This conversation, in detail, is given in letter to author by Thebus 1/5/70.*

8. *This episode is related with the quotation in detail within the official report of CTG 27.5 - NY 119; Pvt. Papers A.L. Lind. Also entered as testimony in army investigations in England, 14th Port—File 560—Modern Military Records, Natl. Archives.*

9. *The "ice cream run" and other details are given within the official Convoy Report under Repair Services Rendered, Encl E—also the log of the USS Powers for that date which specifically notes the ice cream transfer.*

10. *This episode is naturally not found in the official report, but was related to the author by Ballard in a telephone conversation in 12/69, and later in a letter dated 1/1/70. Ballard is uncertain as to whether the tug captain he enlisted was Clarke or Kuiper of the LT 653 but his recollections are that the tug's skipper was not a foreigner which would eliminate Kuiper and therefore automatically pinpoint Clarke as the one who took on the "Guide" role. Captain Clarke died before the author began his research therefore an assumption must be made to serve (in this case) the cause of history. In addition, information concerning this event would not, because of its unofficial nature, be found in the MAUMEE'S log book although there is a notation in the log book of the USS POWERS—(DE 528), that on the 30th of September when the MAUMEE dropped out of her regular position in order to refuel the LTs in other columns, she turned over her official "Guide" role to Clarke's ship which was numbered "61" within the convoy plan. It is therefore accurate to surmise that the LT upon which he officially bestowed this responsibility must have been the one that had been unofficially carrying on that responsibility.*

NOTES — *Chapter IV*

1. *Comments concerning the state of the bilges and their lack of effect on the ST 719's stability are to be found within the survivor interrogations of Papaliolios, Van der Linden and Swartwout; CTG Report; 27.5 - NY 119.*

2. *The activities and actions of the POWERS are taken from that vessel's log book.*

3. *Comdr. Lind's actions are taken from CTG Report 27.5 - NY 119.*

4. *The situation as described aboard the ST 719 is taken from survivor interrogations; CTG Report 27.5 - NY 119 <u>and</u> conversations, letters and tape recordings to be found within ST 719 list of bibliography. The locations of Harding, Scott and Janos are from the testimony of Scott in England; File 560—Modern Military Records, Natl. Archives.*

5. *The exact time when the ST 719 capsized is uncertain. The author has used 0135 as the best average as taken from various sources: POWERS' log book, survivors' testimony, CTG Report and the best circumstantial evidence as related by Thebus, whose watch stopped, presumably by submergence at 0135—Ltr. Thebus 1/5/70.*

6. *Survivor's testimony; CTG Report 27.5 - NY 119.*

7. *There is no testimony as to the exact events concerning Dorwart; other than he was in the galley, he was trapped there, he cut his feet badly, and was treated for it aboard the Powers, and that his screams were heard by Swartwout. These events are related within CTG Report 27.5 - NY 119.*

8. *The quotations are from Ltr. from Thebus 1/5/70.*

9. *For the rescue of Dorwart; Swartwout was given the "Meritorious Service Award" by the War Shipping Administration. The citation is dated Dec. 28, 1945. The citation's recounting of the events of the Dorwout rescue are accurate but the later accounting of the survivors being "rescued by lifeboat from an adjacent vessel" is not, and is obviously an attempt by some typist to have filled space on paper without access to the official record.*

10. *None of the survivors were sure of what was happening on the LT 492 and none, within the record or in conversation with the author, stated that they saw any glow from a cutting torch.*

11. *None of the survivors officially testified that there was any suction; CTG Report; 27.5 - NY 119; Nor later in Army investigative statements given in England. C.V. Harding in conversation with the author 11/69 stated that he was pulled down by suction even though he wore a life preserver. In that event he must have been closer to the derelict hulk than the others who were washed off with him, or possibly he may not have gone over at the same time as the group but rather, a later wave may have pushed him off. The violence of the elements that the survivors were subjected to, understandably could have confused and disoriented them. The fact remains that suction from the sinking ship was not noticeable except in the isolated case of Harding who may have been over-powered by a large wave and mistook it for something else.*

12. *The sequences of rescue is quite clear and given within CTG Report 27.5 - NY 119.*

13. *Once separated, Leonard and Thebus along with Harding thought they were isolated completely from the others and this effectively points out how wild the night was. In reconstructing the scene it becomes apparent that Swartwout, Scott, Dorwart and Moran must have been quite close, yet once physical contact was lost each survivor became convinced that he was far from anyone else, and in fact, alone in the ocean.*

14. *The hysterical condition of Harding is documented in Ltr. to author; Thebus 1/5/70 <u>and</u> in the Rescue Report of the USS POWERS, Convoy Report CTG 27.5 - NY 119.*

15. *His experiences after being passed up by the ABNAKI and later hearing the "voice", were told to the author by C.V. Harding in a telephone conversation 11/69.*

16. *This graphic account of Swartwout's rescue is given in his tape recording in the custody of The South Street Seaport Museum. It should be mentioned here, that whenever the author has been able to compare Swartwout's taped testimony with factors within the official records and against accounts given by others; the similarity of his retelling of events attest to the accuracy of his tape recorded statements. It therefore is the author's belief that the Swartwout recording is completely authentic in all respects.*

17. *Convoy Report; CTG 27.5 - NY 119.*

NOTES — *Chapter V*

1. *Taken from Ltr. to author from Charles H. Buswell, survivor of the ST 720, 12/14/69. The spoiled meat and poultry situation aboard the ST 720 was roughly the same as it had been aboard the ST 719 and it is known that food was jetisoned before the Convoy had reached a point abeam of Bermuda. It is logical to assume that all the STs had the same experience since the facilities were identical aboard all of them. Buswell also remembers bread, stored in his cabin, molding beyond use and potatoes sprouting early in the trip. The prominent ration according to Buswell's memory was spam and green apples. During the trip he lost between 20 and 30 lbs. The testimony of Joseph D. Holliday, survivor of the ST 511 also states that the fresh meats were jetisoned off that tug when four days out of N.Y. The ST 511 did have some hams which they saved by hanging in the open air from the mast rigging.*

2. *In the official Convoy Report; CTG 27.5 - NY 119: Within the introductory remarks on page 4, par. 10, is a reference to this episode which mistakenly refers to the ST 718 as the ST 720. That entry within the report as given is obviously an error since the ST 720 was consistently in the company of the LT 538 either under tow or when she was not so—and was traveling alone—she was never with any other vessel capable of towing her. The author has checked all enclosures of the official report and the log books of the escort vessels and knows this to be correct—therefore the author's description of the events of the morning of September 26th, are believed to be accurately stated.*

3. *Derived from Operation Order; CTG 27.5,- NY 119, Annex E; Characteristics of Craft in Convoy; Personal Papers, A.L. Lind.*

4. *The weather data as given is from Encl. G - Convoy Report; CTG 27.5 - NY 119. Encl. G is a weather summary that was prepared by the Meteorologist aboard the O'Toole on CTG's staff. It is an average of the weather conditions of each day. Occasionally the author refers within this history to specific weather remarks entered within the log books of particular vessels. When this is done, the source is usually stipulated—otherwise the reader may assume that the data is derived from the CTG Report.*

5. *Log of the USS POWERS.*

6. *Only one LT was refueled that day, the others were refueled on Oct. 2nd, 3rd and 4th; Encl. F—Convoy Report CTG 27.5 - NY 119. Also conversation with Beagly.*

7. *Log of USS MASON, 0000-0400 watch entry.*

8. *War Diary of the USS O'TOOLE and The Log Book of the USS MASON.*

9. *An embarrassing attack in ASW terms, is one usually not pinpointed but designed to harrass an enemy or possible enemy, in order to disrupt his intended tactical attack approach—usually used when contact was in close proximity to a convoy. Lind's Operation Order; CTG 27.5 - NY 119 specified such a plan when the circumstances were similar to that of the event of the afternoon of Oct. 3rd as related.*

10. *Taken from Encl. E, Convoy Report CTG 27.5 - NY 119, page 12. Therein the PRETEXT is referred to by her code name, "Soda".*

11. *Convoy Report; CTG 27.5,- NY 119, Encl. E, Hull casualties.*
12. *The method used by the LT 581 to effect this towing hook-up is not described in the Official Record but is a technique the author has witnessed and is the most probably one that took place—therefore the author has inserted it for the edification of those not familiar with such procedures.*

NOTES — Chapter VI

1. *The boarding party landed on the BCF via rubber raft as it was still too rough to put a tug alongside. Summary of Loss and/or Damage to Vessels; CTG 27.5 Report; Page 5.*
2. *Letter to the author from Charles Buswell dated 12/14/69.*
3. *The education and employment records for some of the crew members aboard the Army vessels are contained within a report addressed to the author by Mr. M.D. Davis, Chief, Civilian Reference Branch; General Services Administration, St. Louis, Missouri; Dated 12/11/69.*
4. *Ltr. Buswell to author 12/14/69.*
5. *Summary of Loss and/or Damage to Vessels; CTG 27.5 Report; Page 6.*
6. *Letter to the author from Edward P. Edmunds, Captain USNR 12/29/69. The incident is also mentioned in the War Diary, USS O'TOOLE. Although the Diary entry does not comment on the entrance of salt water into the ST 676's tanks, there is ample comment of the problem generally throughout the report of CTG. The author has photographs of this specific transfer operation and they illustrate the partial submergence of at least the fantail deck of the ST.*
7. *This episode is amply described in Damage to Vessels CTG 27.5; The log of the POWERS; The War Diary of the O'TOOLE.*
8. *CTG 27.5 Report, Para. 10.*
9. *Logbook of the POWERS, 1600-1800 watch entry signed by John W. Keefe USNR.*

NOTES — Chapter VII

1. *Logbook of the POWERS.*
2. *War Diary of the O'TOOLE. Within the same entry, Lt. Commander Mauldin makes mention of passing mail to the MAUMEE, the contents of which were probably operational orders from CTG. Mauldin found the maneuver to be extremely dangerous with the rough seas and at such a slow speed. He advises that such transfers should not be attempted while traveling at less than 7-8 knots unless sea conditions are good.*
3. *Told to the author by Stanley Pasko in a telephone conversation. Pasko at the time of this research (1969-70) was the only alumnus of NY 119 who was known to be still going to sea. He was then employed as a Bosun with the U.S. Military Sea Transport Service.*
4. *From a letter written by Captain A. Lind to Ambassador Robinson McIllvaine dated 11/22/69. Also CTG 27.5 Report.*
5. *At the time of the Convoy transit, the areas considered most dangerous for submarine attack were the approaches to the English Channel and the Irish Sea—Although the schnorkle submarine blitz did not start until December of 1944, lasting through the early part of April 1945. At that time, the attacks concentrated around the British Isles.*
   The next small craft convoy to follow NY 119 was CK 4 which arrived in England in early December. CK 4's escort's return voyage was highlighted by the torpedoing of the task group's flagship, the USS FOGG: an event which took place

north of the Azores. Additionally, the LST 359, under tow of an Army LT was torpedoed and sunk during the same attack. The attacker was the U 870, the southern most of three picket U boats which were on station to transmit weather reports which were instrumental in the German offensive known as the Battle of the Bulge. The U 870 later met her end during an allied bombing raid on the submarine pens at Bremen, Germany.

6. The complete list of the fourteen BCFs is to be found in the Operation Order CTG 27.5, Annex E.

7. The complete account of the "Engagement Against the Barge" can be found in the log book of the MASON and the War Diary of the O'TOOLE. The humorous highlights are not evident within the typically dry entries in the official records, but were told to the author in a letter from Leonard Barton dated 11/21/69.

8. War Diary—USS O'TOOLE.

9. Related to the author by Lt. Commander John Dodson USN (Ret'd) in a phone conversation on 12/16/69. Dodson later became the Commanding Officer of the MAUMEE.

10. Reference to the replacement of the LT,536's engine-room crew is to be found in: Major Deficiencies of Army Craft and Personnel, CTG 27.5 Report, Pages 2 and 3 Para. b. The reason for relief was given by Lind, "for incompetency to insure the safety of the Convoy." The LT 536 had been under tow for 60% of the time since leaving New York. After the Navy engineers took over there was no further breakdown through to the end of the voyage.

NOTES — Chapter VIII

1. The description of this event is contained in Summary of Loss and/or Damage to Vessels, CTG 27.5, III, Loss of BCF 3204 and BCF 3205. In the latter report however, the date of the ABNAKI picking up the barge is given as the (14th). This is an obvious error since the log of the POWERS puts it on October 13th. The text therefore reflects the correct date of October 13th.

2. The pressure was caused by the waves forcing their way through the gap in the planking with insufficient space available for drain off before the next wave would strike which in effect would drive the first mass of water between the upper and lower barges. Liken the situation if you will to the sea striking a steep rocky coast wherefrom a line of waves has not time to recede before the next line rolls in—the combers are then forced vertically against the rock face.

3. Log of the POWERS.

4. Letter from Charles Buswell to author 12/14/69.

5. Within the testimony later given in England by the survivors (see File 36622, Modern Military Records Div., Nat'l Archives) by 1st Asst. Engineer Lamude: There is emphasis placed on the controversy over the vessels speed. Lamude's transcribed words do not definitely indicate a heated argument yet, the author believes it unlikely that the circumstance would have motivated an emotionless conversation.

6. Lowe's words were restated to the author in a telephone conversation with Lt. Commander Kendall Valentine, USNR (ret'd) in October of 1969.

7. The author's deduction that Lamude was first on the raft can not definitely be established either from Lamude's or from Buswell's testimony since both men were in severe shock from the combination of their debilitated condition and the cold water and fear.

8. The quotation is from a letter to the author by Lt. Henry C. Wenzel III, USNR (ret'd) dated 11/20/69.

9. Log book of the POWERS.

NOTES — *Chapter IX*

1. *Log of the MASON 1200-1600 watch 14 Oct. '44.*

2. *The sighting by radar is from the Log of the MASON. At the time of NY 119's passage, the submarines which formerly worked in force from the West Coast of France had been removed to Norwegian bases. If the "target" was in fact a submarine, it probably was working south to off the approaches to Gibralter.*

3. *Summary of Loss and/or Damage to Vessels, CTG 27.5 Report; IV Loss of BCF 3211.*

4. *Log of the MASON. 1600-2000 watches, 16 Oct. '44. Also CTG 27.5 Report, Encl. J, 18 Oct.*

5. *War Diary, USS O'TOOLE, 17 Oct. '44.*

6. *Message File, CTG 27.5, 17 Oct. '44. There is some difference of opinion among former naval officers of TG 27.5 as to whether or not the Convoy was under CTG control via radio at this point. Lind insists that at no time for periods of more than an hour or so did he lose overall command supervision even though parts of the Task Group were operating separately. Research through the log books of different escort vessels bear this out. In fact the busy radio traffic eminating from CTG to the strung out Task Group almost pre-empted the British emergency channel which was being utilized—this later brought a complaint from Admiralty.*

7. *Log of the MASON 1800-2000 watch, 17 Oct. '44.*

8. *As told to the author by B.W. Clarke in a phone conversation. Mr. Clarke remembers his brother Captain Clarke telling the story prior to his death.*

9. *CTG 27.5 Report, Encl. D, V par. 2.*

10. *The best description of conditions to be found aboard the ST 511 prior to capsizing can be found in the author's "Declassified Records File"; from Modern Military Records, Nat'l Archives, File 560, Hq. 14th Port, Sinking 511.*

11. *Taken from the War Diary, USS O'TOOLE, 18 Oct. '44.*

12. *The description of what happened in the engine room of the O'TOOLE while attempting the ST 511 survivor's rescue and the effect the air box explosion had on the ship's steerage way along with what happened to the men alongside, are contained in a letter to the author from Captain Edward P. Edmunds, USNR ret'd. The letter is within the author's O'TOOLE file. Captain Edmunds at the time of the Convoy was a Lieutenant and the O'TOOLE's Engineering Officer. Neither the O'TOOLE's War Diary or CTG 27.5 Report mentions the air box explosion with its relevancy to the loss of the survivors.*

13. *The interview conducted by Lind with Joseph D. Holliday is to be found as an attachment to CTG 27.5 Report, Encl. D. The Editorial comments following some of Holliday's answers are provided by the author as are the spelling corrections which were included so as to avoid confusion on the part of the reader. The author had available to him the personnel records of ATS crewmen which Commander Lind and/or his Yeoman did not when transcribing the interview.*

14. *The sighting of the ST's deck house is mentioned in The War Diary, USS O'TOOLE.*

15. *The fact is that the LTs did become dispersed from their former tows. The reasons for it are actually undocumented but the probability of "why" is as stated.*

16. *Author's Declassified Records File; taken from File 91011, Modern Military Records, Nat'l Archives.*

17. *The fact that Falmouth, or more correctly its satellite estuary, the River Helford, was used for home basing a Free French Trawler fleet engaged in the support of espionage became known to the author upon visiting there in the summer of 1970. The author gathered the information through conversation with locals involved in the port's wartime activities. Other than this, there is no written documentation*

which has been consulted for confirmation of the Free French activities.

18. *The history of the 343rd and the parent Major Ports, the 13th and the 14th, give very little detail as to the barge building program at Truro. The author however has visited the construction site at Truro which by 1970 had been made into a public park. There is also a detailed description of the project when it was under the earlier control of the 329th Harbor Craft Company, Transportation Corps, U.S. Army. The 329th was in charge of the barge project according to a privately published history, by April of 1944. It relinquished this role shortly following the invasion in June. For a detailed description of the earlier 329th activities at Truro and Falmouth, see History of the 329th Harbor Craft Company—World War II, published by Albert Love Enterprises. A known copy of the history is in the possession of The Transportation Museum, Ft. Eustis, Va.*

19. *According to File A56-312, Box 219, 2/51 49.2, Modern Military Records, Nat'l Archives; The official history of the 13th Major Port states that the command switch to the 14th Major Port occurred on 13 Oct. 1944. It is known to the author from conversations with Colonels Perry C. Euchner and C.A. Noble, both formerly of the 13th Major Port, that Hurst was at Falmouth engaged in stevedore supervision at the time of the Normandy Invasion in June of 1944. Also there is mention of Hurst being in command at Falmouth in the report of Convoy NY 78 which entered that port in April of 1944. From the above factors the author has reconstructed the command structure existing at Falmouth on the 18th of October, 1944.*

   It is of interest, that both Euchner and Noble, although not claiming to be personal friends of Hurst, praised that officer's record for fast loading of vessels during the rushed period of early June through July of 1944 when Falmouth held the record for efficiency among 13th Port commands.

20. *The author has not been able to definitely establish the responsibility of the 343rd Harbor Craft Company in any role that they would have been expected to play in receiving a convoy such as NY 119. None of the messages included within the Message File of CTG 27.5 include any which assured CTG of "Falmouth" coopera- tion or even allude to that port being made aware of any task it was expected to assume.*

21. *Report of CTG 27.5, Encl. J, 1 (a).*

22. *Letter from Russ V. Bradley to author dated Dec. 1, 1969.*

23. *Report of CTG 27.5, Encl. J, 1 (c).*

24. *What Commander Lind actually said to them is contained in a letter from Lind to author dated Dec. 13, 1969, the pertinent text of which is reproduced as follows: "If your ships and crews cannot take the punishment ours have been taking for some 30 days you would be of no value to us. Permission granted. Over and Out." The message might seem unduly harsh but it is an understandable reaction coming from a Task Group Commander who had given his all for the last thirty days to try and get in a convoy which he could now visualize disintegrating before his eyes. On the other hand, to the Britishers, hardened as they were after five years of the war at sea, the loss of a few barges must have hardly seemed worthwhile putting one's vessel in jeopardy for.*

25. *Log of the MASON, 2000-2400 watch.*

26. *Log of the POWERS gives reference to turning on the navigational lights in an entry made by the midnight to 0400 Watch Officer, Lt. (jg) John W. Keefe USNR, OOD. The reference to the unreliability of the radar because of "spin-drift" is the assumed reason. The author's own experience with surface radar during the early years following its introduction, proved that heavy breaking seas causing "spin-drift" could often obscure a target's clarity on the cathode ray tube. Even a model in use on a U.S. Naval Transport as late as 1952 exhibited this fault (USNS Callan).*

27. *Log of the POWERS, 1600-1800 watch. The Log of the MASON also records this*

rather minor but significantly location orienting event, within three minutes of the other's entry.

28. *Report of CTG 27.5, Encl. J, 2 (f).*

29. *Report of CTG 275, Encl. J.2 (e). In his report in the paragraph, Lind refers to the BCF 3207 as the BCL 3209 while later in paragraph 10(c) he refers to it again but designated it as the BCF 3207, which the author believes was the correct designation. BCL 3209 is thought to have been the lighter which had been lashed atop the BCF 3207 at the time of the shelling and therefore its number would have been in more visual prominence than the lower and water-logged car float's would have been. The tandem unit when examined from the O'TOOLE showed it had been punctured with "some 20 projectiles in addition to having been depth charged by the ROCHESTER.*

30. *From a letter to author from Baily Cowan dated Oct. 27, 1969. Cowan was the Executive Officer of the POWERS at the time of NY 119.*

31. *The description of the POWERS taking water down her ventilators along with the description of the heavy seas that dawn, are taken from a letter to the author written by Lt. Henry G. Wenzel III, USNR Ret'd., dated Nov. 30, 1969. The quotations shown are his.*

32. *War Diary of USS EDGAR G. CHASE, 20 Oct. '44.*

NOTES — Chapter X

1. *Leatham displayed a good sense of humor when he laughed over the target practice that had been earlier engaged in by the HMS ROCHESTER. He told Lind that, "I will have to see that they improve their shooting."*

2. *The experiences of Commander Lind at Falmouth are taken in their entirety from CTG Report, Convoy NY 119, TG 27.5 - Encl. J, pages 6, 7, dated for 23 Oct. '44*

3. *CTG Report, Encl. J, 23 Oct. (b)*

4. *From letter to the author from McIlvaine, dated 12 Nov. 1969 (page 3). To be found in BERMINGHAM file; (Note—see Bibliography.) Ambassador McIlvaine probably heard this radio conversation either before or sometime following 23 Oct. 1944—On that date there were no U boats sunk by Royal Naval vessels. The incident may have arisen from an attack against the U 1006 on 16 October by HMCS ANNAN north of the British Isles.*

5. *Letter to author from Bradley, dated 12/1/69.*

6. *This message is reproduced from CTG Report, Encl. J, page 8, dated for 24 Oct. '44.*

7. *Documentation for this can be found in CTG Report, Encl. J and in the Log Book of the POWERS for 24 Oct.*

8. *Looking at things twenty-six years after the fact, it becomes apparent that there were a great many wrecks which although reported to the Admiralty were either not in turn reported to vessels at sea or those vessels did not up-date their charts from the issued "Notice to Mariners" or possibly such "Notices" were not issued for sometime following receipt of reports from vessels at sea.*

   Concerning the sound contact made by the O'TOOLE on 24 and 25 October; there is no such wreck located on a coastal chart of the British Isles—Number 4431 and dated February 1946. However the earlier sound contact which the O'TOOLE made on October 19th and held into the 20th, had been reported to Admirality as a wreck as was an earlier contact made by the O'TOOLE on the 19th. Both these wrecks were reported in June of 1944 by HMCS WASKESIU while on a search and find mission. It was then assumed that they were ships sunk some days earlier (June '44). The names of the wrecks are not known to Admiralty. Notice of their locations were issued in 1631/1944. One wreck may have been that of HMS MOURNE sunk by a U boat on June 15, 1944 and reported as having gone down in the area of the O'TOOLE contact.

See letter from H.M. Hydrographic Office to author dated 28 Nov. '69—Misc. NY 119 File. Also Die U-boot Erfolge by Jurgen Rohwer for information on the MOURNE.

9. *At about the time of NY 119's arrival was the beginning of the German "Schnorchel" submarine offensive. The offensive did not get into full swing until December when it concentrated its main thrust in the Western Approaches and the Irish Sea. The "last gasp" attacks on the Antwerp bound convoys were carried on by smaller coastal and midget subs along with E boats.*

For the best account of the Schnorchel offensive, the student is referred to Roskills', The War at Sea as Morison covers it only lightly; the reason being that the concentration against it was mainly a British responsibility.

10. *CTG Report, Encl. J.*

GLOSSARY

AB — Able Bodied Seaman

ASW — Anti Submarine Warfare

ATS — Army Transport Service; later in 1943, became officially the Army Transportation Corps — Water Division; but the civilian manned fleet continued to be unofficially referred to as "A.T.S."

BCF — Barge, Car Float

BCL — Barge, Cargo Lighter

CIC — Combat Information Center; Nerve center for operational activity on Naval vessels.

CTG — Commander, Task Group (In the case of Convoy NY 119—Cmdr. Lind was CTG).

DE — Destroyer Escort; Smaller than a conventional destroyer. Built for U.S. Navy from 1943 onward. This class of vessel has been lauded as one of the more decisive factors in turning the Battle of the Atlantic in favor of the Allies.

DOPPLER EFFECT — Pitch variations which indicate on sonar an increasing or decreasing range to target.

EASTERN SEA FRONTIER — U.S. Navy designation for its command control of the United States East Coast.

FO'C'SLE — Common seagoing term for crew's living quarters.

FOXER GEAR — Noise making device towed to foil acoustical torpedoes. Most often used by Naval vessels; rarely by Merchant ships.

HAWSER — Heavy line of fibre or wire; a towing hawser; any line over 5 inches.

HEAD — Lavatory aboard ships.

LT — Army designation for "Large" or seagoing tug.

MILITARY TIME SYSTEM — The European system whereby time is told by the 2400-minute method. One minute past midnight is 0001; one minute before midnight is 2359.

NIP — Sharp bend or turn in a rope or wire.

NYPOE — New York Port of Embarkation; U.S. Army term for its port of New York command entity.

PAD EYES — Steel rings or fixed loops, most usually welded to a ship's deck.

PORT — The left side of a ship when the observer on the vessel is facing toward the bow (front) of a vessel.

PORT CAPTAIN — The administrative officer of a port; usually a former ship's master. The Army had such an official in its civilian command structure at each port where it had shipping interests. He was overseen by a military officer.

SCHNORCHEL — A device by which a submarine breathed in air through an extended mast and at the same time vented engine exhausts. This device was introduced by the Germans for use on their U boats during the last months of the War. Theoretically, it enabled a submarine to operate submerged, except for the "schnorchel," during most of its operational patrol. There were flaws in the device which often blocked exhaust fumes' exit or shut off air, the latter causing a severe vacuum effect within the submarine. The "schnorchel" was, though, a vast improvement for the U boat, and boats so equipped did create havoc within the seas surrounding the United Kingdom during even the last few weeks of the War.

ST — Army Small Tug, or harbor tug.

STARBOARD — The right side of a ship when the observer on the vessel is facing toward the bow (front) of the vessel).

TBS — Voice radio set. A radiotelephone limited in wattage for short-range communication within a convoy. Wattage was deliberately limited so radio traffic could not be picked up by enemy listeners.

TC — Transportation Corps, U.S. Army.

TG — Task Group; refers to a Naval unit. In the case of NY 119: the escorts, the Navy oiler, and any other Naval vessels operationally assigned, i.e., the ABNAKI.

TOWING BRIDLE — In the case of a "towed" vessel: Refers to two cables leading from each side of the towed ship to a point forward of the bow where they shackle to a ring from which leads the main towing cable forward to the stern of the towing vessel.

Y BOAT — Army harbor and coastal tanker; similar in design to U.S. Navy "Yard Oilers." Were discontinued as a vessel class following World War II.

BIBLIOGRAPHY

BACKGROUND PERIOD READING

The Battle of the Atlantic: Sept. '39 — May '43 by Samuel Eliot Morison

The Atlantic Battle Won: May '43 — May '45 by Samuel Eliot Morison

The War at Sea: Volume I thru III part II by Captain S.W. Roskill

U.S. Army in World War II — Technical Services: The Transportation Corps: Movements, Training and Supply by Chester Wardlow; The Transportation Corps: Operations Overseas by Bykofsky and Larson

CONVOY NY 119

Individual Vessel Files: (Correspondence and Recorded Interviews)

LIND and CTG STAFF — ABNAKI — BERMINGHAM — EDGAR G. CHASE — MASON — MAUMEE — O'TOOLE — POWERS — LT and Y BOATS — STs

File of "Salvage Operations" 4) 21st Oct. 1944 thru 8) 25th October 1944; Pages 5, 6, 7, 8.

Misc. File on NY 119

File on US Army T.C. — WD; mainly correspondence

File on ST Design and Specifications

British Coastal Charts — Scillys to Dover

File of Declassified records (conformed copies) of Army records concerning NY 119. Originals are in the Modern Military Records Center, National Archives, Suitland, Maryland.

File of Photographs — NY 119

*As of the publishing date the above files are in the possession of the author who intends within the future to place them in the custody of South Street Seaport Museum.

"Declassified" CTG Report, Convoy NY 119 14 Aug. — Oct. 27, 1944.

Message Report, NY 119

War Diarys — O'TOOLE, CHASE, MASON, relating to period of Convoy and in the case of the MASON from Jan. 1st — Jan. 12, 1945.

Log of the USS POWERS — 18 Sept. — 25 Oct. 1944

Log of the USS MASON 18 Sept. — 30 Nov. 1944

*The above records will be part of those placed in custody of The South Street Seaport Museum. They are however also available through application to the Office of Naval History.

Log Book of the USS ABNAKI (excerpts) Sept. — Oct. 1944

*This can be seen at the National Archives — however the "excerpts" from it are within the ABNAKI vessel file.

Personal Message File — A.L. Lind Sept. — Nov. 1944 *Private papers, Captain A.L. Lind

Operation Order — CTG 27.5, NY 119* Private Papers, Capt. A.L. Lind

The Schumberg Collection — Mason Scrapbook, N.Y.C. Public Library

OTHER SMALL CRAFT CONVOYS

Convoy Reports and Message Files of: Convoys CK 1 — CK 2 — CK 3 — CK 4 — NY 78 — NY 118

*Obtainable through the Office of Naval History

INDEX

THE ORDEAL OF CONVOY NY 119

NOTE: Bold Face indicates reference to a photograph, chart or statistical listing.

(Over)